KNOW YOUR ANCESTORS

KNOW YOUR ANCESTORS

A Guide to Genealogical Research

by

ETHEL W. WILLIAMS, PH.D

CHARLES E. TUTTLE COMPANY
Rutland, Vermont

Representatives

Continental Europe: BOXERBOOKS, INC., Zurich
British Isles: PRENTICE-HALL INTERNATIONAL, INC., London
Australasia: PAUL FLESCH & CO., PTY. LTD., Melbourne
Canada: HURTIG PUBLISHERS., Edmonton

Published by the Charles E. Tuttle
Company, Inc., of Rutland, Vermont and
Tokyo, Japan
with editorial offices at
Suido 1-chome, 2-6, Bunkyo-ku, Tokyo

Library of Congress Catalog
Card No. 60-15252

International Standard Book No. 0-8048-0344-7

First printing, 1960
Twentieth printing, 1974

Printed in Japan

TABLE OF CONTENTS

FOREWORD

It is with a feeling of profound humility that this work is presented, in the hope that it may serve a useful purpose until something better is developed. It is designed to provide a guide for Family History classes in the Kalamazoo Community School for Adults, and is based upon the lectures given before the first class in 1958–1959.

The course is intended to give fundamental instruction in scientific methods of tracing ancestry and compiling family history. The family is considered as the basic unit of society, and its relationship to history, both local and general, is featured.

Family research in public records, on local, county, state, and national levels, is outlined. Books and other library materials are discussed and evaluated, and a comprehensive bibliography of available source material is included, as well as a glossary of terms and abbreviations in common usage. Church records, internal migrations, and research sources in the principal states from whence the pioneers migrated westward are considered.

While the primary purpose of this book is to acquaint the student, or reader, with the principles of original research in American genealogy, the chapters on research in Canada and the British Isles, and on Heraldry, which are really beyond the scope of this work, were included by request.

Grateful acknowledgment is made to Mrs. Esther Loughin of the Michigan State Library for abstracting the probate laws.

To the members of the first Genealogy class who so faithfully endured the winter storms of 1958–1959 to reach Central High School each Wednesday evening, this work is affectionately dedicated.

Ethel W. Williams

1. INTRODUCTION TO GENEALOGY

INTRODUCTION TO GENEALOGY—DEFINITION AND EXPLANATION—
ATTRIBUTES OF A GENEALOGIST—HISTORY OF GENEALOGY IN THE
UNITED STATES—TEXTS AND GUIDES.

The word GENEALOGY is derived from two Greek words—
"Genea," meaning descent, and "logos," meaning discourse. It is the
vital branch of history, and is catalogued as one of the social sciences.
In the narrowest sense, it is the study of individuals and their relationship, wherein complete identification is established; in its broadest
sense, it is a scientific study which contributes to and coordinates with
many cognate fields of learning, such as history, biography, geography, sociology, law, medicine, and linguistics, to name but a few.

We will consider genealogy in its broadest sense, because we want
to know more about our ancestors than mere names and dates. We
want to know the stories of their lives, and just how they were interwoven into the fabric of history.

Complete identification is sometimes difficult to establish. For
example, in Hebron, Connecticut, in 1708, two girls were born. Each
one was surnamed Skinner, and christened Rachael. One was the
daughter of Thomas, and the other of John Skinner. In 1728, each of
these two Rachaels married an Ebenezer Root, one of whom was the
son of Aaron, and the other of Jesse. Then, along came the children
of these two couples, and to make identification even harder, they
were all baptized in the same church.

Relation to history. Family history is the basis of all history. The
combined history of families makes up the community history,
whether that community is a village, city, town, or county. The combined county histories make up the state history, and the combined
state histories make up the national history. Thus, genealogy and

history go hand in hand, each one contributing richly to the other.

Biography. Genealogy adds background to biography which, in turn, often furnishes the genealogist with the clue he seeks.

Geography. Genealogy and geography are closely affiliated. It is a fact that when people migrate to a foreign country, they seek a location as nearly like their homeland as possible. Scandinavians go north where the climate resembles their own, and the waters abound in their native food. People who have been accustomed to live in the mountains quite naturally seek land of a similar topography. Geography affected early migrations and settlements more than any other natural factor. Virgin soil was an inducement to the pioneers to travel, but mountains were barriers to travel. Waterways were the great transportation routes of the pioneers; hence the first settlements were along the eastern seaboard, and the next ones along the great inland rivers. The opening of the Erie Canal on October 26, 1825, was one of the greatest factors in the early settlement of Michigan, because it provided a shorter, safer, and cheaper route from New York State.

Sociology and genealogy are closely interlocked. Behind migrations there was always a social factor. Americans, unlike the English, have always been an actively mobile people. Why, for example, was there a migration, in 1859–1860 from the South to the North? Simply because some southern families were not in sympathy with the cause of slavery, and life in the South was almost unbearable for them, so they came North to find more agreeable neighbors. Sometimes people migrated for religious reasons. The Mormons, who were persecuted from New York State to Utah, are an example, as are also the Quakers, who were terribly persecuted in New England. Some states passed intolerable laws that imposed taxes which people were unable to meet, and this caused them to seek new homes elsewhere. Because of poor land in many parts of New England and New York, many went west to seek the virgin soils of Ohio and Michigan. After the American Revolution, many men who had served were given bounty land in other states, and they migrated to take up this land.

Law and genealogy are associated through heredity. The genealogist can establish the exact relationship of a person to the deceased in heirship problems; and the attorney can establish the legality of the claim, according to the laws of descent and distribution.

Medicine and genealogy are interrelated. The investigations of heredity by medical science are borne out in the findings of the alert genealogist. That is the reason photographs are so important. Physical characteristics, even facial expressions, continue for generations in a family, and the study of these often gives you a clue.

The study of linguistics often affords helpful clues to nationality and place of residence. For example, the early American "porch," in Dutch sections of New York and New Jersey, was called a "stoop," from which "step" was derived; in Italian sections it is called a "veranda," and in Anglo-Indian countries, a "piazza."

The attributes of a genealogist. A good genealogist has an innate pride in family and country, and recognizes his duty to search out and record the truth. He becomes, first of all, a full-time detective, a thorough historian, an inveterate snoop, and at the same time, a confirmed diplomat, a keen observer, a hardened skeptic, an apt biographer, a qualified linguist, a part-time lawyer combined with quite a lot of district attorney, a studious sociologist, and—above all, an accurate reporter.

People who are interested in genealogy fall largely into two distinct groups—those who are interested in joining hereditary societies where membership is based upon the achievements of their ancestors, and others who, in appreciation of what their ancestors have accomplished, are inspired and dedicated to make their own contribution to the preservation of local and family history. Whatever motivates an individual to explore his own background, the interest invariably grows with the passing years, and he discovers that he has a fascinating life-time hobby. Youthful Americans who develop an interest in genealogy become better citizens through the knowledge gained of community history, and they have a better appreciation and understanding of the American way of life after they have discovered the part their own ancestors played in building the commonwealth.

CHRONOLOGY OF DEVELOPMENT

1783: The first patriotic society was founded, and it still endures. It was called the Society of the Cincinnati. The founders were officers of the American Revolution. George Washington was the society's first president.

1820:   John Farmer wrote "A Genealogical Register of the First Settlers of New England." This was a great stimulus to the development of genealogy in the United States.

1845:   The New England Historic-Genealogical Society was founded. In January, 1847, it began the publication of the New England Historical and Genealogical Register, a quarterly which is currently being published in its 112th year.

1860:   James Savage, a famous antiquarian of Boston, published "A Genealogical Dictionary of the First Settlers of New

1862:   England," in four volumes. For its time, it was a masterpiece, and is still a valuable reference work. His critics should remember that he was a pioneer in his field, and had no vital records or other guides to follow.

1871:   The first family genealogy was published in the United States. It was "The Genealogy of Mr. Samuel Stebbins and Hannah, His Wife, from the Year 1707 to 1771."

1876:   The centennial of the signing of the Declaration of Independence was celebrated, and was a great impetus to the search for family history. This led to the organization of a number of hereditary-patriotic societies, some of which soon died out.

1889:   The Sons of the American Revolution was organized.

1890:   The Daughters of the American Revolution and the Society of Descendants of Mayflower Passengers were organized, and were very popular among the social leaders of Boston, New York, Philadelphia, and Newport, when proof of lineage was not so painstakingly checked as it is today.

1890:   During the 1890's, a great interest in family history developed in Virginia, where, unfortunately, many of the early records were destroyed during the Civil War. The Virginia Historical Society was founded at Richmond, in 1831, and reorganized in 1847. It has published a quarterly, "The Virginia Magazine of History and Biography," since 1893.

1920:   War is one of the greatest factors in kindling anew the flame

1960:   of patriotic fervor which promotes the desire to delve into the family background. In this "era of wars," interest in family history has become widespread in the United States. It is further stimulated at this time (1960) by the preparation of the centennial commemoration of the Civil War.

Texts and Guides

For a list of published texts and guides to genealogical research, please turn to Chapter 28, and consult *Beginner's Guides,* in the bibliography. It should be remembered, when selecting a book of this nature, that each author has been motivated by his personal interests to write his book; and by following his guidance in solving your problems, you will be considering them through his angles of approach. Each of the guides has some outstanding feature.

Several of the more recent books were written primarily for the use of members of the Mormon Church, the doctrines of which make genealogical research mandatory. So, naturally, these works, excellent as they are, are slanted to the philosophy of the church.

Mr. Gilbert Doane's *Searching For Your Ancestors,* is, without doubt, still the most comprehensive work in this field. An excellent feature of this book is the group of appendices which include bibliographies carefully arranged by states, census records missing and on file, and a bibliography of lists, registers, and rosters of Revolutionary War soldiers. The work is so delightfully presented that one wishes one could know Mr. Doane and sit down and chat with him. In speaking to the reader, Mr. Doane says: "To those of you who read this book and are thereby led into the pursuit of your ancestors, I owe both congratulations and condolences: condolences because I know that you will never be able to rid yourselves of the desire to search out one more ancestor: and congratulations because I know that you will have found an absorbing hobby which will profit you in many ways. And so, good digging!"

Mr. Jacobus, in his *Genealogy As a Pastime and a Profession,* writes from his vast knowledge of the subject, and cites many examples of misleading and erroneous statements, and gives a number of interesting case histories.

Mr. Kirkham's *A. B. C's of American Genealogical Research* is easy to read, and helpful to the beginner. *Research in American Genealogy,* by the same author, contains some valuable reprints of out-of-print material. It also contains the history of county origins of the United States, state by state. While this is helpful, it should be used with extreme caution, and checked against official records.

"Search and Research" is slanted more to the use of public records, and is, therefore, an important contribution. It is now out of print, but a new edition is in progress. Mr. Stevenson is an attorney and the legal aspects are somewhat emphasized.

Mr. Archibald Bennett's *Guide to Genealogical Research* expounds the doctrines of the Mormon Church, gives sources in foreign countries, and is an all-round scholarly work. The above works are recommended as guides, but you alone must find the solution to your problems.

2. WHERE TO BEGIN

WHERE TO BEGIN—FIRST STEPS IN EXPLORING YOUR BACKGROUND
—HOME SOURCES—TRADITIONS AND HOW TO HANDLE THEM—
SURNAMES.

Your family tree. Consider its importance and influence in
your life, and in the lives of your descendants. Have you ever thought
to what extent your talents and abilities are the fruit of generations
of ancestors, whose very characteristics, by environment or heredity,
have given meaning and direction to your life? It is a fact that these
ancestors are all a part of your background, and have contributed not
only to your physical appearance, but to your philosophy of life as
well. The study of the lives of these men and women in your past is
the first step towards a better understanding of yourself.

Men of all races and creeds have always shown a desire to know
and preserve their ancestry. The Bible has the Begats, the Egyptians
their Rosetti Stone, the Druids had their Bards, the British Heralds
their Visitations, and the American Indians their Totem Poles—to
mention but a few. Today, the Mormons, a people dedicated to genealogy by the very doctrines of their church, are spending one million
dollars each year to collect and preserve their ancestry.

If you have never attempted to trace your lineage, and would enjoy
an interesting and fascinating adventure that may well develop into
a family project, and lead to a lifetime avocation, I heartily recom-
mend that you inaugurate a search for your very own family tree
which is located somewhere in the great forest of humanity. I can almost hear you ask: "Where do I start?" Start right in your own home
where you will find evidences of family history all about you.

There is no magic formula to follow in tracing family history because each search presents different problems, and the solution of

one problem usually leads to several new and unsolved ones. You simply take a logical approach, as in any other field of research, and work from the known facts to the unknown. *Time* and *place* are the basic factors in the solution of all genealogical problems.

There are two main classes of source materials used in genealogical research. These are primary sources and secondary sources. Your research work will develop by three stages: (1) Home work; (2) Library Work; (3) Archives Work.

Primary source material is original material, and therefore it is the most authentic. For example, if a man writes, or causes to be written, his will, that is primary source material. On the other hand, the same will abstracted or copied into a family history becomes secondary source material. A photographic copy, such as a photostat or microfilm, is just as authentic as the original record, because it is an exact copy, but, if it is written or printed in a foreign language, the camera doesn't translate. A family history, pieced together, bit by bit, from original records, presents a true and accurate account of that family, whereas a history of the same family copied from secondary sources which are not backed by sound evidence is inaccurate and misleading and would be better left unwritten.

First Stage of Research—Homework

In the home you will find many records, both primary and secondary. The first thing to do is to talk to as many of your immediate relatives as you are able to contact. Then, set up your family history, one generation at a time, starting with yourself, and write it down. Never make the mistake of starting with some one whom you assume to be your immigrant ancestor, and working down to yourself. Remember, you work, always, from the known to the unknown. You base your calculations upon the facts you know in order to determine the facts you do not know, just as in solving a problem in mathematics, you let X equal the unknown factor.

Write down on paper your family history, as far as you can go, setting it up as follows:

YOUR NAME—birth, date and place; marriage, date and place, and to whom. This is your first generation.

YOUR FATHER'S NAME   YOUR MOTHER'S MAIDEN NAME
  birth; date and place   birth; date and place
  marriage; date and place   death; date and place; place of
  death; date; place; place of   burial.
  burial.

You now have two generations. Then continue working back, generation to generation, in this same way. Always keep in mind that the
number of ancestors you have will double with each generation, because each individual has two parents—it is as simple as that. In ten
generations you will have 1022 ancestors. Ten or twelve generations
of American ancestry is about as far as one can go, for that will take
you back to the time of the Jamestown Settlement in Virginia (1608),
or to the landing of the Mayflower (1620).

It is always well to contact all your oldest living relatives as soon
as possible. Try to interview your great-aunts and uncles, grandparents, great-grandparents, or old people who have been long time
friends of the family, while they are still here and able to give you the
information. If you can interview them personally, take along a
notebook and pencil and carefully write down all they tell you, and
if they are not sure of some of their facts, make a note of that, too.
The ideal way to conduct such an interview is with the use of a tape
recorder.

If the relatives or family friends you would contact live too far away
to be personally interviewed, then the next best thing is to carefully
type out a questionnaire, leaving ample space for them to fill in the
answers, and being sure to enclose a self-addressed, stamped envelope.
Place the most important questions at the beginning of your questionnaire, because old people may grow weary or become confused before
they reach the end of a long series of questions.

Bible Records

One of the first places to look for family records in the home is in the
family Bible. Family records have been found in Bibles since the time
of Gutenberg. They are usually found on pages between the Old and
New Testaments. In the United States some family records were kept
in Bibles from the early seventeenth century, but most of them date

from the era of the large family Bible—that is, between 1790 and 1890.
These large Bibles are cumbersome and many have been lost or destroyed. They are frequently found in secondhand stores or second-
hand book stores. That is always sad because it indicates that family
records, precious to someone, have fallen into disinterested hands.
The very least that any one who finds such records can do is to get
permission from the owner to copy the family record and place it in
some suitable depository.

The value of a Bible record depends largely upon who wrote the
record, and if he was contemporary with the events recorded. That is
what really determines whether a Bible contains "Jury Truth," or
just "Gospel Truth." For example, a man was born in 1773; he was
married in 1795; he died in 1859; his children's births are recorded
from 1796 to 1805. All the records are in the same handwriting except the man's death in 1859, so the conclusion is drawn that he wrote
the records. Now, take a look at the date of publication of this Bible.
It was published in 1886. So, obviously, a man who died in 1859
did not write this record. Had it been published in 1800, it would
probably have been acceptable as "Jury Truth."

In copying Bible records, be sure to note the following items:

Place of publication of the Bible.

Date of publication of the Bible.

Name of publisher.

Name of printer, if different from publisher.

Name and address of present owner, and name of original
owner.

Copy any other information such as obituary or marriage
notices that you find in the Bible, written on loose sheets,
or in newspaper clippings.

Primary Records in the Home

Look around your home for original records. You are apt to find land
deeds, marriage certificates, diaries, family letters, account books, and
many other items. Often pioneers kept diaries or journals of their
travels from New York and New England, when they came to seek
new homes in the Michigan wilderness. There are soldiers' diaries
kept during the Civil and other wars. Account books were kept by

people in all kinds of business and the professions; these often contain much more information than just accounts. Justice of the Peace records often contain a gold mine of information. They were not public records which had to be turned in to some county official, but were the property of the individual. If one of your ancestors happened to have been an early innkeeper, search for the "Register of Guests." It was a "Friendship Quilt," with names and dates embroidered upon its blocks, which finally established one lineage of the Standish family, descendants of Captain Myles.

If someone in your family was the sexton of a cemetery, a pioneer minister, or a circuit rider, and you have access to his papers, their contents may contain a wealth of information. The account books of early physicians often contain birth and death records that have never been registered. Early surveyors often kept records, not only of the land surveyed, but also of the families who owned the land. Early school records, such as report cards, awards of merit, and registers, all contain family records. Look also for engraved silver and napkin rings; you may even find a family coat of arms.

In the 1880's and 1890's photography was a young art. Candid and motion picture cameras were unknown, and "sitting for one's picture" (that's what they called it), was an event in one's life. When a photograph was given to friends or relatives, the donor often wrote his name, age, and the date, on the back. So, look in the attic for the plush-covered album with the heavy clasp, then slip out the pictures and look for inscriptions on their backs. If you have no idea where this ancestor resided, look for the photographer's mark. If it is "Heath, Kalamazoo, Michigan," then you know that this person lived within "buggy riding" distance of Kalamazoo. On the back of baby pictures look for the name and birth date of the baby, and the parents' names; on wedding pictures you are apt to find the names of the bride and groom and the date of the wedding.

Look for inscriptions in gift books. For example, on the fly leaf of "Little Women," you may find something like this: "To Margaret on her 16th birthday, June 9, 1896, with love from Aunt Mary." So now you know that Maggie was born June 9, 1880. If, among your attic treasures you find a sampler, even though it may be falling apart, it quite possibly may reveal some family history, for, besides the numerals and letters of the alphabet, it will probably give the name and age of the maker, and the date, as: "Dora Brown, aged 13, 1858," and there you have an original record in Dottie's own best cross-stitch. These are but a few examples of items which reveal family history. You will find many others, some much more interesting, especially if your ancestral home has housed several generations of your family.

Tombstones may or may not be primary records. Many stones were placed long years after the death occurred. Burial records are now kept in the cemetery office, and they do not always agree with the gravestone record. In the early days there were no cemetery offices and the records were kept by the sexton or the minister. When they moved to other fields the records often went with them. When you visit a cemetery to look for the inscriptions on the stones of your departed ancestors, it is a good idea to take along some chalk, some fine steel wool, a blunt-edged knife, and a camera. If the inscription is weatherbeaten and hard to decipher, scrape off the loose dirt with the blunt knife and steel wool, then go over the inscription with the chalk, and take a snapshot. It will be much more satisfactory to study this inscription in an air-conditioned room than among the brambles, wasps, mosquitoes, and possibly snakes, in an old overgrown cemetery on a hot August day. Also, you may change your conclusions upon further study; perhaps what first appeared to be a figure 3 is really the remains of a partly eroded 8. If no stones are found, then your next move is to check place indexes to determine if inscriptions from this cemetery have been copied and published. Perhaps someone has been there before you and copied all the inscriptions before the disintegration of the stones took place. They may have been published in a genealogical periodical covering the area, or they may be found in a typescript in the local or state library.

Traditions and How to Handle Them

Family traditions are tales relating to the history of a family, which have been handed down through successive generations, by oral communication, without having been committed to writing. Most traditions contain a nucleus of truth, but often the story has been enlarged with each retelling, and successive generations have added their own interpretations, until it has become greatly distorted.

Traditions should be preserved, as such, but never stated as facts. They add color to your narrative, and we love them for what they are. They have value but should be evaluated. For example, few of us believe the story of George Washington and the cherry tree, but it is part of our national folklore. We love it and wouldn't think of giving it up. In interviewing various kinsfolk it is not uncommon to uncover several versions of the same story, but never let that throw you—it only adds grist to your mill.

There is no set rule as to what may or may not be accepted as fact. Certainly, it is not wise to accept as the truth traditions that predate grandparents. A statement of fact is good only to the extent that the fact is within the personal knowledge of the person making the statement.

Make a record of the story just as it was told you, and record by whom it was told. One of the most common errors that creeps into family traditions is that a story is credited to the wrong side of the house. It may be told of the paternal side when it was actually on the maternal side. Another common mistake that is made is in the generation. A man from California wrote me that his grandfather was killed in the Massacre of Cherry Valley. The dates of his grandfather's life did not check with that statement, but those of his great-grandfather did, and the fact that his great-grandmother appeared in Oneida County, New York, soon afterward, as a widow with three young children, added a further clue which was later confirmed by research.

Some common traditions are: that the family is of royal descent; that there is a large estate, usually complete with castle, in the native country; that the immigrant ancestor was kidnapped and brought to this country; or that the family is of the same lineage as that of some prominent person of the same name.

Spelling of Surnames

Your family name was probably not always spelled as it is today. Until about one hundred years ago, ours was a phonetic language, and a name was spelled as it sounded to the individual who was writing it, and it often sounded different to different individuals. For example, the common name of Jones was spelled in nine different

ways: Jones—Joans—Joanes—Johns—Johnes—Joahns—Jonse—
Jhons—Jhonse. Surname history is a fascinating study. Almost all
family names have undergone many changes in orthography, the study
of which is most intriguing to those bearing the name. Many times
the identity of the original name is completely lost in the modern
version. For example, the surname Travis was originally Brieveres,
according to one authority.

What's in a Surname

"What's in a name?" asked the Bard of Avon. But have you ever
asked yourself what's in your name? There may be romance in your
name. It is your most intimate possession, which symbolizes your
personality, and forms the latest link in the historical chain of ancestral
sequence.

Where did your name originate? Was it in the bonny braes o'
Scotland, in Flanders' fields, beside the blue Danube, in an Alpine
village or on the Isle of Capri? It may have been along the white
cliffs of Dover, in the land of dykes and windmills, among the Scandinavian fiords, or where the river Shannon flows; perhaps it was in a
gypsy camp in Bohemia, or in a little Spanish town.

What is the meaning of your name? What changes in orthography
has the passing of time wrought? Is it found interwoven into the warp
and woof of history? Perchance an earlier link may have borne the
name of a Knight of the Round Table, a Viking, a Magna Charta
Baron, or one who wore a royal crown. Your family crest may have
been worn by an armored knight in the War of the Roses, or perhaps
your family coat of armour is charged with a crusader's cross.

Your romantic ancestry may be revealed in the history of your surname, and of the men and women who forged the earlier links in
your ancestral chain. You are a part of all those who have gone before,
and whose spiritual faith, talents and abilities have come down to
you, link by link, through the ages.

History of Names

Old Testament names expressed religious sentiment or some circum-
stance of birth, as Isaac (laughter), Jacob (supplanter), or Hannah

(favor), and were the names preferred by the English Puritans and Scottish Covenanters. The most unique system of nomenclature was that of the ancient Chinese race. Twelve hundred years B. C., each clan head was compelled to frame a verse, and members of the clan took the first word of this verse as a middle name, the second generation took the second word, and so on, explaining, perhaps, why it is said that "all Chinese are cousins."

Surnames were not used by the Hebrews, Egyptians, Assyrians, Babylonians, Persians, Greeks, and early Romans, but later, every Roman citizen had three names. The praenomen, or personal name, was placed first, and was usually abbreviated, as C. for Caius; this was followed by the nomen, the name of the gens or clan, as Julius, to indicate Julian gentes; and lastly came the cognomen, or family name, as Caesar. Early Greek and Roman names were filled with meaning; for example, Apollodorus meant "gift of Apollo," and Cicero, "vetch-grower." Celtic and Teutonic names were equally significant, like Gottfried, meaning "God's peace."

So it is that personal or Christian names are as old as mankind. They were conferred at baptism, and date back to the beginnings of the Christian church, while surnames which are the family or tribal names, inherited from the male parent, were added, at various times, as a matter of convenience, when the population had increased to such an extent that it became confusing to use one name only. Personal names indicate the history of a people, for the chief events of a nation are reflected in its nomenclature. Following the Civil War, Lincoln, Sherman, Grant, and Lee became popular given names for boys, and after World War I many girls, whose fathers had served "over there," were named Lorraine, just as Washingtons and Deweys were legion after the American Revolution and the Spanish-American Wars, respectively.

The study of surnames also parallels the study of history. Among English-speaking people, surnames came into use following the Norman Conquest, in 1066. The first census, known as the Domesday Survey, necessitated the use of surnames, and about the time the Feudal system was inaugurated in England, the custom of using surnames came into practice in France and Germany, and a little later in Scandinavia. Thus surnames came into general use in the eleventh and twelfth centuries.

Origin of Surnames

The principal sources from which hereditary surnames are derived are: patronymics or sire-names; rank; place names; professions or trades; animals; natural objects and nicknames.

The earliest surnames were simply coined by adding "son" to the father's name, as Robertson and Adamson. This custom was later further simplified by adding an "s" to the father's name, as Roberts and Adams. The Welsh equivalent of the English "son" is "ap," and when used before a name beginning with a vowel, often becomes incorporated with it, as ap Rice which has given us Price; ap Howell, Powell; and ap Richard, Prichard. The Norman patronymic was "fitz," a corruption of the French "fils" (son) which has given us a whole category of names such as Fitzgerald, Fitzpatrick, and Fitzwalter. So, the Gaelic "mac," also meaning "son," is prefixed to Scottish names, as MacDonald. The Anglo-Saxon patronymic "son" was not only added to the original name but to an abbreviation; for example, from David, we get Dave or Daw, and from these came Davison and Dawson; Walter was abbreviated to Watt, and from that we got Wattson and Watson. O' meaning "descendant of," was prefixed to ancient Irish family names, and was followed by the genitive case of the name of the ancestor, as O'Neill (nominative Niall), a descendant of Niall. The apostrophe is due to the mistaken idea that O stands for "of." The German affix -shon or -son, the Scandinavian -sen, and the Russian -vitch, are all equivalents of -son, as are also the Hebrew ben (Solomon ben David) and the Arabian ibn (Abraham ibn Ezra). The Saxon suffix -ing, also signifies "son of," in names such as Browning, Harding and Whiting.

Many surnames are derived from personal characteristics, as Black, White, Short, and Long, while from rank we get such names as King, Prince, Pope, Bishop, and Knight, and from the trade or profession of the family, Smith, Farmer, Shepherd, Baker, Taylor, Carpenter, and Wright. In fact these names form a catalogue of primitive occupations. The names Hill, Dale, Wood, Forest, Brooks, Rivers, and Field, with their many compounds, reflect the topography of the ancestral land. From animals are derived such names as Horsley from the equine species; Kinley, Cowley, and Oxley, from the bovine; while from the deer we get Hartley, Hindley, and Rowley; besides such names as Wolf, Fox, and Roebuck. Many names come from locations, as Atwell, a dweller near a well; Bywater, one living beside a lake or stream; Beecher or Beechman signified a resident in or near a grove of Beech trees. Townsend was applied to one who lived at the end of a town, and Kirkman, to one who lived near a church.

Another source of surnames is from nicknames, from which national figures have developed into graphic personalities; noted examples are John Bull and Uncle Sam. The latter was first known as "Brother Jonathan," an epithet applied to Governor Jonathan Trumbull by George Washington. Governor Trumbull was a tall, gaunt, sharp-featured, bewhiskered gentleman who, for full dress, wore a swallow-tailed coat and striped trousers of homespun.

Because the United States is a country made up of all nations, we have a greater variety of surnames than any other country on the globe, but all our surnames had their beginnings in Europe, since the custom of having surnames originated before the settlement of America. Although time and events have changed their spelling, the evolution of each family surname has a romantic, interesting, sometimes adventurous, often historical background. The study of surnames is closely tied in with the study of history, as our surnames were all developed from the various conditions which surrounded the people of the Old World during the thousand years which followed the time of the Saviour.

"How am I to determine where my family originated?" you ask. Go to your library, consult a good surname book, and learn the history and meaning of your surname. The following bibliography of books on surnames may help you to locate yours.

Bibliography of Books on Surnames

ANDERSON, WILLIAM: *Genealogy and Surnames*. Scotland. 1865.

BAILEY, ROSALIE FELLOWS: *Dutch Systems in Family Naming, in New York and New Jersey*. Pubs. of National Genealogical Society, No. 12. 1954.

BARBER, HENRY: *British Family Names—Their Origin and Meaning*. London. 1902.

BARDSLEY, CHARLES W.: *A Dictionary of English and Welsh Surnames, with Special American Instances*. London. 1901.

BARDSLEY, CHARLES W.: *Our English Surnames, Their Sources and Significations.* n. d.

BARING-GOULD, SABINE: *Family Names and Their Story.* London. 1910.

BLACK, GEORGE F.: *The Surnames of Scotland, Their Origin, Meaning, and History.* (Bulletin of the N. Y. Public Library, August 1943 to September 1946).

BRECHENMACHER, JOSEF K.: *Deutsche Sippennamen.* Gorlitz. 1936. 5 v. in 3. The best source for German surnames.

CARNOY, ALBERT: *Origines De Noms De Familles En Belgique.* Louvain, 1953. Belgian Surnames.

CHAPUY, PAUL: *Origine De Noms Patronymiques Française.* Paris. 1934. French Surnames.

DAUZAT, ALBERT: *Dictionnaire Etymologique Des Noms De Famille et Prénoms De France.* Paris. 1935.

DELLQUEST, AUGUSTUS WILFRID: *These Names of Ours.* New York. 1939.

DIXON, HOMER: *Surnames.* 1855. Pub. in U.S.

EVEN, CECIL L'ESTRANGE: *A Guide to the Origin of British Surnames.* London. 1938.

FERGUSON, ROBERT: *Surnames as a Science.* London. 1883.

FERGUSON, ROBERT: *Teutonic Name System.* London. 1864.

FERNOW, BERTHOLD: *New Amsterdam Family Names and Their Origin.* In Historic New York; Second Series of the Half Moon Papers. 11: 211–240. New York. 1899.

FINLAYSON, James: *Surnames and Sirenames.* London. 1889.

FUCILLA, JOSEPH F.: *Our Italian Surnames.* Evanston, Illinois. 1949.

GARDNER, JOHN ENDICOTT: *List of Chinese Family Names.* n. d.

GATES, SUSAN YOUNG: *Surname Book and Racial History.* Salt Lake City, Utah. 1918.

GOTTSCHALD, MAX: *Deutsche Namenkunde.* Berlin. 1954.

GUERIOS, ROSARIO F. N.: *Dicionario Etimologico De Nomes E Sobrenomes.* Curitiba. 1949. Portuguese names.

GUPPY, H. B.: *The Homes of Family Names.* n. d.

HARRISON, HENRY: *Surnames of the United Kingdom.* London. 1912.

HUIZINGA, A.: *Encyclopedie Van Namen.* Amsterdam. 1955.

HUIZINGA, A.: *Encyclopedie Van Voornamen.* Amsterdam. 1956.

INNES, COSMO: *Concerning Some Scotch Surnames.* Scotland. 1860.

JENTRY, THOMAS G.: *Family Names.* 1892. Pub. in U. S.

KELLY, PATRICK: *Irish Family Names, with Origins, Meanings, Clans, Arms, Crests, and Mottoes.* Chicago. c1939. Reprinted 1958.

LEITE DE VASCONCELLOS PEREIRA DE MELLO, Jose: *Antropopimia Portuguesa.* Lisbon. 1928. Portuguese names.

Les Noms De Familles Suisses. Zurich. 1940. 2 v. (Lists names of families residing in the French, German, and Italian sections; also lists dates when the family name first appeared in the various Swiss Cantons.)

LOWER, MARK ANTHONY: *Patronymica Britannica*. London. 1860.

LOWER, MARK ANTHONY: *Historical Essays on English Surnames*. London 1843.

MAC LYSAGHT, EDWARD: *Irish Families, Their Names, Arms and Origins*. Dublin. 1957.

MATHESON, ROBERT E.: *Varieties and Synonyms of Surnames and Christian Names in England For Guidance of Registration Office and the Public in General, in Searching the Indexes of Births, Deaths and Marriages*. Dublin. 1890.

MATHESON, ROBERT E.: *Surnames and Christian Names in Ireland*. Dublin. 1901.

MENCKEN, H. L.: The American Language, Chapter X, p. 474: *Origin, Meaning and Usage of Proper Names in America, Including Surnames, Given Names, and Place Names*.

MOORE, A. W.: *Manx Surnames*. n. d., n. p.

NEW ENGLAND HISTORIC & GENEALOGICAL REGISTER: *When Waits Became Wrights*, October, 1953.

PHILLIMORE, W. P. W., AND FRY, E. A.: *An Index to Change of Names, 1760–1901*. n. d.

SCHETTER, CLARENCE: *Does Your Name Identify You?* In Social Forces, 21: 172–176.

SIMS, CLIFFORD S.: *The Origin and Signification of Scottish Surnames*. Albany. 1862.

SMITH, ELDSON C.: *Dictionary of American Family Names*. New York. 1956.

SMITH, ELDSON C.: *The Story of Our Names*. New York. 1950.

WEEKLEY, ERNEST: *The Romance of Names*.

WEEKLEY, ERNEST: *Surnames*. Third ed. New York. 1937.

WOULFE, PATRICK: *Irish Names and Surnames*. Dublin. 1923.

YOUMANS, CHARLES L.: *Dicionario De Apellidos Castellanos Origen Y Significado*. La Habana. 1955. Spanish names.

3.   CHARTS AND CHARTING

CHARTS AND CHARTING—THE AHNENTAFEL—CHANGES IN TIME
AND PLACE—JULIAN VS GREGORIAN CALENDARS.

After you have located several generations of ancestors, it is
well to make a chart. This is a graphic representation of your knowledge of your background, and places your family in its true perspec-
tive. You may either draw a chart or buy one from a supply house.
They can be ordered from:

American Historical Co., Inc., 80–90 Eighth Ave., New York 11,
New York. (Fan chart)

Everton Publishers, Logan, Utah. (Issue chart catalog)

Goodspeeds Book Shop, 18 Beacon St., Boston 18, Mass. (All
types of charts—issue a book catalog 35¢)

Charles E. Tuttle Co., Rutland, Vermont. (All types including a
real tree chart—book catalog free)

The chart is not a family history in any sense of the word. It is
a work sheet which enables you to see at a glance how much you
really know about your lineage. It serves merely as an index to your
individual ascendants, and gives only their names, dates of birth,
marriage and death, and principal places of residence. There is no
place on the chart for collateral lines (brothers and sisters). Everton
Publishers sell a family group sheet which has spaces for the complete
records of each individual family, and its use, in connection with
your chart, greatly simplifies your preliminary work.

The most practical chart to use, in class or research work, is the
one shown here, and it may be purchased or drawn. It is 8½ × 11
inches, and is indefinitely expansible. By this time you should have
two notebooks, one for copying the information you accumulate, and
the other, a standard sized (8½ × 11) loose-leaf type into which you

transcribe your notes for permanent record, of which these charts are a part. Each sheet of the chart has space for 31 names. They are left unnumbered as the numbering depends upon which line you extend.

Instructions for Filling in Chart

Your first chart is to be numbered 1 at the top. Your own name is filled in on the line numbered 1, and that is YOUR number. Your father is number 2, and your mother is number 3. Your father's father is number 4, and your father's mother is number 5. Your mother's father is number 6, and your mother's mother is number 7. Your father's ancestry is all above the center line, and your mother's ancestry is all below the center line.

To extend any line beyond the limits of Chart Number 1, use another blank chart and mark it "Chart Number 2, Continuation of Chart Number 1," inserting the ancestor's name whose line is to be extended, in the position of number 1 on chart 1. Insert numbers on Chart Number 2, following the same arrangement as on Chart Number 1. For example, if Ancestor Number 24's line on Chart Number 1 is to be extended, then fill in his name and dates on the center line (which on Chart 1 was Number 1), but transfer his number (24) to that line on Chart Number 2. An ancestor's number is never changed, regardless of the position it takes on the chart. Ancestor Number 24's father becomes Number 48, and his mother Number 49. Opposite Ancestor Number 24 on Chart 1, mark "See Chart 2."

Note that one's own number is 1. Every father's number is twice that of his child, and every wife's number is her husband's number plus one. With the exception of Number 1, all men's names carry even numbers, and all women's names odd numbers. This chart shows one's lineal ascendants only.

Do not regard your chart as a family history. It is only a work sheet. Remember that all of the ancestors you have charted here were real people who lived full lives, and whose biographies you will want to record in another section of your family history.

The Ahnentafel

Another type of chart which is useful especially in collecting informa-

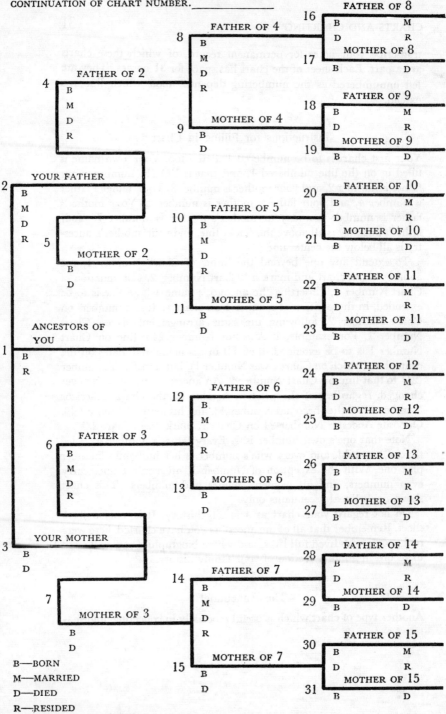

FATHER OF 8
16
B   M
D   R
MOTHER OF 8
17
B   D

FATHER OF 4
8
B
M
D
R

FATHER OF 9
18
B   M
D   R
MOTHER OF 9
19
B   D

4
B
M
D
R

FATHER OF 2

MOTHER OF 4
9
B
D

YOUR FATHER

2
B
M
D
R

FATHER OF 10
20
B   M
D   R
MOTHER OF 10
21
B   D

FATHER OF 5
10
B
M
D
R

5

MOTHER OF 2

FATHER OF 11
22
B   M
D   R
MOTHER OF 11
23
B   D

B
D

MOTHER OF 5
11
B
D

ANCESTORS OF
YOU

1
B
R

FATHER OF 12
24
B   M
D   R
MOTHER OF 12
25
B   D

FATHER OF 6
12
B
M
D
R

6
B
M
D
R

FATHER OF 3

FATHER OF 13
26
B   M
D   R
MOTHER OF 13
27
B   D

MOTHER OF 6
13
B
D

YOUR MOTHER

3
B
D

FATHER OF 14
28
B   M
D   R
MOTHER OF 14
29
B   D

FATHER OF 7
14
B
M
D
R

7

MOTHER OF 3

FATHER OF 15
30
B   M
D   R
MOTHER OF 15
31
B   D

B
D

MOTHER OF 7
15
B
D

B—BORN
M—MARRIED
D—DIED
R—RESIDED

tion by correspondence, is the Ahnentafel. Literally, the word is
derived from two German words, "ahnen," meaning ancestors, and
"tafel," meaning table, hence *table of ancestors*. The ahnentafel is
really a skeleton genealogy (but not the family skeleton) for it reveals,
at a glance, all that is known to a person of his family tree, without
the decorations.

While the Ahnentafel is, in no sense, a family history or genealogy,
it serves a very useful purpose in that it is a great timesaver. Many
ancestor hunters have set up their ahnentafels and made either car-
bon or mimeographed copies. Then when they discover a kindred
soul working on the same lines, they mail him a copy. Some genealogical periodicals are publishing the ahnentafels of their subscribers.
The ahnentafel is really a list, by generations, of one's known ancestors, giving names, dates of birth and death, and principal places of
residence, separating generations by a double space.

The following form is used to set up an ahnentafel. There is but one
simple rule to keep in mind. The same rules as to numbering apply
as in the previous chart.

Your Ahnentafel

1. Ahnentafel of—Your Name and Address.
2. Your father   (birth and death dates) Residence(s)
3. Your mother   „   „   „   „   „
4. Your father's father   „   „   „   „   „
5. Your father's mother   „   „   „   „   „
6. Your mother's father   „   „   „   „   „
7. Your mother's mother   „   „   „   „   „
8. Your father's father's father   „   „   „   „
9. Your father's father's mother   „   „   „   „
10. Your father's mother's father   „   „   „   „
11. Your father's mother's mother   „   „   „   „
12. Your mother's father's father   „   „   „   „
13. Your mother's father's mother   „   „   „   „
14. Your mother's mother's father   „   „   „   „
15. Your mother's mother's mother   „   „   „   „

The above outline covers four generations and may be continued in this way back to the immigrant. Fill in the names, dates, and places you know, and leave the other lines blank. Your correspondent will know at a glance which ancestors you have, and those you do not have. If 28 is blank, he immediately turns to 14 as that is where your stalemate began.

Time and Place

Time and place are two of the most important factors in solving research problems in family history. That these two factors have not always been stable complicates the solution to the answers of *when* and *where*. Time is now measured by the number of days, hours, minutes, and seconds required for the earth to make one complete revolution around the sun. In earlier periods it was impossible to reckon the solar year accurately and this resulted in conflicting calendars. In 45 b.c., Julius Caesar decreed that by the Roman calendar a year should be 365 days and 6 hours, with one day added to February every fourth year. This was known as the Julian Calendar, and continued in use until the fall of the Roman Empire, in 1582. In that year the Roman calendar was proved defective by 10 days, as the vernal equinox fell on the eleventh instead of the twenty-first of March. To correct this error, Pope Gregory XII, in 1582, abolished the Julian calendar in all Catholic countries and introduced the Gregorian calendar. By his edict, October fifth was reckoned as October fifteenth, thus compensating for the ten days gained by the Julian calendar. In order to understand the time element in genealogical research, it is important to know when various countries adopted the Gregorian calendar.

In Great Britain and its American Colony which later became the United States, double dating was used over a period of 170 years (1582–1752). This was due to the conflict between the historical calendar by which the first day of the year fell upon January first, and the ecclesiastical calendar which recognized March twenty-fifth as the first day of the year. Therefore, double dating is used only between January first and March twenty-fifth in the intervening years from 1582 to 1752. It must be borne in mind that these dates apply only to England and British possessions. All dates before the change were called Old Style (O.S.), and after the change New Style (N.S.). Double dates were written as 1750/51. For example, George Washington was born February 11, 1732, (O.S.) or February 22, 1732, (N.S.).

That *time* and *place* are the basic factors in genealogical research cannot be reiterated too frequently or emphasized too strongly. Changes in time and place often paralleled each other, and changes in political divisions left their imprint upon historical geography. For example, residents of the area which embraces the present State of Vermont, in 1789, were living in New York State which then held jurisdiction over the territory to the Connecticut river, but in 1791 the same region was in the Vermont we know today. The study of maps, atlases and gazetteers of different periods is sometimes quite a revelation.

Charts and Charting

Dates of changes from the Julian calendar to the Gregorian calendar in countries outside the British Empire, took place as follows:

Austria and	:	
Bohemia	:	January 7, 1584 became January 17, 1584.
Denmark	:	February 19, 1700 became March 1, 1700.
England and	:	
British pos-	:	September 3, 1752 became September 14, 1752.
sessions	:	
Finland	:	February 18, 1753 became March 1, 1753.
France	:	December 10, 1582 became December 20, 1582.
Germany—	:	
Protestant	:	
States	:	February 19, 1700 became March 1, 1700.
Germany	:	Augsburg—February 14, 1583 became February 24, 1583.
Catholic	:	Lausitz and
States	:	Silesia—January 13, 1584 became January 23, 1584.
	:	Paderborn—June 17, 1585 became June 27, 1585.
	:	Prussia—August 23, 1612 became September 2, 1612.
	:	Pfalz-Neuburg—December 14, 1615 became December 24, 1615.
Greece	:	Stabilized the calendar in 1923.
Hungary	:	Stabilized the calendar in 1587.

Italy	:	October 5, 1582 became October 15, 1582.
Lorraine	:	Stabilized the calendar October-December, 1582.
Netherlands	:	
Catholic	:	
Sector	:	December 15, 1582 became December 25, 1582.
Netherlands	:	
Protestant	:	
Sector	:	Stabilized the calendar in 1700.
Norway	:	February 19, 1700 became March 1, 1700.
Poland	:	October 5, 1582 became October 15, 1582.
Portugal		October 5, 1582 became October 15, 1582.
Russia	:	Stabilized the calendar in 1918.
Spain	:	October 5, 1582 became October 15, 1582.
Sweden	:	February 18, 1753 became March 1, 1753.
Switzerland	:	
Catholic	:	Stabilized the calendar in 1583.
Cantons	:	
Switzerland	:	
Protestant	:	
Cantons	:	Stabilized the calendar in 1701.
except	:	
St. Gallen	:	Stabilized the calendar in 1724.
Glarus	:	
Appenzell	:	Stabilized the calendar in 1798.
Graubuenden	:	Stabilized the calendar in 1798.

PLACE. A geographical location remains fixed but the political division in which it is located may undergo changes. For example, Annville Township in Lebanon County, Pennsylvania, was at one time attached to Lancaster County, and at another time it was part of Dauphin County. Therefore, county records of a family residing on the same farm through several generations will be found in three different counties.

4. INTRODUCTION TO LIBRARY RESEARCH

INTRODUCTION TO LIBRARY RESEARCH—REFERENCES AND METHODS OF RECORDING THEM—BIBLIOGRAPHY.

Now that you have gathered all the information you can from relatives and family records, the ideal way to proceed would be to go, personally, to the place where your ancestors lived, and start searching the records there, but as that is seldom possible, you will instead, go to the nearest library.

Before you go to the library, organize your work and analyze your problems. By this time you have many of them, but don't try to work on them all at once. Follow one line at a time, taking one ancestor and one generation at a time. Have a definite knowledge of what you are looking for.

In considering an ancestor, ask yourself these questions—what do I know about him that I can prove? What do I know about him that I cannot prove? What do I know about him that is purely hearsay? Perhaps you have always pictured great-grandfather as having been born in New York State. Do you really have proof of where he was born, or do you just surmise that was the case because you have been told that he came from there? Have you ever located him in a census or by any other means that would give you positive proof of his residence? In other words, how far back do you really have proof of your ancestry? Documenting ancestry is apt to bring forth a great many surprises.

First, get acquainted with the library and its genealogical collections, and also with the librarian in charge. Find out how their books are catalogued, and what special collections and indexes they have.

Libraries catalog by book title, author's name, subject and place. Some have further breakdowns. Some libraries also have analytic cards which index the allied families in a genealogy, as well as the principal family. Most family genealogies contain considerable information on intermarried families which can be readily found by the use of analytic indexes. In town or county histories you may find one branch of a family in Connecticut, another branch, or the same one later on, in Ohio, and still later, in Texas or on the West coast; all of these are readily picked up by means of analytic cards.

Remember that the person in charge of genealogical collections in the library is a librarian, but seldom a genealogist. It is only his or her function to see that you get books to use. You must do your own thinking and your own research. Remember, too, that people you meet in the library are also there to do research, and are not interested in hearing the story of your ancestry, so don't take their time and embarrass them by inflicting it upon them, for they, too, have ancestry.

Many genealogical books are old, out of print, and worn, so be careful of them—handle them as you would your own and then the library will not hesitate to extend to you the privilege of using their rare books. First, find out if a genealogy of your family has been published; if there is one, the next step is its evaluation, which will be discussed further.

Now that you are doing library research you will need to adopt a systematic procedure of keeping references. A good rule to follow is to write down your reference before you start to copy the material, otherwise you may become so absorbed in what you are reading that you will forget it.

Reference Work Sheet

BOOKS AND PAMPHLETS:

Author's, editor's, or compiler's full name—surname first, as Jones, John James.

Title—complete as listed on title page. Unimportant words may be omitted by indicating thus (. . . . .).

Publisher's name, place and date of publication. If no date is given, and book has been copyrighted, list the date thus: c1910. If there is no date and no copyright, list it n.d.

If there is more than one volume, state the number of volumes in the set.

If there has been more than one edition, state which, as "3rd ed." State volume and page as, 5: 72–89.

GOVERNMENT DOCUMENTS:

In addition to the information above, include series, title and number, and if it is a Congressional document, state the number of the Congress and of the session.

MANUSCRIPTS OR COLLECTIONS OF PERSONAL PAPERS:
Author's name.
Title as catalogued in library or depository.
Page or file number.

It is well to develop some system of keeping your references organized and indexed. One method is to set up the family names on cards (either 3 ×5 or 4 ×6, as you prefer). Let us say one of your families is Brainard. Place the name BRAINARD at the top of the card, and below it all the references you have found to that family. As you look them up, adopt some sort of a check mark to indicate whether or not you have completed that reference. If you have done some work on it but have not completed it, you might use half an X, and when completed, add the other half. You will save yourself a lot of duplicated effort, as the years go by, if you adopt some such system.

Unfortunately, printed genealogies are not standardized as to format, and you will find many unique presentations on library shelves. There is a recognized system of setting up a genealogy which is used by the American Society of Genealogists, and which has been generally adopted by the better publications. This will be discussed later on. However, most of the genealogies that are already on library shelves do not follow this pattern, and some have such complicated numbering systems that a "Philadelphia lawyer" would be utterly confused. It will help you greatly if you will take the time to read the Preface (sometimes called the Foreword), for in that the author explains what he has done, and what unique system of numbering he has developed. Read this carefully and you will gain a good idea of the value of the work he has done, for he may tell you to what records he had access. Also, read the Table of Contents, and look over the index or the indices. It is now considered better journalism to have one consolidated index, but many genealogies have several. Sometimes there is one index of all the individuals having the family surname, and another index of those individuals who have married into the family, and sometimes there are also place and subject indexes, as well.

Bibliography

It is necessary for you to familiarize yourself with various types of reference books that you will use over and over. It is well to become familiar with the books which are listed in Chapter 28.

After you have found 25 or 50 ancestors, you will need to devise some system of keeping track of the biographical material you have accumulated so that it is readily available. I will describe my system; you may have something better. I use a 4 × 6 card or slip. A paper slip is just as well because it is a temporary record that you will destroy after your family history is complete. The advantage of slips is that if you have more information than a 4 × 6 card can accommodate, the paper slip can be cut 6 × 8 and folded. These slips may be filed numerically (using ancestor's number on chart), or alphabetically by name. Always be sure to document these records.

Here are a few suggestions on presenting the biographical material in your family history. Record the place and date of the father's birth and death, and place of burial, with gravestone record, if possible. State the name of his parents, and give the name of his wife, date and place of her birth and death, and place of her burial. State the date and place of marriage, names of her parents and their place of residence. If she was a widow, the names of her other husbands should be stated, and if she remarried after the father's death, record the name of her husband. Enter all the vital records in the first paragraph. This is standard procedure as it saves the reader's time in identifying the ancestor he is seeking.

If the father married more than once, the story of each wife and her family may be given a separate paragraph. Give the complete list of children and number them consecutively, regardless of the number of wives a man may have had. Write up the family migrations and deal with the various places of residence as fully as possible. State the man's occupation and education, and record his civil and military service. Record family traditions as such, unless you have definite proof of their authenticity. An abstract of his will should be included, if possible. Be sure to document each statement you make, and a hundred years later, his descendants may bless you for so doing.

5.   FURTHER LIBRARY RESEARCH

FURTHER LIBRARY RESEARCH—EVALUATION OF LIBRARY MATERI-
ALS—USE OF GUIDES AND INDEXES—MAPS AND OTHER TOOLS—
NEWSPAPERS CARRYING GENEALOGICAL COLUMNS.

When you go to a library the important thing is to have an
objective. Know exactly what you are looking for, and work with
that purpose in mind. When you go to a library for the first time, ask
the librarian what special collections and indexes they have. All
libraries, even small ones, have collections of regional material. If
they have a special collection that you want to use, find out how it
is indexed. Below are a few examples of such collections:

DENISON COLLECTION in the Burton Historical Collection of the Detroit Public Library, consists of 30 volumes of genealogies of early
French settlers of Detroit.

INDEX TO STATE CENSUS RECORDS OF ILLINOIS, made by the State Historical Society, is in the Illinois State Library at Springfield.

FAMOUS NAME INDEX AT NEWBERRY LIBRARY, CHICAGO. In the early
days before so many genealogies had been published, each name in
every genealogy was indexed.

NEW YORK STATE LIBRARY, ALBANY, AND VIRGINIA STATE LIBRARY,
RICHMOND, both have photostats of the early church records of
their respective states.

WISCONSIN STATE LIBRARY at Madison has a "Graveyard" which is an
enormous file of obituaries of Wisconsin families, since 1850. They
also have the *Draper Mss. Collection of Southern Families*. Draper was
a circuit rider who traveled on horseback through Kentucky, Tennessee, and the Carolinas, and kept diaries of his travels.

VOSBURGH COLLECTION OF EARLY NEW YORK CHURCH RECORDS. Typescript compiled by the New York Genealogical & Biographical

Society. Copies are at the State Library, Albany, in the Library of the N.Y.G. & B. Society, in the Library of Congress, and probably elsewhere.

MICHIGAN BIOGRAPHICAL INDEX, compiled by the Detroit Public Library, indexes every individual upon whom five or more lines of copy are found, in any Michigan County History. Copies are in the Burton Collection, Detroit, and in the Michigan State Library, Lansing.

THE FRANK WILLING LEACH COLLECTION of Descendants of the Signers of the Declaration of Independence, the *Gilbert Cope Collection of English Quaker Records,* and the *Mervine Collection of early Pennsylvania and New Jersey Families* are all to be found in the library of the Genealogical Society of Pennsylvania at Philadelphia.

THE WILLIAM WADE HINSHAW COLLECTION OF QUAKER RECORDS is at Friends Library at Swarthmore, Pennsylvania, and is well indexed.

So always be on the lookout for any special collections that may simplify your work. Unless you make inquiries you may not be told about them.

If the library has a genealogy of your family, find out also if they have town or county histories covering the places of residence of your family. Having found these, the next thing to do is to evaluate the work of the authors. The more experience you gain, the simpler will be the matter of evaluation. Just as in buying merchandise you learn to look for certain brand names that may always be depended upon for high quality, so in time, you will learn to differentiate authors, in this field in the same way.

How does one evaluate a family genealogy? The first step is to read the preface and learn how the author collected his material. He will probably tell you to what records he had access. Did he base his work upon family tradition and hearsay, or did he really do a good job and consult original records? However he did his work, copy the pedigree as given in your line, and use it as "clue material" if it is not documented. If he documented each item, then you are really in luck.

If, on the other hand, he lists at the end of each chapter, such references as "Family Records," or "Bible Records," without stating who owns these records and where they may be found, you cannot accept them. Of course, if the author is living, you can write and ask him where such records are located. If he "guessed" he probably won't reply. If he is dead there isn't much more you can do except to keep in mind that such records may be in existence, but it is hardly worth while to waste time in trying to find them. In that case you can only treat his work as you would a tradition, as clue material, and start from scratch.

Perhaps you will not find a published family genealogy, but you may find a reference to your grandfather in a county or town history. Then you will have to do some historical research. Find out when the county was organized and first settled. Look in the historical section of the book to find where the settlers came from. In pioneer days one family did not struggle through the wilderness alone. Migrations followed definite patterns and the settlers came in groups. Often relatives and sometimes a whole congregation "came West" in a group, under the leadership of their pastor. Vermontville, Michigan was settled by such a migration. The entire congregation of the East Poultney, Vermont Congregational Church migrated to Eaton County, Michigan, in 1836, under the leadership of their pastor, bought land, settled the town, and named it, as was the custom, for their native state. Your search then increases in interest because you are placing your family in its proper historical setting.

There is but one basic rule for evaluating the evidence of a book. *A statement of fact is good only to the extent that the fact is within the personal knowledge of the person making the statement.* Applying this rule to a family genealogy, it is evident that statements may be accepted within the generation of the author, or the generations immediately preceding his generation, since his information on these generations was no doubt furnished him by persons then living, but for earlier generations the statements in a published genealogy can only be accepted if references which can be checked are stated. A genealogy, in order to be acceptable, must give specific references to volume and page for every statement made, otherwise it can be used only as "clue material" for which evidence must be found.

Guides and Indexes

More and more guides and indexes are being authored and published to aid the genealogical researcher. It is very important that you should become familiar with these, and learn how to use them. In the Bibliography Section of this work, Chapter 28, will be found a list of the more helpful ones, under the heading of GUIDES AND INDEXES. These are briefly described here, and are discussed fully in class work. These are the tools that will help to simplify your work. Learn how to use them. Scholars agree that next to knowing the facts the most important thing is knowing where to find them.

Maps and Atlases

Attempting to do genealogical research without maps is like trying to steer a ship, without a rudder, or to find your way through a dense forest without a compass.

County atlases, properly called cadastral maps, are those prepared for taxation purposes. They give the names of the land owners, and the acreage, and are usually scaled 25 inches to the mile. These are to be found in the Library of Congress, and in some state and county libraries. These maps were produced during the period of 1860 to 1890. They were first made in New York and Philadelphia, and by 1870 were being produced on a nation-wide scale.

The largest publisher of county atlases was G.A. Ogle & Company of Chicago. The most important cartographer of that time was Henry F. Walling (1825–1888), Professor of Engineering at Lafayette College, who produced more than twenty state atlases. Then, also, there were several Beers Companies—Daniel, Frederick. J. B., J. H., and S. N.

Some of the atlases for the western states, for 1890, gave quite a lot of early history. Some of them even gave the date and place of birth of the land owner, and the place from whence he migrated. Some are listed as illustrated, historical, statistical, and geographical, and some show pictures of the early homesteads or farms, and the early settler, with his signature beneath his picture.

Maps may be obtained from almost every government agency. The Government Printing Office issues a catalog of maps—PL 53. For this, write to the Superintendent of Documents, Washington 25, D. C. It is free. These maps sell from 25¢ to 75¢ each. Maps may also be obtained from the General Land Office; The Coast & Geodetic Survey; The National Geographic Society; Public Roads Administration; State Highway Departments; State Conservation Departments, and many other state and national agencies. The county highway department maps often show churches, schools and cemeteries. For Canadian maps, write to The Legal Surveys and Map Service, Ottawa, Ontario, Canada.

It is very helpful to use the $8\frac{1}{2}'' \times 11''$ outline maps in your research. These may be purchased at office supply stores, and sell from 10¢ to 25¢ each. Some have towns printed upon them, and others show only the county boundaries and the county seat. With the latter it is easy to fill in the places of residence of your ancestors, and plot their migrations. In "A Century of Population Growth—1790–1900," published by The Bureau of the Census, Washington, D. C., are maps which show the changes in county lines, 1790–1900. This work is now out of print, but is to be found in most reference libraries.

Newspapers Carrying Genealogical Columns

THE ADVOCATE, MT. STERLING, KENTUCKY, carries a column by Harry Willard Mills, 4805 Twentieth Street, North Arlington 7, Virginia, titled, "*Early Families of Montgomery County.*" (Weekly)

BEAUREGARD NEWS, DE RIDDER, LOUISIANA, carries a weekly local history column titled, "*Parish History.*" (Weekly)

THE BOSTON EVENING TRANSCRIPT published a page of "*Genealogical Queries and Answers*" (1872–1940). The Boston Public Library, Boston 17, Mass., has a complete file. Mr. Richard G. Hensley, Chief Librarian, Reference Department, has answered letters and looked up names in the master index. (Weekly; twice weekly for many years)

CONSERVATION NEWS, JACKSON, MISSISSIPPI, has a genealogical column called "*Your Family,*" which carries queries, and in 1954 was publishing the 1822 tax rolls for Hinds County. Address queries to Mrs. Robert B. Price, 932 North President Street, Jackson, Mississippi.

THE HARTFORD TIMES, HARTFORD, CONNECTICUT, is currently publishing a weekly page of *Genealogical Queries and Answers*. This feature was begun January 27, 1934, and appears in the Saturday edition.

HOBBIES—a monthly magazine, has carried a feature "*At the Sign of the Crest,*" since 1938. This feature is authored by Mrs. Hazel Kraft Eilers, 2522 Thayer Street, Evanston, Illinois.

LODI TIMES, LODI, CALIFORNIA, publishes a genealogical query column called *"An Interview with the Past."* This appears the fourth Thursday of each month.

MACON COUNTY TIMES, LAFAYETTE, TENNESSEE, publishes *"Cal's Column,"* in which Elder Calvin Gregory, editor and publisher of the paper, gives some lengthy accounts of early settlers of the region. The column does not appear in every issue. Subscription $2.50 per year.

THE NORTHWEST SUNDIAL, PORTLAND, OREGON, carries a column written by Barbara Elkins, titled *"Northwest Ramblings—Bits of Lore from Days of Yore."* Portland history.

ROCHESTER, NEW YORK, DEMOCRAT & CHRONICLE, in 1954 carried a column titled *"Your Name Quiz,"* conducted by Ven Pitoni.

SAN ANTONIO LIGHT, SAN ANTONIO, TEXAS, carries a feature called *"Twigs and Trees,"* authored by Mrs. Lucille Stewart Krisch.

THE SUN, HAMMOND, LOUISIANA, carries a feature called *"Family History,"* which gives local information and publishes queries and answers. Subscription $2.50 per year. The first volume *"Hunting Forebears,"* was reprinted and is for sale at $1.50.

THE VIRGINIA GAZETTE, WILLIAMSBURG, VIRGINIA, publishes a weekly genealogical page. The editor is Dorothy Ford Wulfeck, 51 Park Avenue, Naugatuck, Connecticut.

6. PUBLIC AND NON-PUBLIC RECORDS

OWNERSHIP OF RECORDS — OFFICIAL, SEMI-OFFICIAL, AND UN-OFFICIAL RECORDS AS TOOLS IN GENEALOGICAL RESEARCH.

The definition and use of records, as well as the differentiation as to whether a record is to be considered as public or non-public, is regulated by state law, the sources of which are statutes, court decisions, official regulations, and opinions of Attorneys General. As these sources differ in various states, a record may be public in one state and non-public in another.

New Jersey has a statute which defines public records as follows: "any written or printed book, document or paper, map or plan which is the property of the state or of any county or municipality or part thereof, and in or on which any entry has been made or is required to be made by law, or which any officer or employee of the state, or of a county or municipality, has received or is required to receive for filing or recording."

The following states have statutes which define public records: California; Delaware; Idaho; Illinois; Kansas; Louisiana; Maryland; Massachusetts; Montana; New Jersey; North Carolina; Oregon; Tennessee; Texas; Utah.

Florida has a statute which defines the right of inspection of public records as follows: "all state, county, and municipal records shall, at all times, be open for a personal inspection of any citizen of Florida." The states which define a general right of inspection of public records are: Alabama; Arizona; California; Florida; Georgia; Idaho; Illinois; Iowa; Kentucky; Louisiana; Massachusetts; Michigan; Minnesota; Montana; Nebraska; Nevada; New Hampshire; New Mexico;

New York; North Carolina; Oklahoma; Oregon; South Dakota; Utah; Virginia; West Virginia; Wisconsin.

INSPECTION AND USE OF PUBLIC RECORDS IN MICHIGAN, from the compiled laws of Michigan, 1948, Section 750,942 (Penal Code). "Any officer having the custody of any county, city, or township records in this state, who shall when requested fail or neglect to furnish proper and reasonable facilities for the inspection and examination of the records and files in his office and for making memoranda or transcripts therefrom during the usual business hours, which shall not be less than four hours per day, to any person having occasion to make examination of them for any lawful purpose, shall be guilty of a misdemeanor provided that the said custodian of said records and files may make such reasonable rules and regulations with reference to the inspection and examination of them as shall be necessary for the protection of said records and files and to prevent interference with the regular discharge of the duties of such officer."

OWNERSHIP: Following the meeting of the Michigan Historical Commission in June 1942, the following letter and enclosure were released: To the Heads of all State Departments, Boards, Commissions, and Institutions: In regard to old records of state offices and in connection with the duty of the Michigan Historical Commission under Section 5 of Act No. 271, Public Acts of 1913 (Section 8118 Compiled Laws of 1929) to collect all such records, documents, files, books and papers as are not less than 30 years old and valuable for historical purposes, and to retain the same in its custody and possession for use of the public, we are forwarding to you an opinion from the Attorney General's office relative thereto, with assurance that we shall be pleased to examine for historical value such records as may be referred to the historical commission for such purpose. Very Respectfully, The Michigan Historical Commission, George N. Fuller, Secretary.

OPINION FROM THE OFFICE OF THE ATTORNEY GENERAL: This will acknowledge receipt of your letter of March 24, 1942, in which you ask the following question: "What is the extent of legal power which a public officer, state or local, may exercise, to keep or destroy public documents which originate in his office, or which come into his office from any public source over which the state has jurisdiction?"

It is a recognized rule of law that public records or public documents being property of the state, or some political subdivision thereof, can only voluntarily be removed from the place where by law they are designated to be kept, or may be voluntarily mutilated or destroyed only when such removal, mutilation or destruction is authorized by the same authority which in the first instance required said record to be made and kept. This rule is well stated in 23 ruling Case Law, p. 169, which reads: "as heretofore stated, public records and documents are the property of the state and not of the individual who happens, at the moment, to have them in his possession; and when they are deposited in the place designated for them by law, there they must remain, and can be removed only under authority of an act of the legislature and in the manner and for the purpose designated by law. The custodian of a public record cannot deface it or give it up without authority from the same source which required it to be made."

The rule above stated was recognized by the legislature of the State of Michigan by enacting Act 6, Public Acts of Michigan, 1851, which Act, as amended being section 17018, compiled laws of 1929, provides as follows: "All books, papers or records, belonging or in anywise appertaining to the offices of clerk, treasurer, register of deeds, or judge of probate of the several counties, and also all books, papers and records belonging or in anywise appertaining to the offices of the several townships and school district officers of this state, are hereby declared to be public property, belonging to the people of the State of Michigan, to be used and preserved by and under the direction of said officers, and be by them preserved during their continuance in office.

"Any person who shall wilfully carry away, mutilate or destroy any such books, papers, records or any part of the same, and any person who shall retain and continue to hold the possession of any books, papers or records or parts thereof belonging to the aforesaid offices of clerk, treasurer, register of deeds, or judge of probate, of the several counties, or to the offices of the several township and school district officers of this state, and shall refuse to deliver up said books, papers, records, or parts thereof, to the proper officer having charge of the office to which the said books, papers or records belong, upon demand being made by such officer, shall be guilty of a misdemeanor, punishable by imprisonment in the state prison not more than two (2) years or by a fine of not more than one thousand ($1,000) dollars."

From the foregoing it is apparent that where a record is one required by law to be kept, or it is necessary that it be kept by a public officer in the discharge of the duty imposed on him by law, or the same is a writing required to be filed in a public office, or is a written memorial of a transaction of a public officer made in the discharge of his duty, the same is a public record and may not be disposed of, mutilated or destroyed without express authorization from the proper legislative body. Very truly yours,

Herbert J. Rushton, Attorney General.
R. Glenn Dunn, Deputy Attorney General.

Public Records as Tools in Genealogical Research

OFFICIAL RECORDS

A. MUNICIPAL, TOWN, AND VILLAGE RECORDS
1. Vital records (births; marriages; deaths)
2. Court records
3. Land records kept in some towns and cities
4. Miscellaneous records

B. COUNTY RECORDS
1. Court records
   a. Criminal (custodian—county clerk)
   b. Civil (custodians, county clerk and register of probate), include actions for possession of property, real and personal; for partition of property; to quiet title; foreclosures; divorces and others.
   c. Probate (custodian—judge of probate)
      1. Wills
      2. Petition for probate of will
      3. Letters testamentary
      4. Petition for letters testamentary
      5. Letters of administration
      6. Petition for letters of administration
      7. Bond of executor or administrator

8. Inventory and appraisement
9. Notice to creditors
10. Miscellaneous affidavits
11. Petitions to determine heirship
12. Decree of distribution
13. Releases signed by heirs
14. Guardianship papers (minors and incompetents)
15. Adoption proceedings
16. Sale of real estate of intestates
17. Antenuptial agreements
18. Delayed birth certificates
19. Marriage waivers
20. Change of names
21. Secret marriages
22. Escheat proceedings

2. Land Records (custodian—register of deeds)
   a. Deeds
   b. Mortgages
   c. Leases
   d. Recorded wills
   e. Contracts pertaining to real property
   f. Powers of attorney
   g. Miscellaneous affidavits
   h. Judgments and decrees affecting real property
   i. Maps and plats

3. Vital Records (custodian—county clerk)
   a. Birth certificates
   b. Marriage licenses and intentions to marry
   c. Marriage license returns
   d. Marriage records
   e. Death certificates

4. Miscellaneous records
   a. Assessment and tax rolls
   b. Register of voters
   c. Miscellaneous records pertaining to land
   d. Coroner's files
   e. Minutes of Board of Supervisor's meetings
   f. Naturalization records

C. STATE AND TERRITORIAL RECORDS
1. Territorial Papers (in process of publication)
2. State Papers (published for many states)
3. State Archives (published and unpublished)
4. Appellate Court Papers and File
5. Secretary of State (custodian of many early records)
6. State Census Records
7. Vital records (births; marriages; deaths)

D. FEDERAL RECORDS
1. Census: (in National Archives)
   a. 1790 published; available in most libraries
   b. 1800 to 1880 in National Archives; microfilm copies in many libraries
   c. 1890 destroyed; 1900 and later in Census Bureau
2. Land Records
   a. Patents in General Land Office and National Archives
   b. Bounty Land Papers (applications, affidavits, and warrants) in National Archives
3. Court Records
   a. U.S. District Court
   b. Circuit Court of Appeal
   c. U.S. Supreme Court
4. Military Records
   a. Service records all U.S. Wars (National Archives)
   b. Pension applications and files all U.S. wars (National Archives)
   c. General Accounting Office Records (death records of pensioners; now in National Archives)
5. Miscellaneous Records
   a. Shipping and Passenger Lists (National Archives)
   b. Immigration records (Incomplete) (Nat. Archives)
   c. Passport records and applications (1791–1879) (National Archives)

SEMI-OFFICIAL RECORDS

A. CHURCH RECORDS
1. Baptisms

2. Marriages and Banns
3. Burial records
4. Membership rolls
5. Cemetery records
6. Churchwarden's accounts
7. Quaker Meeting Records
    a. Marriages
    b. Burials
    c. Certificates of Removal
    d. Disownments
    e. Manumissions
    f. Sufferings

B. SCHOOL AND COLLEGE RECORDS
    1. Roster and rolls
    2. Biographies

UNOFFICIAL RECORDS

A. FAMILY RECORDS
    1. Bible and other family records
    2. Diaries and journals
    3. Letters
    4. Samplers and autograph albums
    5. Photographs
    6. Engraved jewelry and silverware
    7. Newspaper clippings
    8. Unprobated wills
    9. Lodge records
    10. Insurance papers
    11. Social Security papers
    12. Employment records
    13. Items from genealogical columns of newspapers
    14. Memory books
    15. Inscriptions in gift books

7. RESEARCH IN COUNTY RECORDS

RESEARCH IN COUNTY RECORDS—VITAL RECORDS—THEIR USE AND VALUE—WHERE AND HOW TO OBTAIN THEM—HOW TO PROVE YOU WERE BORN IF YOUR BIRTH IS NOT ON RECORD.

Now it is time to visit the courthouse and compare the facts gathered from family sources and printed material in the libraries, with official records. If the information sought is in a distant courthouse it will be necessary to write to the official in charge. Among the records that should be searched for family history are vital records, land records, probate, tax and poll lists, census and naturalization records.

Vital Records

Vital records are records of births, marriages and deaths. Laws requiring the registration of vital records were not enacted and put into effect until many years after a state was settled, nor were they uniform. Only eighteen states registered vital records before 1900.

1779—Vermont
1842—Massachusetts
1843– New Jersey
1852—Connecticut
1853—Hawaii; Rhode Island;
    Virginia
1861—Delaware
1865—Florida

1867—Michigan
1880—Arizona; Iowa; New
    Hampshire; New York
1887—Illinois
1892—Maine
1893—North Dakota
1898—Maryland

Fortunately, early American pioneers were a religious people, and, for the most part, kept good church records which pre-date vital re-

cords by many years. Vital records for several New England States
have been published to 1850. See Vital Records in Bibliography,
Chapter 28. There are many inaccuracies in early vital records.
When registration laws were first enacted there were no State Boards
of Health to make it mandatory for the attending physician or the
hospital to report the birth within a stated time, as is done today.
There were few hospitals, most births occurred at home, and the attending physician was too busy to report them.

In Michigan, for example, the State Registration Law was enacted
in 1867, but until the early 1900's births were reported but once a
year. This information was gathered by the City or Township Tax
Assessor who was paid five cents per head for all births reported. He
naturally inquired at each residence he visited about any children
born within the year, and consequently many infants who were born
in other states, and had migrated with their parents to Michigan,
during their first year, were erroneously reported as having been born
here; these people may have birth records in two states.

Early marriage records were collected in the same way. In Territorial days the officiating clergyman or Justice of the Peace stopped
in the courthouse and reported the marriage at his convenience. Many
were never reported. The law requires that a death certificate be
filled in before a burial permit is granted. The family history on the
death certificate, such as the birthplace and date of the deceased, his
parents' names including maiden name of mother, and their birth-
places, is often inaccurate unless it is given by a member of the family
who knows the family history.

To obtain a certified copy of a birth, death, marriage, or divorce
record in the United States and Territories, proceed as follows: For
births and deaths of United States citizens occurring within the
boundaries of the Continental United States or its Territories, write
or go to the vital statistics office of the State or Territory where the
event occurred, the addresses of which follow.

In making application for a birth or death certificate, give the following information:

(1) FULL NAME of person whose birth or death certificate is sought.
(2) DATE on which birth or death occurred; if unknown, state
     approximate date.
(3) PLACE at which birth or death occurred.

(4) SEX AND RACE of person who was born or who died.

(5) PARENTS' NAMES (especially for birth certificates, including maiden name of mother).

Citizens of the United States born outside of the limits of its states, territories or possessions, may obtain copies of their birth records in the following ways:

(1) By sending a request to the official vital statistics office of the county where the birth occurred.

(2) By requesting the Passport Office, Department of State, Washington 25, D.C., to issue a copy of the report filed by the United States Consul in the country of birth.

(3) By obtaining, if person is judged to have citizenship status, a "Certificate of Citizenship," from the Immigration and Naturalization Service, Department of Justice, Washington 25, D.C., in case the birth was not reported to the United States Consul in the country of birth.

(4) For births of persons in the United States Army and Air Force hospitals, the Commanding Officer, Kansas City Records Center, 601 Hardesty Avenue, Kansas City 24, Missouri, will, upon request and when it is not otherwise feasible to obtain a record of the birth, issue a statement of birth which will suffice for many purposes.

The record of the death of a United States citizen who died in a foreign country may be obtained in one of two ways:

(1) Each country has its own registration system, and a copy of the death certificate issued by the country in which the death occurred may be obtained by writing to the vital statistics registration office in that country.

(2) United States Consular Officers obtain information on deaths of all United States citizens which occur in their districts. To obtain copies of death records prepared overseas for civilians and merchant seamen, write to the Office of Special Consular Services, Department of State, Washington 25, D.C.

For deaths which occurred on U.S. Army installations (both military and civilian), write to the Adjutant General, Department of the Army, Washington 25, D.C. For deaths which occurred on U.S. Naval installations (including Coast Guard and Marine Corps person-

nel) write to the Bureau of Medicine and Surgery, Department of the
Navy, Washington 25, D.C.

MARRIAGE RECORDS. In 38 states and some of the larger cities, marriage
records are filed in a central registry. In writing for a certified copy
of a marriage record, the following information is necessary in order
to correctly identify the record:

(1) Full name of bride and groom (including nicknames).
(2) Residence addresses at time of marriage.
(3) Ages at time of marriage (or dates of birth).
(4) Places of birth (state or foreign country).
(5) Date and place of marriage.

DIVORCE RECORDS. In 33 states and 4 independent registration areas,
divorce records are filed in a central registry. When writing for a
certified copy of a divorce record, include the following information,
in order to identify the correct record:

(1) Full names of husband and wife (including nicknames)
(2) Present residence address
(3) Former addresses (as in court records)
(4) Ages at time of divorce (or dates of birth)
(5) Places of birth (state or foreign country)
(6) Date and place of divorce
(7) Type of final decree

Vital Records of the United States
Its Territories and Possessions

The following information was compiled from official sources. Fees
are stated as given, but are always subject to change.

ALABAMA

CENTRAL REGISTRY	State Department of Health, Bureau of Vital Statistics, Montgomery 4, Alabama.
BIRTHS AND DEATHS	Records since 1908. Fee $.50 payable to the State Registrar of Vital Statistics, No records prior to 1908 except those established by delayed certificate.
MARRIAGES	In central registrary since August 1936. Fee

$.50. Prior to August 1936, write Probate Judge of county where license was issued. Fee $.75.

DIVORCES
Write Clerk or Register of Courts of Equity in county where divorce was granted. Fee $1.00.

ALASKA

CENTRAL REGISTRY
Bureau of Vital Statistics, Alaska Department of Health, Fourth and Main Streets, Juneau, Alaska.

BIRTHS AND DEATHS
In central office since 1913. Fee $2.00. Some records in churches and towns which date back to the early 1800's.

MARRIAGES
Central Registry. Fee $2.00.

DIVORCES
Central Registry since 1950. Fee $2.00. If not there, write to the Clerk of the U.S. District Court, Judicial Division where the divorce was granted; First Division—Juneau; Second Division—Nome; Third Division—Anchorage; Fourth Division—Fairbanks.

AMERICAN SAMOA

CENTRAL REGISTRY
Clerk of High Court, Pago Pago, American Samoa.

BIRTHS AND DEATHS
Central Registry. Fee $.50.

MARRIAGES
Central Registry. Fee $.50.

DIVORCES
Central Registry. Fee $.50.

ARIZONA

CENTRAL REGISTRY
State Department of Health, Division of Records and Statistics, Phoenix 18, Arizona.

BIRTHS AND DEATHS
Central Registry since July 1, 1909. Some counties hold records back to 1887. These were transferred to the state office in 1935. Fee $1.00.

MARRIAGES
Write to Clerk of Superior Court where license was issued. Fee varies with county.

DIVORCES
Write to Clerk of Superior Court where divorce was granted. Fee varies.

ARKANSAS

CENTRAL REGISTRY	Bureau of Vital Statistics, State Board of Health, Little Rock, Arkansas.
BIRTHS AND DEATHS	Central Registry has records from February 1, 1914. For records previous to that date, in Little Rock, Fort Smith or Texarkana, write City Clerk where birth or death occurred; for other places the County Clerk. Fee $1.00.
MARRIAGES	Write County Clerk where license was issued. Fee $1.00. Copy of partial record available since 1917 at Central Registry. Fee $.50.
DIVORCES	Write Clerk of County or Chancery Court in county where divorce was granted. Fee varies. Since 1923 copy of partial record available from Central Registry. Fee $1.00.

CALIFORNIA

CENTRAL REGISTRY	Bureau of Records & Statistics, State Department of Public Health, 631 J Street, Sacramento 14, California.
BIRTHS AND DEATHS	Central Registry since July 1, 1905. Some cities and counties have records dating back to 1857. If birth or death occurred prior to 1905, write to city health officer if born in an incorporated municipality, otherwise to the County Recorder. Fee $1.00.
MARRIAGES	Central Registry. Fee $1.00.
DIVORCES	Write Clerk of Superior Court in county where divorce was granted. Fee varies with county.

CANAL ZONE

CENTRAL REGISTRY	Statistical Clerk, Vital Statistics Unit, Administration Branch, Balboa Heights, Canal Zone.
BIRTHS AND DEATHS	Central Registry since May 1904. Fee $1.00.
MARRIAGES	United States District Court for the District of the Canal Zone; Deputy Clerk of Court, Cristobal, Canal Zone; or Clerk of Court, Balboa Heights, Canal Zone. Fee $1.00.

DIVORCES	Same as marriages. Fee $1.00 minimum.

COLORADO

CENTRAL REGISTRY	State Department of Public Health, Records and Statistics Section, State Office Bldg., Denver 2, Colorado.
BIRTHS AND DEATHS	Central Registry has records since 1907. Fee $2.00. For records prior to 1907, write local Registrar of Vital Statistics at county seat or town of birth.
MARRIAGES	Write County Clerk of county where license was issued. Fee varies.
DIVORCES	Write Clerk of District Court or Clerk of County Court in county where divorce was granted. Fee varies.

CONNECTICUT

CENTRAL REGISTRY	Bureau of Vital Statistics, State Department of Health, 165 Capitol Avenue, Hartford 15, Connecticut.
BIRTHS AND DEATHS	Central Registry has records since July 1, 1897. For records prior to that date write to the Registrar of Vital Statistics of the town or city where the birth or death occurred. Fee $1.00.
MARRIAGES	Central Registry since July 1, 1897. Previous to that date write Registrar of Vital Statistics in town where license was issued. Fee $1.00.
DIVORCES	Write Clerk of Superior Court in county where divorce was granted. Fee $3.00.

DELAWARE

CENTRAL REGISTRY	Division of Vital Statistics, State Board of Health, Dover, Delaware.
BIRTHS AND DEATHS	Central Registry has records since 1861, except for a period of 1863 to 1881. Fee $2.00.
MARRIAGES	Central Registry. Fee $2.00.
DIVORCES	Write Prothonotary of County where divorce was granted. Fee $1.00.

DISTRICT OF COLUMBIA

CENTRAL REGISTRY	Vital Statistics Section, Department of Public

	Health, District of Columbia, 100 Indiana Avenue, N.W., Washington 1, D.C.
BIRTHS AND DEATHS	Central Registry has records since 1871. Fee $.50.
MARRIAGES	Marriage License Bureau, United States District Court, Washington 1, D.C. Fee $1.00.
DIVORCES	Clerk, United States District Court, Washington 1, D.C. Fee varies.

FLORIDA

CENTRAL REGISTRY	Bureau of Vital Statistics, State Board of Health, P.O. Box 10, Jacksonville 1, Florida.
BIRTHS AND DEATHS	Central Registry has records beginning January 1, 1917, with some dating back to 1865. Fee $1.00.
MARRIAGES	Central Registry has records since 1927. Fee $1.00. If year is unknown, fee ranges from a minimum of $1.00 for each calendar year to be searched, to a maximum of $10.00.
DIVORCES	Same as marriages. Prior to 1927, write Clerk of Circuit Court in county where divorce was granted.

GEORGIA

CENTRAL REGISTRY	Division of Vital Statistics, State Department of Public Health, 1 Hunter St., S.W., Atlanta 3, Georgia.
BIRTHS AND DEATHS	Central Registry has records since January 1, 1919. For records prior to that date, in Savannah and Atlanta, write City Health Office. Fee $1.00. For delayed certificates write Court of Ordinary.
MARRIAGES	Write County Ordinary of county where license was issued. Fee $2.00.
DIVORCES	Write Clerk of Superior Court in county where divorce was granted. Fee varies.

GUAM

CENTRAL REGISTRY	Office of Vital Statistics, Division of Public Health, Division of Medical Services, Government of Guam, Agana, Guam.
BIRTHS AND DEATHS	Central Registry.

MARRIAGES Central Registry. Fee $.50.
DIVORCES Write Clerk, Island Court of Guam, Agana, Guam. Fee varies.

HAWAII

CENTRAL REGISTRY Bureau of Health Statistics, Department of Health, Kapuaiwa Bldg., Honolulu, Hawaii.

BIRTHS AND DEATHS Central Registry has records since 1853. No records elsewhere. Also "Certificates of Hawaiian Births" (in effect Delayed Certificates) are on file in office of Secretary of Hawaii. Fee $1.50.

MARRIAGES In Central Registry since 1853. Fee $1.50.

DIVORCES Central Registry since July 1, 1951. Prior to that date write Circuit Court of county where divorce was granted. Fee varies.

IDAHO

CENTRAL REGISTRY Division of Vital Statistics, State Department of Public Health, Boise, Idaho.

BIRTHS AND DEATHS Central Registry has records since 1911. For records from 1907 to 1911, write County Recorder in county where birth or death occurred. Fee $.50.

MARRIAGES Write County Recorder of county where license was issued. Fee $1.00.

DIVORCES Write County Recorder. Fee varies.

ILLINOIS

CENTRAL REGISTRY Bureau of Statistics & Records, Illinois Department of Public Health, Springfield, or County Clerk of county where birth or death occurred, or Local Registrar in city where birth or death occurred.

BIRTHS AND DEATHS Central Registry has records since July 1, 1915. County Clerks have copies of records filed since July 1, 1915, and original records previous to that date. Local Registrars in cities have records since 1916. Delayed birth certificates may be secured from the County Clerk. Fee $1.00.

MARRIAGES	County Clerk of county where license was issued. Fee $1.00.
DIVORCES	Clerk of Court in which divorce was granted. Courts having jurisdiction are the Circuit Court of each county, the Superior Court of Cook County, and certain city courts. Fee varies.

INDIANA

CENTRAL REGISTRY	Division of Vital Records, State Board of Health, 1330 W. Michigan St., Indianapolis 7, Indiana.
BIRTHS AND DEATHS	Central Registry has records since October 1, 1907. For records prior to that date, write local health officers of the city or county. Fee $1.00.
MARRIAGES	Clerk of Circuit Court or Clerk of Superior Court in county where license was issued. Fee $1.00.
DIVORCES	County Clerk of county where divorce was granted. Fee varies.

IOWA

CENTRAL REGISTRY	Division of Vital Statistics, State Department of Health, Des Moines 19, Iowa.
BIRTHS AND DEATHS	Central Registry has records since July 1, 1880. Fee $1.00.
MARRIAGES	Central Registry since July 1, 1880. Fee $1.00.
DIVORCES	Central Registry since July 1, 1880. Fee $1.00.

KANSAS

CENTRAL REGISTRY	Division of Vital Statistics, State Board of Health, Topeka, Kansas.
BIRTHS AND DEATHS	Central Registry since July 1, 1911. For records previous to that date, write county clerk. Fee $1.00.
MARRIAGES	Central Registry since May 1913. Fee $1.00.
DIVORCES	Central Registry since May 1913. Fee $1.00.

KENTUCKY

CENTRAL REGISTRY	Bureau of Records & Statistics, State De-

partment of Health, 620 South Third St., Louisville 2, Kentucky.

BIRTHS AND DEATHS
Central Registry since January 1, 1911, and for Louisville, earlier. For Covington records before 1911, write City Health Department. Fee $1.00.

MARRIAGES
Clerk of county court where license was issued since July 1, 1958. Prior to that date, write Central Registry. Fee varies.

DIVORCES
Clerk of District Court, or Clerk of Circuit Court where divorce was granted. Since July 1, 1958 in Central Registry. Fee varies.

LOUISIANA (EXCEPT NEW ORLEANS)

CENTRAL REGISTRY
Division of Public Health Statistics, State Department of Health, Civil Courts Bldg., New Orleans 7, Louisiana.

BIRTHS AND DEATHS
Central Registry has records since July 1, 1914. For records previous to that time, write Parish Clerk of the parish where the birth or death occurred. For Shreveport records before 1914, write Caddo Shreveport Health Unit, Shreveport, La. Fee $1.00.

MARRIAGES
Write Clerk of Court in parish where license was issued. Fee varies.

DIVORCES
Write Clerk of Court in parish where divorce was granted. Fee varies.

LOUISIANA (NEW ORLEANS)

CENTRAL REGISTRY
Bureau of Vital Statistics, City Board of Health, 1903, City Hall, Civic Center, New Orleans 12, Lousiana.

BIRTHS AND DEATHS
Central Registry has records since 1790. Fee $1.00.

MARRIAGES
Central Registry. Fee $1.00.

DIVORCES
Clerk of Parish Court. Fee $1.00.

MAINE

CENTRAL REGISTRY
Division of Vital Statistics, State Department of Health, Augusta, Maine.

BIRTHS AND DEATHS
Central Registry has records since 1892. For

earlier records write Town Clerk where birth or death occurred.

MARRIAGES   Central Registry since 1892. Fee $1.00.

DIVORCES   Clerk of Superior Court in the county where divorce wasg ranted. Letter verifying place and date available from Central Registry. Fee $1.00.

MARYLAND (EXCEPT BALTIMORE CITY)

CENTRAL REGISTRY   Division of Vital Records & Statistics, State Department of Health, 2411 North Charles St., Baltimore 18, Maryland.

BIRTHS AND DEATH   Central Registry has records since 1898. Fee $1.00.

MARRIAGES   Central Registry has records since June 1, 1951. For records prior to that date, write Clerk of Circuit Court in the county where the license was issued. Fee $1.00.

DIVORCES   Clerk of Circuit Court in the county where divorce was granted. Fee $1.25.

MARYLAND (CITY OF BALTIMORE)

CENTRAL REGISTRY   Bureau of Vital Records, City Health Department, Municipal Building, Baltimore 3, Maryland.

BIRTHS AND DEATHS   Central Bureau has records since 1775. Fee $1.00.

MARRIAGES   Write Clerk of Court of Common Pleas, Baltimore, Md. Fee varies.

DIVORCES   Write Clerk of Circuit Court of Baltimore City, or Clerk of the Circuit Court No. 2, Baltimore, Maryland. Fee varies.

MASSACHUSETTS (EXCEPT BOSTON)

CENTRAL REGISTRY   Division of Vital Statistics, 272 State House, Boston 33, Massachusetts.

BIRTHS AND DEATHS   Central Registry has records since 1850. For records prior to 1850, write clerk in city or town where birth or death occurred. Fee $.50.

MARRIAGES   Central Registry or City or Town Clerk. Fee $.50.

DIVORCES   Clerk of Superior Court or Register of Probate in county where divorce was granted. Fee varies.

MASSACHUSETTS (CITY OF BOSTON)

CENTRAL REGISTRY   City Registrar, Registry Division, Room 1004, City Hall Annex, Boston 8, Mass.

BIRTHS AND DEATHS   City Registrar has records since 1639. Fee $1.00.

MARRIAGES   City Registrar. Fee $1.00.

DIVORCES   Write Clerk of Superior Court or Register of Probate, Boston, Mass. Regular certificate fee $.50; if certificate is signed in longhand, fee $.90.

MICHIGAN

CENTRAL REGISTRY   Vital Records Section, State Department of Health, Old DeWitt Road, Lansing 4, Michigan.

BIRTHS AND DEATHS   Central Registry since 1867. Copies of records since 1647 may also be obtained from county clerk. Village and city clerks have records since 1906. Detroit records may be obtained from City Health Department, for births occurring since 1893, and deaths since 1797. Fee $1.00.

MARRIAGES   Central Registry or County Clerk since 1867. Fee $1.00.

DIVORCES   Central Registry or County Clerk, since 1867. Fee $1.00.

MINNESOTA

CENTRAL REGISTRY   Section of Vital Statistics, State Department of Health, 469 State Office Bldg., St. Paul 1, Minnesota.

BIRTHS AND DEATHS   Central Registry has records since 1900. Copies may be obtained from Clerk of District Court of county. Some counties have records from 1870. Minneapolis and St. Paul records date back to 1865. For St. Paul,

Minneapolis, and Duluth, write City Health
Officer. Fee $1.00.

MARRIAGES   Clerk of District Court in county where
license was issued. Fee varies.

DIVORCES   Clerk of District Court where divorce was
granted.

MISSISSIPPI

CENTRAL REGISTRY   Division of Vital Statistics, State Board of
Health, P.O. Box 1700, Jackson 5, Missis-
sippi.

BIRTHS AND DEATHS   Central Registry has records since November
1, 1912. Fee $1.00.

MARRIAGES   Circuit Court of the county where the license
was issued. Since 1926 name of county may
be obtained from Central Registry. Fee $1.00.

DIVORCES   Chancery Clerk of county where divorce was
granted. Since 1926 name of county may be
obtained from Central Registry. Fee $1.00.

MISSOURI (EXCEPT ST. LOUIS)

CENTRAL REGISTRY   Bureau of Vital Statistics, State Department
of Public Health & Welfare, Jefferson City,
Missouri.

BIRTHS AND DEATHS   Central Registry has records since 1910. For
births 1863–1882, write to Recorder of
Deeds, county of birth; for births 1883–1909,
write County Clerk in county of birth. Fee
$.50. For Kansas City write City Health
Department. Fee $1.00.

MARRIAGES   Recorder of Deeds of county where license
was issued. Since 1947 name of county may
be obtained, without charge from Central
Registry. Fee varies.

DIVORCES   Clerk of Circuit Court of county where divorce was granted. Fee varies.

MISSOURI (ST. LOUIS)

CENTRAL REGISTRY   St. Louis Bureau of Vital Statistics, 10 Municipal Court Bldg., St. Louis, Missouri.

BIRTHS AND DEATHS	Central Registry prior to 1910.
MARRIAGES	Recorder of Deeds, City Hall, St. Louis 3, Missouri. Fee $1.50.
DIVORCES	Since 1821 Clerk of Civil Court, Civil Courts Bldg., St. Louis 2, Missouri. Fee varies.

MONTANA

CENTRAL REGISTRY	Registrar of Vital Statistics, State Board of Health, Helena, Montana.
BIRTHS AND DEATHS	Central Registry has records since 1907. Fee $1.00.
MARRIAGES	Clerk of District Court in county where license was issued. Since 1943 name of county may be obtained from Central Registry. Fee $1.00.
DIVORCES	Clerk of District Court in county where divorce was granted. Since 1943 name of county may be obtained from Central Registry. Fee varies.

NEBRASKA

CENTRAL REGISTRY	Bureau of Vital Statistics, State Department of Health, State Capitol, Lincoln 9, Nebraska.
BIRTHS AND DEATHS	Central Registry has records since 1905. If record is not filed write County Clerk of the county where the birth or death occurred. Fee $1.00.
MARRIAGES	Central Registry since 1909. Fee $1.00.
DIVORCES	Central Registry since 1909. Fee $1.00; prior to 1909 Clerk of District Court where divorce was granted. (For some counties). Fee varies.

NEVADA

| CENTRAL REGISTRY | Division of Vital Statistics, State Department of Health, Carson City, Nevada. |
| BIRTHS AND DEATHS | Central Registry has records since July 1, 1911. Prior to that date write County Recorder of the county in which the birth or death occurred. Some counties have records from 1887. Fee $1.00. |

MARRIAGES	Write County Recorder of the county where the license was issued. Fee varies.
DIVORCES	Write County Clerk of the county where the divorce was granted. Fee varies.

NEW HAMPSHIRE

CENTRAL REGISTRY	Division of Vital Statistics, State Department of Health, 61 S. Spring Street, Concord, New Hampshire.
BIRTHS AND DEATHS	Central Registry and city or town clerks from 1640.
MARRIAGES	Central Registry or city or town clerk where license was issued.
DIVORCES	Since 1881 in Central Registry or Clerk of the Superior Court which issued the decree.
FEES	$.50 for minimum search which includes a copy if record is found.

NEW JERSEY

CENTRAL REGISTRY	State Registrar of Vital Statistics, State Department of Health, Trenton 7, New Jersey.
BIRTHS AND DEATHS	Central Registry has records since 1848. Fee $1.00.
MARRIAGES	Central Registry. Fee $1.00.
DIVORCES	Superior Court, Chancery Division, State House, Trenton, New Jersey. Fee $2.00.

NEW MEXICO

CENTRAL REGISTRY	Division of Vital Statistics, State Department of Public Health, P.O. Box 711, Santa Fe, New Mexico.
BIRTHS AND DEATHS	Central Registry has records since January 1, 1920. (A few from 1907). Fee $1.00.
MARRIAGES	Write County Clerk of the county where the marriage was performed. Fee varies.
DIVORCES	Write Clerk of the District Court in the county where divorce was granted. Fee varies.

NEW YORK (EXCEPT NEW YORK CITY)

CENTRAL REGISTRY	Office of Vital Statistics, State Department of Health, Albany 1, New York.

BIRTHS AND DEATHS — Central Registry has records since 1880. If the birth or death occurred prior to 1914, in Albany, Buffalo, or Yonkers, or before 1880 in any other city, write to the Registrar of Vital Statistics in the city where the birth or death occurred. For rest of state, except New York City, write to Central Registry. Fee $2.00.

MARRIAGES — Central Registry has records from 1880 to 1907 and since May 1915. If the marriage occurred in Albany or Buffalo, apply to the city clerk, and if in Yonkers, to the Registrar of Vital Statistics. Fee $2.00. From 1908 to April 1915, apply to the county clerk in the county where the license was issued. Fee varies.

DIVORCES — Write County Clerk of the county where the divorce was granted. Fee varies.

NEW YORK (NEW YORK CITY)

CENTRAL REGISTRY — Bureau of Records & Statistics, City Department of Health, 125 Worth Street, New York 13, New York.

BIRTHS AND DEATHS — Records on file since 1847. Records on file for Old City of New York, which was made up of the present Borough of Manhattan, and part of the present Borough of the Bronx. Records of the Boroughs of Queens and Richmond prior to 1898, and records of other areas prior to the annexation of those areas to the city, are on file with the State Department of Health. Fee $1.00.

MARRIAGES — Records on file from 1847 to 1865 at the Municipal Archives & Records Retention Center, New York Public Library, 238 William Street, New York 30, New York. Certified copies not issued. From 1866 to 1907 records are at City Health Department in the Borough where the marriage was performed. Fee $1.00 Bronx Borough—1826 Arthur Ave., Bronx 57, New York, Brooklyn

Borough—295 Flatbush Avenue Extension, Brooklyn 1, New York.

Manhattan Borough—125 Worth St., New York 13, N.Y. Queens Borough—90-37 Parsons Blvd., Jamaica 32, New York.

Richmond Borough—51 Stuyvesant Place, St. George, Staten Island 1, New York.

For records since January 1, 1908, write to the City Clerk in Borough where license was issued. Fee $3.06. $1.00 is payable to the City Clerk; $2.06 is payable to the County Clerk; both fees should be sent to the City Clerk. Depositories of these records are as follows:

Bronx Borough, Old Borough Hall, 177th., at 3rd., New York 57, New York.

Brooklyn Borough, Municipal Bldg., Brooklyn 1, N.Y. Manhattan Borough, Municipal Bldg., New York 7, N.Y. Queens Borough, Sutphin Blvd., Jamaica 35, N.Y. Richmond Borough, Borough Hall, St. George, Staten Island 1, New York.

DIVORCES Write County Clerk of the county where the divorce was granted. Fee varies.

NORTH CAROLINA

CENTRAL REGISTRY Public Health Statistics Section, State Board of Health, P.O. Box 2091, Raleigh, North Carolina.

BIRTHS AND DEATHS Central Registry has records since October 1, 1913. For records prior to that date in cities, write City Board of Health; in counties write Register of Deeds. Fee $1.00.

MARRIAGES Write Register of Deeds of county where marriage was performed. Fee varies.

DIVORCES In Central Registry since January 1, 1958. Fee $1.00. Prior to 1958 write Clerk of Superior Court in county where divorce was granted. Fee varies.

NORTH DAKOTA

CENTRAL REGISTRY Division of Vital Statistics, State Department of Health, Bismarck, North Dakota.

BIRTHS AND DEATHS · Central Registry has records since 1908 and some records from 1893. Fee $1.00. (There are very few original records for the period of 1895 to 1899. Many delayed certificates dating back to 1870 are on file.)

MARRIAGES · Write County Judge of the county where license was issued. Fee varies.

DIVORCES · Write Clerk of District Court in county where the divorce was granted. Fee varies.

Ohio

CENTRAL REGISTRY · Division of Vital Statistics, State Department of Health, G-20, State Departments Bldg., Columbus 15, Ohio.

BIRTHS AND DEATHS · Central Registry has records since December 20, 1908. Most counties have much earlier records. For records prior to 1908 write Clerk of the Probate Court of the county. For records in Cleveland, Columbus, Toledo, Akron, Cincinnati, Dayton, Canton, or Youngstown, write the City Bureau of Vital Statistics. Fee $1.00.

MARRIAGES · Write Probate Judge of county where license was issued. Fee $.75.

DIVORCES · Write Clerk of Court of Common Pleas in county where divorce was granted. Fee $1.00.

Oklahoma

CENTRAL REGISTRY · Division of Statistics, State Department of Health, 3400 North Eastern, Oklahoma City 5, Oklahoma.

BIRTHS AND DEATHS · Central Registry has records since 1908. Fee $1.00.

MARRIAGES · Write Clerk of Court in county where license was issued. Fee varies.

DIVORCES · Write County Clerk in county where divorce was granted. Fee varies.

Oregon

CENTRAL REGISTRY · Vital Statistics Section, State Board of

Health, 1400 S.W. Fifth Avenue, Portland 1, Oregon.

BIRTHS AND DEATHS Central Registry has records since 1903, except Portland records for the period of 1903 through 1915, which are in the Portland City Health Department.

MARRIAGES Central Registry and the County Clerk of the county where marriage was performed have records since 1907. Records prior to 1907 are in the office of the County Clerk of the county in which the marriage was performed. Fee $2.00.

DIVORCES Central Registry since 1925; prior to 1925 in office of clerk of the county where divorce was granted. Fee $2.00.

PENNSYLVANIA

CENTRAL REGISTRY Bureau of Statistics & Records, State Department of Health, South Office Bldg., Harrisburg, Pennsylvania.

BIRTHS AND DEATHS Central Registry since January 1, 1906; Clerk of the Orphan's Court, county where birth or death occurred, 1893–1906. Some cities had municipal registration prior to 1906. Fee $1.00.

MARRIAGES Office of Register & Recorder in the county where the license was issued. Fee $1.00.

DIVORCES Prothonotary of county in which divorce was granted. Fee varies.

PUERTO RICO

CENTRAL REGISTRY Bureau of Registry & Demographic Statistics, Department of Health, San Juan, Puerto Rico.

BIRTHS AND DEATHS Central Office has records since July 22, 1931. For records prior to that date, write the local registrar of the municipality (The Registrador Demographico). Fee $.50.

MARRIAGES Central Registry. Fee $.50.

DIVORCES Corresponding Superior Court where divorce was granted. Fee $.60.

RHODE ISLAND

CENTRAL REGISTRY
Division of Vital Statistics, State Department of Health, State Office Bldg., Providence 2, R.I.

BIRTHS AND DEATHS
Central Registry has records since 1852. For records prior to that date write the Town Clerk.

MARRIAGES
Central Registry or Clerk of the City or Town where marriage was performed. Fee $.50.

DIVORCES
Clerk of Superior Court in county where divorce was granted. Fee varies.

SOUTH CAROLINA

CENTRAL REGISTRY
Bureau of Vital Statistics, State Board of Health, State Office Bldg., Columbia 1, South Carolina.

BIRTHS AND DEATHS
Central Registry has records since January 1, 1915. For records prior to that date in the City of Charleston, write Central Registry for records of deaths from 1821, and for records of births from 1877. Write to the Clerk of the Court of Charleston County for records of births and deaths in the county prior to 1915. For records prior to 1915 in any other part of the state, write to the Clerk of the Court in the county where birth or death occurred. In Berkley, Lexington and Sumter counties, the County Health Department has replaced the Clerk of Court. For records of Spartanburg, write to the Director of Vital Statistics and Special Auditor for Spartanburg County. Fee $1.00.

MARRIAGES
Central Registry since July 1, 1950. From July 1, 1911 to July 1, 1950, write Probate Judge of county where license was issued. No records prior to 1911. Fee $1.00.

DIVORCES
Clerk of Court of County where petition was filed. Fee varies.

SOUTH DAKOTA

CENTRAL REGISTRY   Division of Public Health Statistics, State
                    Department of Health, Capitol Bldg., Pierre,
                    South Dakota.

BIRTHS AND DEATHS   Central Registry has records since July 1,
                    1905; also have access to some earlier re-
                    cords.

MARRIAGES   Central Registry or Clerk of Court in county
                    where marriage was performed. Fee $1.00.

DIVORCES   Central Registry or Clerk of Court in county
                    where divorce was granted.

TENNESSEE

CENTRAL REGISTRY   Division of Vital Statistics, State Department
                    of Public Health, Cordell Hull Office Bldg.,
                    Nashville 3, Tennessee.

BIRTHS AND DEATHS   Central Registry has records since January 1,
                    1914. For records of Nashville, Chattanooga,
                    Knoxville or Memphis, write to the City
                    Health Department. A fee of $1.00 is charged
                    for search and if record is found, one copy
                    is issued without additional cost.

MARRIAGES   Central Registry since July 1945. Fee $1.00;
                    prior to July 1945, County Court Clerk of
                    county where license was issued. Fee $.50.

DIVORCES   Since July 1945 in Central Registry. Fee
                    $1.00. Previous to July 1945, Clerk of Court
                    where granted. Fee varies.

TEXAS

CENTRAL REGISTRY   Bureau of Vital Statistics, State Department
                    of Health, Austin 1, Texas.

BIRTHS AND DEATHS   Central Registry has records since 1903; for
                    records prior to 1903, write County Clerk or,
                    in cities of more than 2500, write City Clerk.
                    Fee $1.00.

MARRIAGES   County Clerk of county where license was
                    issued. Fee varies.

DIVORCES   Clerk of District Court in county where
                    divorce was granted. Fee varies.

TRUST TERRITORY OF THE PACIFIC ISLANDS

MARRIAGES	Clerk of Court in district where marriage occurred. Fee $.25.
DIVORCES	Records since early 1950; Clerk of Court in District where divorce was granted. Fee varies.

UTAH

CENTRAL REGISTRY	Division of Vital Statistics, State Department of Health, Salt Lake City, Utah.
BIRTHS AND DEATHS	Central Registry has records since 1905. Records from 1890 through 1904 in Salt Lake City or Ogden. Write to City Board of Health. For records elsewhere in the State, from 1898 to 1904, write the county clerk. Fee $1.00.
MARRIAGES	County Clerk of county where license was issued.
DIVORCES	Clerk of District Court in county where divorce was granted. Fee varies for both marriages and divorces.

VERMONT

CENTRAL REGISTRY	Commissioner of Health, 115 Colchester Avenue, Burlington, Vermont.
BIRTHS AND DEATHS	Secretary of State, Montpelier, Vt.; Town or City Clerk. Some records as early as 1740. Earliest law requiring registrations of births passed in 1779. Fee $.75.
MARRIAGES	Office of Secretary of State, Montpelier, or Clerk of Town or City where license was issued. Fee $.75.
DIVORCES	County Clerk of county where divorce was granted, or Secretary of State. Fee $.75.

VIRGINIA

CENTRAL REGISTRY	Bureau of Vital Statistics, State Department of Health, 1227 West Broad St., Richmond 20, Virginia.
BIRTHS AND DEATHS	Central Registry has records since June 14, 1912, and about 1/3 of the records from 1853

	to 1896. For these records in the larger cities, write the City Health Department. Fee $1.00.
MARRIAGES	Since 1853 in Central Registry. Fee $1.00. Or write Court Clerk of county or city where license was issued. Fee varies.
DIVORCES	Since 1918 in Central Registry. Fee $1.00. Or write Clerk of Court of county or city where divorce was granted. Fee varies.

VIRGIN ISLANDS

CENTRAL REGISTRY	Registrar of Vital Statistics, Charlotte A-malie, St. Thomas, Virgin Islands. (For St. Thomas) Registrar of Vital Statistics, Christiansted, St. Croix, V.I. (For St. Croix)
BIRTHS AND DEATHS	St. Thomas—records of births since July 1, 1906; of deaths since January 1, 1908. Fee $.40 St. Croix—records since 1873. Fee $.40.
MARRIAGES	St. Thomas and St. John—Judge of Police Court, Charlotte Amalie, St. Thomas, Virgin Islands. Fee $.40. St. Croix—Judge of Police Court, Christiansted, St. Croix, Virgin Islands. Fee $.40.
DIVORCES	St. Thomas and St. John—Clerk of District Court, Charlotte Amalie, St. Thomas, Virgin Islands. Fee $2.40. St. Croix—Deputy Clerk of District Court, Christiansted, St. Croix, Virgin Islands. Fee $2.40.

WASHINGTON

CENTRAL REGISTRY	Public Health Statistics Section, State Department of Health, Olympia, Washington.
BIRTHS AND DEATHS	Central Registry has records since July 1, 1907. For records in Bellingham, Everett, Seattle, Tacoma, or Spokane, write the City Health Department. For records before July 1, 1907, write County Auditor. Fee $1.00.
MARRIAGES	Write County Auditor of county where license was issued. Fee varies.
DIVORCES	County Clerk of county where divorce was granted. Fee varies.

WEST VIRGINIA

CENTRAL REGISTRY
: Division of Vital Statistics, State Department of Health, State Office Bldg., No. 3, Charleston 5, West Virginia.

BIRTHS AND DEATHS
: Central Registry has records since 1917. Prior to 1917 write County Clerk. Fee $.50.

MARRIAGES
: County Clerk of county where license was issued. Fee varies.

DIVORCES
: Clerk of Circuit Court, Chancery Side, in county where divorce was granted. Fee varies.

WISCONSIN

CENTRAL REGISTRY
: Bureau of Vital Statistics, State Board of Health, Madison 2, Wisconsin.

BIRTHS AND DEATHS
: Central Registry has records since 1840. Fee $1.00.

MARRIAGES
: Central Registry has records since 1840. Fee $1.00.

DIVORCES
: Central Registry. Fee $1.00.

WYOMING

CENTRAL REGISTRY
: Division of Vital Statistics, State Department of Public Health, Cheyenne, Wyoming.

BIRTHS AND DEATHS
: Central Registry has records since July 1909. Some records are available for the City of Cheyenne during 1897–1900, and 1905–1909, inclusive. Fee $1.00.

MARRIAGES
: Central Registry has records since May 1941; prior to that date write County Clerk of county where license was issued. Fee $1.00.

DIVORCES
: Central Registry since May 1941; prior to that date write Clerk of the District Court in county where divorce was granted. Central Registry fee $1.00. County fee varies.

How to Prove You Were Born if Your Birth is Not on Record

The births of many persons who were born before 1900 are not a matter of record. Many states did not have compulsory registration laws until quite late. Some records were destroyed by fire, and many Southern courthouses were burned during the Civil War. Clerical errors in recording births should be corrected while proof is at hand. For example, a son Clair, born to Henry Holt, may be registered as Clara Holt, female. Obviously Clair Holt must some day furnish the necessary proof to have this error corrected. If he should die before proof of his identity has been established, his heirs may run into difficulties.

Every American born citizen should be able to furnish a birth certificate. To obtain a birth certificate write to the state of birth, not the state of residence, unless they are the same. The first step in obtaining a birth certificate is to communicate with the proper agency in the state of birth. Enclose the statutory fee together with a self-addressed, stamped return envelope.

If a birth certificate is obtained but is incorrect or incomplete, most states have made provisions to correct or complete such records. The laws of some states do not permit original records to be changed, but they do permit affidavits of correction to be attached, so that when certified copies are issued, they will show the original error and the correction.

If no birth record is on file, then an application should be made for a "Delayed Birth Certificate." In order to secure this, such evidence as the following must be secured and presented:

i   Affidavit of the doctor or midwife who attended the mother at the birth of the applicant. Most states require no further proof.

ii Affidavit of one or both parents, or other persons older than the applicant who have knowledge of his birth.

iii Documentary evidence which varies with the states:

1. Health Department record of place of birth.
2. Office record of deceased physician or midwife.
3. Family Bible (original record).
4. Official church records of baptism, christening confirmation, or membership, bearing the seal of the church.
5. Hospital, nursing home, or clinic records of birth.
6. Historical records in libraries of place of birth.
7. Infant's bank account.

8. Baby books or birth announcements.
9. Printed notices of birth.
10. Newspapers and news clippings.
11. Dated letters or telegrams.
12. Census records—federal, state, or local school.
13. Application for marriage license, showing age and birth-place.
14. School records.
15. Employment record.
16. Military record.
17. Genealogical record.
18. Civil Service record.
19. Lodge record.

If no birth certificate or delayed certificate can be obtained, then the only alternative is the use of a Federal Census Record which is not a substitute for a birth certificate but which is accepted as proof in most situations. The demand for such proof has greatly increased in recent times, due to such factors as the tightening of immigration laws, the establishment of social security and old age retirement, and two world wars. To meet this demand the National Archives has established the Age Search Bureau at Pittsburg, Kansas. This houses microfilms of the Federal Census Population Schedules for 1880 through 1950 (except 1890), which list 739 million names. Proof of birth may be obtained by writing Federal Bureau of the Census, Age Search Bureau, Walnut Bldg., Pittsburg, Kansas. Cost of average search, $3.00.

8. LAND RECORDS AS RESEARCH TOOLS

THE PUBLIC DOMAIN—LAND RECORDS AS RESEARCH TOOLS—
PUBLIC LAND SURVEY SYSTEM—ABSTRACT OFFICE RECORDS—TAX
RECORDS.

A very important approach to family history is through land records. These, in most instances, are to be found in the office of the Register of Deeds in the county courthouse. In some places this official is called the County Recorder.

Records relating to the buying and selling of land yield bits of family and local history. The Register of Deeds has two indexes—the Grantor Index and the Grantee Index. The Grantor is the person by whom the grant or conveyance is made. The Grantee is the person to whom the grant or conveyance is made.

When land records are mentioned people are inclined to think only of deeds, but deeds are only one of the documents to be found in land offices. The principal documents, in addition to deeds, are mortgages, leases, liens, contracts, powers of attorney, releases, notices of action, judgments, decrees, and any other documents that affect the title to land.

Much family history may be gleaned through a painstaking search of deeds. Especially is this true in the case of an estate of a person who died without leaving a will. When real estate is involved it becomes necessary to "quiet the title." In other words, the real estate cannot be sold by the administrator until all the living heirs of the deceased are accounted for. When this accounting is complete, it will give the names and places of residence of the living children, as well as mention any children that may be deceased, and also children living in distant places who may be represented by "power of attorney." And, when the releases are signed by the heirs, the wives of the sons, and the husbands of the daughters, will sign also, to make the conveyance legal. So, with this additional information of married names and new places of residence, one has more clues to follow up.

A deed often mentions relationship between the grantor and the grantee. Often a parent deeds property to a child rather than leave it to be probated. It may read something like this: "I, Ebenezer Eaton, for the great love I bear my son, Ebenezer Eaton, Junior, and for his loving care in my advancing years, do convey the property which I received from my honored father, Jeremiah Eaton, being a part of the original grant which he took from the colonial government."

In early times three steps were necessary in order to secure land. The documents in the original land entries are:

(1) APPLICATION
When a man began the process of securing a grant of land from the Colonial Government, he first had to make an application for it. These applications gave his place of residence; length of time he had lived on the land; and often the depositions of several neighbors who stated they had known him for a certain length of time, and knew that he had resided upon the land and built a habitation, and of the crops he had raised or the amount of land he had cleared.

(2) WARRANT
A warrant was issued which conferred the right of a certain amount of land without actually specifying the place. Then a survey was made which set up the boundaries of the land. These surveys often contain a map of the tract, but unfortunately surveying wasn't done in those days as it is now. One boundary may have been a water course, long since dried up, another a red oak stump, and so forth.

(3) PATENT
The patent, which was actually a grant from the Colonial Government to the warantee, was in reality a deed of ownership.

After the United States Government was established similar grants were made by the several states. Sometimes a warantee sold his rights, and then the patent would be indexed under the name of the purchaser, provided he proceeded to take out the patent. Land grants and early warrants are usually found at the state capitol, but in some states are kept at the county seat. In Connecticut and Vermont they are kept in each separate town. Land office documents include, in addition to plats and notes, the Tract Books in which are recorded the names of persons who became purchasers or preemptors of Government Lands, with dates of entry. People who ever owned land cannot fail to be in the public records. In some states the warantee was required to name his land, and these names are often a clue to the place from whence he came. Pennsylvania and Maryland required that a land name be registered.

A Brief History of the Public Domain

Just what is the Public Domain? The Public Domain is the original landed estate of the American people, the property of all the citizens of a great democracy. In its broadest sense it covered three-fourths of Continental United States, including all of Alaska—a total of one billion eight hundred million acres, or two million eight hundred thousand square miles. It embraced practically all the lands in the United States west of the Mississippi River except Texas, north and west of the Ohio River, and south and west of Tennessee and Georgia.

Acquisition

CESSIONS BY THE ORIGINAL STATES

At the successful conclusion of the Revolutionary War, the boundaries of the newly established republic were determined by treaty with Great Britain, but the boundaries of the thirteen original states were not fixed. Seven of these states laid claim to "wilderness areas" lying west of their present boundaries and stretching to the Mississippi River. These claims often conflicted with one another, partly because of the inconsistencies of colonial charters. As a part of the compromises which led to the formation of a strong central government, these states, between 1781 and 1802, ceded to the Federal Government, with certain exceptions and reservations, their claims to their western lands, thus creating a public domain of more than two hundred million acres. More than 95 per cent of the present public domain outside of Alaska is located in the eleven westernmost states. Federal ownership today consists of about 412 million acres of public domain in the states and 365 million acres in Alaska.

ACCESSIONS BY PURCHASE

1803 Louisiana Purchase. Louisiana Territory purchased from France.

1819 Spanish Cession. Florida ceded to United States by Spain, with adjustments in the boundaries of Spanish and American holdings west of the Mississippi River.

1846 Oregon Compromise. Settlement of boundaries of American and British possessions in the Northwest.

1848 Mexican Cession. Cession of the Southwest by Mexico.

1850 Texas Purchase. Purchase from Texas of more than 75 million acres of land north and west of its present boundaries.

1853 Gadsden Purchase. Purchase from Mexico of 19 million acres in the southwest.

1867 Alaska Purchase. Russia sold the entire Territory of Alaska to the United States.

The total acreage of land thus acquired by the Federal Government for the people of the United States amounted to one billion, seven hundred sixty-five million acres.

THE PUBLIC DOMAIN STATES:

Alabama; Alaska; Arizona; Arkansas; California; Colorado; Florida; Idaho; Illinois; Indiana; Iowa; Kansas; Louisiana; Michigan; Minnesota; Mississippi; Missouri; Montana; Nebraska; Nevada; New Mexico; North Dakota; Ohio; Oklahoma; Oregon; South Dakota; Utah; Washington; Wisconsin; Wyoming.

When each public domain state was admitted to the Union it received grants of public lands which it could use or dispose of for public purposes. There were school grants, road grants, canal grants, river grants, railroad grants, swamp grants, desert grants, internal improvement grants, and in 1862, a grant to all states to provide funds for agricultural colleges.

The cash policy of public land disposal was in effect from 1785 to 1891, and the average price was $1.25 per acre, and by 1854 a plan was inaugurated whereby land that had remained unsold on the market for 35 years could be sold at 12½ cents per acre. In 1862, the Five Year Homestead Act permitted settlers to enter as much as 160 acres of public lands, and after constructing a habitable house, reducing a portion of the land to cultivation, and residing thereon for five years, the settler was entitled to a patent. These conditions were reduced to three years by the Homestead Act of 1912.

When the American Colonies revolted in 1776, they promised bounties to induce enlistments, but it was not until 1796 that conditions were favorable to the enactment of granting legislation. The first grants were relatively restricted in scope. But as time went on and as emphasis changed from grants to induce enlistments to grants to reward military service, the grants became more and more liberal. The legislation of 1855 provided for grants for practically all types of military and naval personnel, in practically all United States military engagements, including Indian Wars, and a grant of 160 acres was given for as little as 14 days of service, or engagement in a single battle. No bounty land was granted after 1855, and veterans of the Civil War received grants under the Homestead Act.

The Public Domain was subject to two classes of rights, the legal title of the United States, and the right of occupancy of the native Indians. The Proclamation of Indian Rights, in 1783, prohibited all persons from settling on lands inhabited or claimed by Indians, or from purchasing or receiving lands from Indians without the express authority of the Congress, and this policy has been consistently followed.

The rectangular system of cadastral surveys, inaugurated in 1785, and continued to the present, with improvements, was designed to protect the public lands, and has prevented the confusion and litigation over land titles which resulted from systems of surveys of "indiscriminate locations" used by other governments, with the result that even the government could not determine the boundaries of its own lands. Rectangular surveys tended to promote orderly and compact settlement of the wilderness, and since the survey lines did not follow natural boundaries, forced settlers to take poor lands as well as good lands with their entries.

In 1800 District Land Offices were set up to handle land transactions, and their number and locations varied as conditions changed. The peak number open at any one time was 123, in 1890. There are only thirteen today and these are under the Bureau of Land Management. In 1800 the district land offices were operating units of the Treasury Department. The General Land Office was established in 1812 but was retained in the Treasury until 1849 when the Interior Department was created to handle domestic affairs.

Under less democratic concepts, this vast area could have been relegated to colonial status, for the benefit of the original thirteen states. But it was early decided that the newly acquired lands were to be subdivided into new states and admitted to the Union on an equal footing with the parent states, as soon as local governments could be firmly established. Between 1803 and 1912, the entire public domain, with the exception of Alaska, was carved into new states which were admitted into the Union on an equal basis with all the other states. Upon their admission the public domain states waived all claim to the federal lands within their boundaries.

The Rectangular System of Surveys

The primary unit of the public land survey system is the township. A township is a square, six miles on each side, or a total area of 36 square miles. Townships are laid out with boundary lines running north-south and east-west. The township boundaries tie into the system of land survey coordinates called principal meridians and base lines. A principal meridian is a line running north and south from an initial point, the latitude and longitude of which is known. There are 36 principal meridians which govern the public land surveys. A base line, running east and west, is a line passing through the initial point, and perpendicular to the principal meridian. When using a public land survey map or plat, the township may be identified by locating it in terms of its principal meridian and base line. To do this, count the number of townships north or south from the base line, and then count the number of townships (called ranges) east or west from the principal meridian. The combined results of these counts will locate any township.

There is a shorthand method of describing a township's location.

For example the shorthand description of the second township south of the base line, and the third township, or range, west of the principal meridian, would read, "T 2 S, R 3 W." In formal land descriptions it is necessary to include the name of the principal meridian.

The principal subdivision of each township is an area one mile square and is called a section, of which there are 36, laid out as a checkerboard. Beginning in the northeast corner of the township, the sections are numbered from one through thirty-six. A section of land contains 640 acres. As it is often necessary to describe an area of less than 640 acres, a system of subdividing sections, called "quartering" has been devised. The first quarter section of 160 acres may again be quartered into 40 acre divisions. These, in turn, may be subdivided into 5, $2\frac{1}{2}$, or $1\frac{1}{4}$ acre parcels, and these may be still further subdivided into lots, all of which may be described by legal subdivision. Lots are given numbers. This system is used throughout the United States.

Public land tracts on unsurveyed land are described by a system called "metes and bounds." The description begins with a well-defined starting point such as a large rock, a bridge, or the mouth of a stream, and so continues around all its boundaries.

Abstract Office Records

In the early days land was freely sold with no evidence of title. Then came the public office for the recording of documents affecting real property. In early times, in most localities, the official in charge of the land records could furnish the buyer with sufficient information concerning the title to meet the needs of the time. While this was called an "abstract," it was little more than a "minute sheet."

As the population of the country increased, more and more documents affecting the title of land came into the recorder's office; complications arose resulting in so much confusion that it became apparent that an improved method must be found. In many places this problem was solved by the organization of abstracting firms. They copied the public records and posted the entries into abstract books, arranged geographically, so that all the documents affecting any parcel of land could be brought together.

The first abstracts were based upon the records in the office of the Register of Deeds, and covered only such instruments as mortgages, taxes and so on, and gave no information on the status of the owners. The public demanded all the facts relating to the title and to the legal ability of the seller to convey a good title. To meet this challenge the abstracters began to copy all of the courthouse records, including probate records, judgments, power of attorney, divorce actions, adoption proceedings, antenuptial agreements, vital records, liens, changes of name, and many others. With this added information the abstract covered a great deal of family history. When an abstract is brought up to date it usually includes the tax history for the past seven years, or back to the last previous conveyance. From tax records it can be determined what years a person resided in the area.

Most abstracts begin with government ownership and show to whom the land was originally granted. When an abstract is begun at a date subsequent to government ownership, the date of beginning is stated together with the following words in capital letters—PARTIAL ABSTRACT.

In deeds, the marital status of the grantor is given, as to whether it is a man and his wife, jointly; or a single man; or in the case of a woman, if she is a married woman dealing with reference to her own separate estate; or if she is single, whether she is a widow. Antenuptial agreements are made between a man and the woman he intends to marry, in order that each may retain control over whatever property he or she may have owned prior to their marriage.

Sometimes when people sign legal papers they spell their names differently than they are spelled in the body of the document. The abstracter then makes a note at the end of the record that this is the same person although the name is spelled in a different way.

Many courthouses have burned and the records have been destroyed. In such cases, if the abstracter had copied the records before the fire, his is probably the only record extant and it can be a great help in the solution of family history problems. However, it must be remembered that the records in an abstract office are not public records, but belong to the individual, the partnership, or corporation that owns the abstract bureau.

REFERENCES:

United States Department of the Interior, Bureau of Land Management:

Highlights in the History of the Public Domain, 1770–1950. Revised
  1957.
Our Public Lands, volume 7, number 2.
Small Tracts. Information Bulletin Number 1. 1958.

Tax Records

The next step after public lands were granted to individuals, was the
assessment and levying of taxes upon those lands. The early tax lists
are useful tools in genealogical research, and reveal the following
facts: the name of the ancestor, with its various spellings; the ancestor's
exact place of residence; and the exact time of his residence in this
location. A study of tax records often affords other clues to family
history. For example, if a man is shown as the taxpayer on a certain
farm, in 1790, but his wife is shown as the taxpayer in 1791, the presumption is that the man died during the year, and indicates that the
next step is to search the probate files. Tax lists offer a much closer
check than census records, as taxes were levied annually and there
was a ten-year interval between census enumerations.

9. PROBATE RECORDS

PROBATE   RECORDS—INTERPRETATION—ABSTRACTS—PROBATE
DISTRICTS.

There is probably no source material more important in family
history research than probate records. Probate records consist largely
of wills and administrations and other documents relating to the
settlement of estates of deceased or incompetent persons. They are
deposited in the probate court of the county or district concerned.
Early vital and church records, important as they are, cannot be
assembled into family groups as can probate records. In a man's will
he named his wife and children, or, if he did not leave a will, the court
determined his heirs and distributed his estate to his widow and children. In either case, the family group was determined by sound legal
evidence. A will is primary source material and is presented in the
first person. It is as though the testator is speaking directly to you to
perpetuate a strong spiritual bond between generations past and
present.

In law, a will is a disposition made by a competent person, known
as the testator, of property over which he has the legal power of disposition, to take effect at his death. Technically, the term "Will"
is used to describe a document which disposes of real property (real
estate), while "Testament" is used to describe one that disposes of
personal property, hence, "the last will and testament" includes
both. Broadly, and by common usage, the term "will" covers both
meanings, and is accepted as describing a written instrument that
disposes of both real and personal property.

Wills may be either written or oral (nuncupative). Wills written
entirely by the hand of the testator are good under some statutes without witnesses, and are called holographic or olographic wills. In wills,

the intention of the testator is the important factor; the form is un-important. A will may be written in any form that expresses the inten-tion of the testator. This form of beginning is in common usage: "In the name of God, amen, I, John Doe, being of sound mind, etc." A testator may leave his estate to whomsoever he pleases, even to strangers if he so desires, without mentioning his next of kin. There is a popular belief that he must mention his children and leave each $1.00, to make his will valid, but this is not true.

An estate is said to be testate when there is a will, and intestate when there is no will. A will must be approved by the Court, and if it is not approved, the estate becomes intestate. In his will, the testator names one or more executors to carry out its provisions. If an executor who has been named in a will should die before the testator, the court appoints an administrator "cum testamento annexo," (with the will annexed). In intestate estates the Court appoints an administrator whose duties are similar to those of the executor of testate estates, except that the estate is distributed by the Court in compliance with the laws of descent and distribution.

Wills, to be valid in the United States, except nuncupative wills, must be written and signed by the testator and witnessed by at least two, and in some states, three persons who must sign in the presence of the testator, and of each other, and who are not beneficiaries under the will. When the will is presented in court it is the duty of the witnesses to acknowledge their signatures and to state that, in their opinions, the testator was of sound mind when he made the will in their presence. If a witness is a woman who has been married in the interval between the making of the will and its admission into court, this acknowledgment before the court constitutes proof of her mar-riage.

The testator of a will must be twenty-one years of age, of sound mind and memory, and not under duress to dispose legally of his inter-est in real or personal property at his death. In some states women may legally dispose of their property at the age of eighteen.

A nuncupative will is one which is made by word of mouth, in the presence of witnesses. These were quite common in early America, and were sometimes called "death-bed wills." Oral wills are permitted in the case of soldiers or sailors in service, to which there must be two or more witnesses who shall, within a reasonable time thereafter, reduce the statement to writing and sign as witnesses. A beneficiary is not a competent witness to a nuncupative will.

An inventory is an itemized account of the holdings of the estate. Sometimes, if there was no will, the inventory is the only paper found. In that case, if the man left a widow, look for her will. It is always well to look for her will, anyway, as it is bound to cover the same or some of the same property, and to mention the same or some of the same heirs.

A will may be altered or amended by the testator. The amendment is known as a codicil which must be signed by the testator and witnessed with the same formality as the original will. A will may be revoked by the testator by destroying it, or by making a new will which automatically invalidates all preceding wills. The destruction of a later will revives a former will if it is still in existence, and it will then have full effect. In some states the subsequent marriage of the testator invalidates a will. State laws vary in their provisions for heirs or next of kin.

In intestate estates it is customary for the next of kin, or some near relative, to petition the court to enter the estate into probate. These petitions are valuable as genealogical evidence for they give the names and places of residence of the heirs, and state their relationship to the deceased.

Interpretation of Probate Records

To properly evaluate the evidence found in probate records, it is necessary to become familiar with the social conventions of the times. In Old England the eldest son received the landed estate, but in New England he was given a double share as his birthright. You may find a deed in which Jabez Brown conveyed a one-sixth interest in the estate of his father, Elijah Brown, deceased. Then, according to New England custom, you may conclude that Elijah Brown left five children, each of whom received one-sixth of the estate, except the eldest who received two-sixths or one-third.

The customary rule of distribution in New England gave the widow, as her dower, one-third of the real estate for life, and one-third of the personal property (called "movables"), absolutely. The children received two-thirds of the remainder of the estate, both real and personal, plus their rightful interest in the widow's dower. If there were no children, the brothers and sisters of the deceased usually came in for a two-thirds interest. If the widow was bequeathed less than one-third of the estate by the terms of the will, she could refuse the legacy and demand her legal dower. If the estate was insolvent, the widow could still retain her dower rights, and the remainder went to the creditors.

In colonial New England it was customary for the father to distribute his landed estate among his sons, and his "movables" among his daughters, the presumption being that the sons-in-law would receive as their inheritance from their fathers real estate for a homestead. The daughters received household goods or other movables, which seemed to be an equable arrangement. Sometimes when a daughter married she was given her full share, or at least a part of it, to enable the young couple to establish housekeeping. The father kept a "little black book" in which all items of disbursement to the children were entered, and when the estate was settled this book was produced in probate, as evidence of the amount advanced to each child, and was taken into consideration by the court in settling and distributing the estate. Those children who had received their full shares during the father's lifetime, may not be mentioned in the distribution of the estate, so it is necessary to read the court order, as well as the releases signed by the heirs in order to be sure that all the surviving children are accounted for.

The mother of a man's children could claim her legal dower rights, but it was a common practice among widows and widowers who married in the later years of their lives, to draw up an antenuptial agreement, so that his estate would go to his children, and her estate would go to her children, with certain provisions for each other. These agreements were made to protect the interests of the children of previous marriages, and were legally binding.

When two executors were named in an early will, it usually followed that one was a relative of the husband and the other a relative of the wife. This arrangement sometimes offers clues to family relationships. The law required that an administrator or an executor of an estate should furnish one or more bondsmen as sureties. In those days there were no bonding companies, and the bondsmen were usually relatives. If the widow was executrix of the will, it usually followed that the bondsmen were her relatives, which may afford a clue as to her identity, if her maiden name is unknown. The Court appointed guardians for children under fourteen years of age, and when a child reached the age of fourteen he was allowed to choose his own guardian, subject to the Court's approval. This was not a hard and fast rule but it offers a clue as to the ages of the children. If the widow was guardian of the children, and she remarried, that marriage was shown in the record. Guardianship papers are important because they give the ages of minors, and the trust ends when the youngest child attains a majority. Laws were not standard for all of the colonies and customs differed somewhat.

Probate Abstracts

Many probate abstracts have been published (See Chapter 28—Bibliography—Published Probate Records), and they are of great value in family history research, especially if one does not have access to the original records. The purpose of the abstract is to present a digest of all information relating to the family that is contained in the file. The value of the abstract depends upon the accuracy and experience of the abstracter. Published probate abstracts are valuable tools in genealogical research. However, they do not pick up many details that may point the way to important clues. Therefore, it is always a good idea to send for a photostat of the original records. When abstracting probate records the following information should be included:

> Name of deceased
> Occupation
> Date of death
> Date will was made
> Date entered into probate
> Will or administration; underscore or circle one
> Courthouse in which located
> Recorded on—(liber and page or file number)
> Date or dates of added codicils
> Executor or administrator
> Petitioner
> Witnesses

Bondsmen
Date of division and disbursement
Heirs determined by the Court
Heirs who signed releases

The Surrogate's Court in New York State corresponds, in general, to Probate Courts in other sections. The Probate Court is called the Orphan's Court in Delaware, Maryland, New Jersey, and Pennsylvania. In Connecticut it is called the Court of Probate; in Georgia and early South Carolina, the Ordinary's Court; and in New Mexico, it is the Prefect's Court.

Probate Districts

In most states the county is the probate district. However, in the following states, the probate districts and the counties do not have the same boundaries: Arkansas; Connecticut; Indiana; Iowa; Massachusetts; Mississippi; Montana; Nevada; North Carolina; Rhode Island (town clerk is ex-officio probate clerk); Utah; Vermont; Wyoming.

REFERENCES:

Martindale-Hubbell Law Directory. Pub. by Martindale-Hubbell, Inc., Summit, N. J. 1958. Part 4.

The Probate Counsel. Pub. by Probate Counsel, Inc., Phoenix, Ariz. 17th ed. 1958.

10. TOWN AND MUNICIPAL RECORDS

TOWN AND MUNICIPAL RECORDS—JUSTICE OF THE PEACE RE-
CORDS—TERRITORIAL RECORDS—STATE ARCHIVES.

In town or municipal records are found vital records, tax lists, poll lists, court records, census records, city directories, atlases, and plat maps. In New England, the town rather than the county was the unit of government. Town records include minutes of the Proprietor's Meetings, minutes of the Town Meetings, or Selectmen's Records, constables and vital records.

The Proprietor's Records contained information about the founding families to whom the Colonial Government had granted large tracts of land which descended to later generations, and although it was unrecorded, the courts ruled that the Proprietor's title was valid. Considerable family history is found in these early land records. The Proprietor's Records were the first records of a town, and after these came the Town Meeting records. These contain a gold mine of information, although few of them have been transcribed or published. In them is to be found a record of all the town affairs such as land transactions, birth, marriage and death records, rate lists, removals, constable's returns, warning out notices, copies of court orders, reports of the poor commissioners, military lists, stray animals, ear marks and cattle brands, and marriage intentions.

Vital records were originally entered in town books in family units. When these were transcribed and published the names were re-arranged, alphabetically, and the family unit could no longer be determined. The rate lists, or assessments, were tax lists which were collected by the constables, and filed. Before stock was fenced, ear marks and cattle brands were personal property, and were registered at the courthouse. Unless these were sold to someone outside the family, they were handed down from father to son, and were recorded in the son's name, thus establishing proof of his paternity. If a family was "warned out" of a town, it did not necessarily indicate that they were undesirable citizens. The warning-out law gave the town the authority to return families who had become impoverished and might become dependent upon the town, back to the town from whence they had come, within a period of three years. Histories of many of the towns of New England have been published and are good sources for family history research.

Justice of the Peace Records

Justice of the Peace records contain information that is of great value in genealogical research, especially those covering the period from 1780 to 1880, when the Justice of the Peace was an important official. He performed marriages, confirmed contracts and apprenticeship indentures, and adjudicated minor disputes. In these records, without doubt, lies the key to many an unsolved genealogical problem. A Justice was not required to deposit his records in any courthouse, and so they were regarded, more or less, as private records, and kept by the Justice himself, usually in a little book. Descendants of these early Justices should search through their papers for these records which may bring to light much information on family and local history.

Territorial Records

The Territorial Papers of the United States, edited by Dr. Clarence Carter, are being published. The earlier volumes were under the jurisdiction of the United States State Department, but it has now been transferred to the authority of the National Archives. These papers are taken from the files of the principal executive departments and agencies of the government, and from the two Houses of Congress.

State, county, and other local records accumulated during the territorial period, and preserved in county courthouses and state archives, are definitely excluded from the series, except insofar as such documents, for some reason, were forwarded to Washington, and then they became a part of the Federal Archives.

The Territorial Papers include petitions and memorials sent, year after year, by the inhabitants of the territories for redress of grievances or change of government, and attached to these petitions are long lists of names of subscribers, reproduced from the originals in the files of the Senate, the House, and National Archives. These names constitute a veritable census, not complete, although nearly every citizen signed some kind of a petition during his lifetime.

Territorial Papers have been published for the following states that were formerly territories: Alabama (1 v.); Arkansas (3 v.); Florida (1 v.); Illinois (2 v.); Louisiana (1 v. under title of Orleans Territory); Michigan (3 v.); Mississippi (2 v.); Missouri (3 v.); Ohio (2 v.); Tennessee (1 v. under title of the Southwest Territory); Wisconsin (1 v.). There are two volumes on the Northwest Territory.

State Archives

State Archives begin with the date of admission of the state to the Union. They consist of many records that have no genealogical value and others that contain considerable family history. Many of the older states have published their colonial records and their state archives. Every state has voluminous files of unpublished archives. These are deposited in the State Archives and Records Center, if such has been established. Otherwise, they are usually found in the State Historical Society, the State Library, or the State Historical Commission. The type of records found in state archives varies with the state and its history. Among the records useful in family history research are early marriage licenses, land grants, militia muster and pay rolls, pensions, immigration and naturalization records, tax lists, and many others. A careful study of the archives, published and unpublished, of the state in which your search is centered, will broaden your knowledge of your family background as well as that of the history of the state.

There have been numerous county boundary changes within the states and each state has an official record of such changes. Most states have published a manual or other official report of these changes. This is the best source to check as it is based upon the legislative enactments which authorized the changes. Before the organization of counties, records covering the area are to be found in the province, territory or state, just as national records previous to 1789 are found in colonial documents, such as notarial records, and in the archives of Great Britain.

11. FEDERAL RECORDS IN THE NATIONAL ARCHIVES

The National Archives is the great public record office of the
United States. It was established in 1934 and holds records from 1775.
There are no colonial records. Those are found in Great Britain and
in the records of the separate colonies. It is not a library, and does
not compete, in any sense of the word, with the two great libraries in
Washington which house large genealogical collections. The Library
of Congress and the Library of the National Society of the Daughters
of the American Revolution both have excellent collections. The
National Archives houses material useful to scholars in many fields.
Among its records are large map collections, complete recordings of
all Indian dialects in the United States, photographs of officers of the
Civil War (Union side), nickelodeon shows, and diplomatic correspondence.

Genealogical records comprise but one per cent of all the records
in the Archives, but these records are used by 95 per cent of all the
researchers. Only records useful in family history research will be
discussed in this work.

Population Census Schedules

The first United States census was taken in 1790, and one has been
taken every ten years since. The originals are in the National Archives.

In many instances photostats or microfilms have been made from the originals when the latter have become too fragile to handle. The originals, the photostats and the microfilms may be examined by any one who requests them. These include the schedules of 1790 to 1880, inclusive. Later schedules are deposited in the Bureau of the Census at Suitland, Maryland, and are not open to the public.

The schedules of the 1790 census have been published and indexed, and are to be found in most libraries having a genealogical collection. (See Chapter 28, Bibliography—Published Census Records.) These were published in 1907 and 1908 for all states whose records were extant at the time. The states are: Connecticut; Maine; Maryland; Massachusetts; New Hampshire; New York; North Carolina; Pennsylvania; Rhode Island; South Carolina; Vermont; Virginia. The schedules for some states were destroyed when the British fired the Capitol buildings during the War of 1812. These have been largely reconstructed on the basis of tax records. Parts of Virginia, Kentucky, Georgia, and the District of Columbia relate to tax lists. There is no volume of any sort for New Jersey. The 1790 schedules give meager information—only the name of the head of the household, and the number of free white males and females in certain age groups, and the number of slaves; but their value in genealogical research lies in the fact that they enable one to locate the place of residence of the family. In Vermont, the census was taken in 1791. The 1880 census schedules are the last ones open to the public at this time. Some states took a State census between the Federal census enumerations. When these can be located, it enables one to make a five-year check of the family sought by using it in conjunction with the Federal census.

Information in Federal Census Records
1790: Name of Head of Household; other members broken down 1800: chiefly in 10-year age groups for free whites; number of 1810: slaves listed. All New Jersey records covering these years 1820: were destroyed.
1820: In addition to the above information, show also if a person 1830: was an alien.
1830: Name of Head of Household; other members broken down

1840:	by 5-year age groups under 20; and by 10-year age groups over 20.
1840:	Name and age of any pensioners living in a household were specially enumerated; found to be 80 per cent accurate. This has been published separately.
1850:	First census to state name and age of every free white person in the United States; also lists state, territory, or country of birth; special enumeration of persons who had married within the census year, July 1, 1749 to June 30, 1850.
1857:	A special census was taken in Minnesota.
1860: 1870:	Give about the same information as 1850; 1870 was the first census that enrolled Indians.
1880:	The first census that gives the name and relationship of each individual member of the family to the head of the house; also gives birthplaces of parents of each person enumerated. All 1880 schedules have been microfilmed as they were on poor paper which did not hold up; valuable to locate birthplaces of people born in early 1800's.
1885:	Special census for which Federal Government paid half and the states paid half; many states did not want to pay, so only the following were taken: Colorado; Florida; Nebraska; New Mexico. These are in the National Archives.
1890:	Destroyed by fire except a special census of Union Veterans of the Civil War and their widows. Information contained: Name of veteran (or if he did not survive, names of both veteran and widow); veteran's rank, company, regiment, or vessel; dates of enlistment and discharge; length of service in years, months, and days; disability. Persons enlisted under assumed names are recorded under both the real name and the alias.
1900:	Schedules give exact month and year of birth of every person in the United States, and are the only ones that do. Have not been opened to the public. They are at the Bureau of the Census at Suitland, Maryland. Microfilm copies are at the Age Search Bureau in Pittsburg, Kansas.

The National Archives has the best collection of Indian records in the United States. These date from 1830. Family records, however, can only be traced for the Eastern Cherokees who claimed a great deal of land. In order to obtain this land they had to fill out applications, giving their ancestry back to their great-grandfathers. Indian marriages were not recognized by the United States Government as legal, as they were performed in Indian rites. But many Indians fought in the wars and their widows applied for pensions. The evidence of their marriages had to be obtained from their chieftains.

The migrations of a family can be accurately traced through the use of census records although it sometimes takes a great deal of time and patience.

Mortality Schedules

In 1849 basic legislation was enacted which required enumerators of the censuses of 1850, 1860, 1870, and 1880 to ask a series of additional questions for the Mortality Schedules. For any person who had died in the twelve months previous to the enumeration, as of June first, they recorded the name; age at death; date of death (month); and the state or country of birth. The actual purpose of this was to determine the death rate, disease prevalence, longevity, and so forth. But, it serves a very useful purpose in family history research, as it predates vital records, and these schedules contain 13 per cent of all deaths over a thirty-year period (1849–1880). Some years ago, the Director of the Census was authorized by Congress, to return these schedules to the states to be placed in some authorized depository such as a state library or State Archives. The Michigan Mortality Schedules are in the Michigan State Library at Lansing.

Land Records in the National Archives

There are partial indexes in the Bureau of Land Management and National Archives, as follows:
  (1) Warrants under the Act of 1788 (incomplete)
  (2) Virginia Military Warrants
  (3) Private Land Claims
  (4) Coal and Mineral Entries

(5) Name indexes of land entries arranged by District Land Offices in the states of Alabama, Arizona, Florida, Louisiana, Nevada, Utah and Alaska.

(6) Among the records of the Veteran's Administration in the National Archives, there is an alphabetical index to applications for military bounty land warrants issued under the Acts of 1847, 1850, 1852, and 1855. (Note: applications for warrants before 1880 were lost by fire; the National Archives has only cards for such entries.)

To find any other land entry file in the National Archives it is necessary to know the legal description of the land, or the date, or approximate date of entry, and the name of the land office through which the entry was made. Revolutionary War veterans were granted land according to their rank, under the Acts of 1788, 1799, 1803, and 1806. A Major-General was granted 1100 acres; a Captain 300; Lieutenant, 200; Ensign, 150; Private, 100. There were no bounty land grants after 1855. Union veterans of the Civil War could take Homestead Land, or Donation Land in Oregon and Washington. Confederate soldiers were not allowed to file for land.

Ships' Passenger Lists

From 1790 to 1820 less than one per cent of the records is available. Starting in 1820, passenger lists were required by law to give the name, age, occupation, name of ship, port of arrival, and port of embarkation. The National Archives has lists from 1820 to 1873 which were made from duplicate lists in the customhouses at the port of entry, for tax collection purposes. The majority of these came through the Port of New York. The fiscal section of the National Archives has passenger lists from 1875 to 1919. After 1919 these records are in the Department of Immigration and Naturalization.

Location of Passenger Lists

BALTIMORE, MARYLAND: lists from 1820 to 1897 are indexed and available through the Field Office of Immigration and Naturalization Service, Postoffice Building, Baltimore 2, Maryland. These lists are missing from 1821 to 1836 and from 1850 to 1855.

PHILADELPHIA, PENNSYLVANIA: lists from 1798 to 1899 are indexed and are in the National Archives. See also, Bibliography—Strassburger and Hinke, Chapter 28.

NEW YORK CITY: lists from 1820 to December 31, 1919 are in the National Archives.

BOSTON, MASSACHUSETTS: early lists, 1813–1883, were destroyed by fire; lists from January 1, 1883 to January 1900 are in the National Archives.

MOBILE, ALABAMA: lists from 1830–1862 are in the National Archives.

NEW HAVEN, CONNECTICUT: lists from 1820–1899 are in the National Archives.

SALEM AND BEVERLY, MASSACHUSETTS: lists from 1798–1800 are in the National Archives.

GALVESTON, TEXAS: lists from 1846–1871 are in the National Archives.

KEY WEST, FLORIDA: lists from 1837–1868 are in the National Archives.

WILMINGTON, DELAWARE: lists from 1820–1849 are in the National Archives.

SAN FRANCISCO, CALIFORNIA: almost all, including those of the 1800's, were destroyed by accident in 1940.

ATLANTIC AND GULF PORTS: lists from 1819–1919 and some from 1798 are in the National Archives.

IRISH RECORDS: the National Archives Library has received from the Public Record Office of Northern Ireland, at Belfast, typed transcripts of Irish records of immigrants to America from 1833–1835.

By correspondence, the National Archives will search the partial indexes to transcripts of lists for Atlantic and Gulf Ports, 1819–1844; the original lists of Philadelphia, 1798–1900; and the indexed transcripts for New Orleans, 1813–1861, and 1864–1867, if you have the following information: full name of passenger; port of arrival; and approximate date of arrival. Since the lists are so large and not alphabetized, they can only undertake further research, if, in addition to the above information, you are also able to supply the name of the vessel.

Naturalization Records

Naturalization records identify the immigrant. There were not many naturalizations during the Colonial period as all the colonists were British subjects and only Continental Europeans were naturalized. In 1740 the English Parliament passed a naturalization law affecting the colonies. This required a seven years' residence in a colony and an oath before a magistrate, or, in the case of Quakers, an affirmation.

In the Publications of the Huguenot Society of London, volume 24, are found lists of persons naturalized in American Colonies, under this 1740 Act, as follows: Jamaica, 1740–1750; Maryland, 1743–1753; Massachusetts, 1743– ; New York, 1740–1770; Pennsylvania, 1740–1772; South Carolina, 1741–1748; Virginia, 1743–1746. The majority of these naturalizations took place in Pennsylvania.

The states handled their own naturalizations from 1775–1790. In 1790 the first naturalization law was enacted in the United States. It affected white people only, and required two years' residence, until 1798 when the period of residence was raised to 14 years. In 1802 it was again revised and five years' residence required, and this is still in effect. In 1906 there was a complete revision of the naturalization laws, brought about by the Irish vote frauds in New York City. This law required an alien to go before a court of record and make formal application.

There are three parts to a naturalization record: (1) Declaration of Intention; (2) Proof of residence in the United States for five years; (3) Certification of naturalization. A naturalization record contains the following information:

NAME	AGE	NATIVITY
Allegiance to what country? Arrived at (place and date). Declaration of Intention (place and date). Witnesses.		Emigrated from (place and date). Proof of residence (place and date). Naturalization granted (place and date).

Naturalization records are found in county courts and are usually in the custody of the county clerk, but they are under the jurisdiction of the Department of Justice. To secure information concerning a naturalization record, write the clerk of the county for records previous to September 27, 1906; for records after that date, write either the clerk of the county court in the county where the oath of naturalization was taken, or to the Commissioner of Immigration and Naturalization, Washington 25, D.C.

The National Archives has no naturalization records except for the District of Columbia, from 1802 to 1926. A clue to the ship upon which the immigrant took passage may be found in his naturalization record, as an alien was required to state the date and place of his entry into the United States, upon his application. As a rule, naturalization records may be abstracted but not copied verbatim, or photostated, as a security measure, to prevent fraud.

Military Service Records

The National Archives has military service records from 1775–1912. These cover the American Revolution, the War of 1812, Indian Wars after 1817, the Mexican War, the Civil War, Union side and captured Confederate records, and the Spanish-American War. Records of later wars are at the present time in the custody of the Veteran's Administration.

Pension Records

Pensions were granted in the United States for military service in the various wars, on the basis of several legislative enactments by the Congress of the United States. In 1790 some of the states paid pensions to invalid soldiers.

Acts	Provisions
	Recently found among the records of the War Department (now in the National Archives under Record Group 107), is a volume entitled "War Office Letter Book, 1791–1794," but instead of containing letters it contains additional

ACT OF 1792	claims filed under the Act of 1792, for disability. These claims were published in volume 46 of the National Genealogical Society Quarterly (1958). Not in American State Papers.
ACT OF 1818	Granted pensions to Revolutionary War veterans who were not disabled, but many did not survive to receive this pension. A minimum of nine months' service was required, and evidence that the veteran was in need.
ACT OF 1832	Six months' service in any branch of the military was required in order to obtain this pension.
ACT OF 1836	The veteran's widow could apply for a pension but had to show proof of her marriage to him before the end of the Revolution.

If a pension record cannot be located, it doesn't necessarily mean that the man did not render military service. He may not have been able to qualify under any of the Acts that were in effect during his lifetime. He may not have needed the pension, or he may have received bounty land. The United States Government did not grant pensions to Confederate soldiers of the Civil War but some of the Southern States did.

Many veterans of the Revolutionary War who would have qualified for a pension under the Act of 1818 did not survive to apply for it. This was especially true of officers who were older men. A great deal of family history is sometimes found in the pension files, especially those applications filed under the Act of 1836, under which the widow could apply for a pension. Proof of her marriage was often difficult to establish, and many times the family Bible records were used as evidence. Of these, the National Archives has quite a collection. She was also required to furnish depositions of friends and relatives to support this evidence and these are fruitful sources of family history. If the veteran survived to apply for a pension, he often gave a detailed account of his service. This story, in his own words, will add a great deal of interest to your family history.

In the early years of our country's history, the United States Government was short on cash but long on land—the one commodity of which Uncle Sam had plenty.

Bounty Land

Bounty land was granted to soldiers of the early wars for their service
to the country, under specific Acts:

Acts:	Provisions and Wars
ACT OF 1847	Under this Act bounty land was granted for service in the Mexican War.
ACTS OF 1850 and 1855	Applications for bounty land under these Acts are in the National Archives. By 1850 many veterans of the War of 1812 had migrated West, and their declarations made under these Acts, applying for Bounty Land, show their residences, ages, places of enlistment, and sometimes the wife's name. The Warrant issued to the soldier is deposited in the Natural Resources Division, General Land Office of the National Archives, and shows where and when the soldier settled on Federal lands. In cases where the soldier died just after the issuance of the Warrant, his wife and other heirs are shown. Bounty lands were also granted under these Acts for services in the various Indian Wars and the Patriot's War of 1838 (a New York border disturbance), as well as for the War of 1812.

For an index to Revolutionary Pension and Bounty Land applications see Bibliography—Guides and Indexes—Hoyt.

Records may be obtained from the National Archives in any one of three different ways. The best way is to visit the Archives and do your own research. Another way is to employ a researcher who lives in the Washington area. The National Archives will send you a list of persons who have registered with them to do research. Or, you may write them and request a copy of Form 288, and when this is received fill it in and return with the small fee requested, for photostat copies of the records. This latter method is probably the most convenient and satisfactory. The charge is very nominal and you have the entire record instead of an abstract, to study at your leisure.

12. CHURCH RECORDS

Church records had their beginning in England in 1538, when Henry VIII, after a dispute with the Pope, established the Church of England. He ordered his archbishop to require the priests (Episcopal), to keep a record of baptisms, marriages and burials. The law was enacted twenty years later, so that in 1558 church records were begun in thousands of parishes throughout England. In 1598 the bishop of each diocese, in England, was required to receive copies of records, and these are the predecessors of state records.

The entries in church records are baptisms, not births. The baptismal date is not far from the birth date, in England, for according to the Episcopal creed, a child was baptized immediately. Unless the weather was bad, baptism took place within a few days after the birth of a child.

The Church of England kept only records of members. Non-conformists had to keep their own records, and that is why George Fox started the Quakers to keeping records about 1658. Friends recorded births, marriages and burials. Quakers do not believe in baptism, so their records are of births, while the Episcopalians record baptisms.

Parish Registers, which are the records of the Church of England, contain records of christenings, marriages and burials. Many of the parish records of England have been published and are found in libraries having collections of genealogical records. In searching parish records it is good practice to copy all the records relating to the family around which your search centers, so that you may assemble the family as a unit, for further study.

The Church of England was the established church in the American Colonies until after the Revolution. Records of baptisms kept in the colonial churches are a great boon to family history research as they antedate vital records by some 200 years. Most church records are kept by the church clerk, minister, or some other official. A few denominations have a central registry. One of the historical projects of the Works Projects Administration was to make an inventory of church archives, and while it was never completed, a great many volumes were published and are to be found in libraries.

Many church records are kept in the churches. A great number of these have been published, both as separate publications, and serially, in genealogical periodicals. For the latter, see Index to Genealogical Periodicals by Donald Lines Jacobus, 3 volumes, under Place Index. Some denominations have central depositories, but for most denominations, records have to be located in the specific church.

In the early days of our country, before churches were organized, "preachers" traveled through the country on horseback, ministering to the spiritual needs of the people, preaching the Gospel, baptizing infants, performing marriage ceremonies, and administering the last rites to the dead. These men were known by various names. The Methodists called them "Circuit Riders" and the Baptists were known as "Gospel Rangers." Whatever their title, they performed a much needed service. They kept the records of their missions in little books in their saddle bags. An itinerant minister named Draper traveled through Tennessee, North and South Carolina, Virginia, Kentucky, and Southern Illinois, where he ministered to many people and wrote his interviews in his notebooks which became the property, through will, of the Wisconsin Historical Society, at Madison.

Following is a partial list of church record depositories in the United States:

CALIFORNIA
San Francisco Theological Seminary, San Anselmo, California. (Presbyterian archives).

CONNECTICUT
Connecticut State Library, Hartford, Connecticut. (Connecticut church records and Vosburgh Records of New York)

DELAWARE
Hall of Records, Dover, Delaware.

DISTRICT OF COLUMBIA

Daughters of the American Revolution Library, 1776 D St., N.W., Washington D.C. (Mss. records for United States)

Howard University Library, Washington, D.C. (Negro).

Library of Congress, Washington 25, D.C. (Protestant Episcopal records of Maryland).

ILLINOIS

Baptist Association of America, 2561 North Clark St., Chicago 14, Illinois.

Illinois State Historical Society and Archives, Springfield, Illinois.

Wheaton College, Wheaton, Illinois. (Congregational).

INDIANA

Goshen College, Goshen, Indiana. (Mennonite).

Indiana Historical Society, Indianapolis, Indiana.

Indiana State Library, 140 N. Senate Ave., Indianapolis 4, Indiana.

Taylor University, Upland, Indiana.

KENTUCKY

Filson Club Library, 118 W. Breckenridge, Louisville, Kentucky.

Kentucky Historical Society, Old State House, Frankfort, Kentucky.

Presbyterian Theological Seminary, Louisville, Kentucky.

Southern Baptist Theological Seminary, Louisville, Kentucky.

MARYLAND

Maryland Diocesan Library, 17 E. Mt. Vernon Place, Baltimore, Maryland.

The Hall of Records, St. Johns College Campus, Annapolis, Maryland.

The Maryland Historical Society, 201 W. Monument St., Baltimore, Maryland.

MICHIGAN

Detroit Public Library, Burton Historical Collection, 5201 Woodward Avenue, Detroit 2, Michigan.

Kalamazoo College Library, Kalamazoo, Michigan. (Baptist).

Michigan State Library, Lansing, Michigan.

MINNESOTA

Minnesota Historical Society, Capitol Hill, St. Paul 1, Minnesota.

St. Olaf College, Northfield, Minnesota. (Lutheran).

NEW HAMPSHIRE

New Hampshire Historical Society, 30 Park St., Concord, New Hampshire.

NEW JERSEY

Diocese of New Jersey, New Jersey Diocesan House, 816 Berkley Avenue, Trenton, New Jersey (Protestant Episcopal).

Drew Theological Seminary, Madison, New Jersey. (M. E. College).

Newark Diocesan House, 99 Main St., Orange, N. J. (Prot. Epis.)

Rutgers University Library, New Brunswick, New Jersey.

State Department of Education, Division of the State Library, Archives and History, State House Annex, Trenton 7, N. J.

NEW YORK

American Irish Historical Society, 991 Fifth Avenue, New York 21, New York.

Buffalo and Erie Counties Public Library, Grosvenor Reference Division, 383 Franklin St., Buffalo 2, New York.

Colgate University Library, Hamilton, New York. (Baptist records for North America).

Cornell University Library, Ithaca, New York.

Cortland County Historical Society, Cortland, New York.

Green County Historical Society, Coxsackie, New York.

Holland Society of New York Manuscript Collection, 90 West Street, New York, N. Y. (Dutch Ref.)

Jewish Theological Seminary Library, 3080 Broadway, New York, New York.

Keeper Joint Committee on Records, 221 E. Fifteenth St., New York 3, New York. (Quaker records for New York, New Jersey, and Vermont)

Long Island Historical Society, Pierpont & Clinton Sts., Brooklyn 2, New York. (Long Island records)

Montgomery County Department of History and Archives, Old Court House, Fonda, New York.

New York Genealogical & Biographical Society, 122 E. 58th., Street, New York 22, New York.

New York Historical Society, 170 Central Park West, New York 24, New York.

New York Public Library, Fifth Avenue at 42nd., St., New York 18, New York.

New York State Historical Association, Fenimore House, Cooperstown, New York.

New York State Library, Albany, New York. (New York records
including Vosburgh records; New Jersey records)

Queens Borough Public Library, Jamaica, New York. (Long Island
records).

Schenectady County Historical Society, 13 Union St., Schenectady,
New York. (Large collection of Dutch church records).

Schoharie County Historical Society, Schoharie, New York.

Syracuse Public Library, Syracuse, New York.

NORTH CAROLINA

The Carolina Discipliana Library of the Historical Commission,
North Carolina Disciples of Christ, Box 1164, Wilson, North
Carolina.

Duke University Library, Durham, North Carolina.

Guilford College Library, Guilford College, North Carolina
(Quaker depository).

Historical Foundation of the Presbyterian and Reformed Churches,
Montreat, North Carolina. (Presbyterian Archives).

Moravian Church in North Carolina, 224 S. Cherry Street, Win-
ston-Salem, North Carolina. (North Carolina Archives).

North Carolina Department of Archives and History, Raleigh,
North Carolina.

OHIO

Anderson State College, Wilberforce, Ohio. (Negro).

The Cincinnati Historical Society, Eden Park, Cincinnati, Ohio
45202.

Oberlin College Library, Oberlin, Ohio.

Ohio Historical Society, Ohio State Museum, Columbus 10,
Ohio.

Ohio State Library, 65 Front Street, Columbus 15, Ohio.

Presbyterian Historical Society, Lancaster, Ohio.

The Western Reserve Historical Society, 10825 East Blvd., Cleveland 6, Ohio.

PENNSYLVANIA

American Catholic Historical Society, 715 Spruce St., Philadelphia,
Pennsylvania.

Department of Records, 302 Arch St., Philadelphia, Pennsylvania. (Quaker records for Pennsylvania and New Jersey).

Friends General Conference, 1515 Cherry St., Philadelphia 2, Pennsylvania.

Friends Historical Library, Swarthmore College, Swarthmore, Pennsylvania. (Quaker; depository for Hinshaw Collection).

Genealogical Society of Pennsylvania, 1300 Locust St., Philadelphia, Pennsylvania. (Pennsylvania; New Jersey).

Historical Society of Berks County, Reading, Pennsylvania.

Historical Society of Dauphin County, Harrisburg, Pennsylvania.

Historical Society of the Evangelical and Reformed Church, Fackenthal Library, Franklin & Marshall College, Lancaster, Pennsylvania. (Pennsylvania, New Jersey, and Virginia)

Historical Society of the Lutheran Ministerium of Pennsylvania, Lutheran Theological Seminary, Mt. Airy, Philadelphia, Pennsylvania.

Historical Society of Montgomery County, Norristown, Pennsylvania.

Historical Society of Pennsylvania, 1300 Locust St., Philadelphia, Pennsylvania.

Historical Society of York County, 225 E. Market St., York, Pennsylvania. (York and Adams Counties).

The Lutheran Historical Society Library, Gettysburg, Pennsylvania.

The Lutheran Theological Seminary Library, 7301 Germantown Avenue, Philadelphia 19, Pennsylvania.

Moravian Historical Society, Bethlehem, Pennsylvania. (Church Archives).

The Pennsylvania German Society Library, Norristown, Pennsylvania.

Pittsburgh-Zenia Theological Seminary, Pittsburgh, Pennsylvania. (Presbyterian Archives).

Presbyterian Historical Society, Witherspoon Bldg., Philadelphia, Pennsylvania. (Presbyterian Archives).

Wyoming Historical and Genealogical Society Library, 69 South Franklin Street, Wilkes-Barre, Pennsylvania.

RHODE ISLAND

Brown University Library, Providence 1, Rhode Island.

Rhode Island State Historical Society Library, 52 Powder Street, Providence 6, Rhode Island.

SOUTH CAROLINA

Furman University Library, Greenville, South Carolina.

The Historical Commission of South Carolina, Columbia, South Carolina.

McKissick Memorial Library, University of South Carolina, Columbia 19, South Carolina.

South Carolina Historical Society, Charleston, South Carolina.

State Library, Columbia, South Carolina.

TENNESSEE

American Baptist Theological Seminary, White Creek Pike, Nashville, Tennessee.

Chattanooga Public Library, 601 McCallie Ave., Chattanooga 3, Tennessee.

Dorgan-Carver Library, Baptist Sunday School Board, 125 9th., Avenue, Nashville, Tennessee.

East Tennessee Historical Society, Knoxville, Tennessee, c/o Lawson-McGhee Library.

Ocoee Baptist Association, Temple Court Bldg., Cherry St., Chattanooga, Tennessee.

Tennessee Baptist Convention, 148 Sixth Avenue, North, Nashville, Tennessee.

Tennessee State Library, Nashville 3, Tennessee.

University of Tennessee Library, Knoxville, Tennessee.

TEXAS

The Church Historical Society of the Protestant Episcopal Church, 406 Rathervue Place, Austin 5, Texas. (Protestant Episcopal Archives for the United States).

UTAH

Genealogical Society of the Church of Jesus Christ of Latter Day Saints, 80 North Main Street, Salt Lake City. (Mormon Archives).

VERMONT

Diocesan Library, Protestant Episcopal Church, Rockpoint, Vermont.

University of Vermont Library, Burlington, Vermont.

Vermont Historical Society Library, Supreme Court Bldg., Montpelier, Vermont.

VIRGINIA

Virginia Baptist Historical Society, Richmond, Virginia.

Virginia Historical Society Library, 707 E. Franklin St., Richmond, Virginia.

Virginia State Library, Richmond, Virginia.

William and Mary College Library, Williamsburg, Virginia.

WISCONSIN

Wisconsin Genealogical Society, 938 North 28th Street, Milwaukee, Wisconsin.

Wisconsin State Historical Society Library, University of Wisconsin, 816 State Street, Madison 6, Wisconsin. (Wisconsin and Draper Mss.).

CANADA

Institut Genéalogique Drouin, 4184 St. Denis Street, Montreal, Quebec, Canada. (Complete Catholic Archives).

13.   QUAKER RECORDS

THE SOCIETY OF FRIENDS—VALUE OF QUAKER RECORDS IN
GENEALOGICAL RESEARCH—MEETINGS AND RECORDS—RELA-
TION OF QUAKERISM TO HISTORY—WILLIAM WADE HINSHAW—
FRIENDS' HISTORICAL LIBRARY OF SWARTHMORE COLLEGE—
INDIANA QUAKER RECORDS—ENGLISH FRIENDS' RECORDS—
BIBLIOGRAPHY.

Who are the Quakers and why are they so important in
American genealogy? The Society of Friends was founded in England
about 1650, at a time when there was a great deal of religious unrest.
The founder, George Fox, at the age of 19, in seeking a satisfying faith,
based the movement upon the conviction that every individual is
endowed by his Creator with a measure of the Divine Spirit which
he called "The Inner Light." It is around this principle of the divine
element in human personality that the Quaker faith has developed.
George Fox lived from 1624 to 1691, and most of his followers were
young people. The Society of Friends was really "The Youth Movement" of those times. Theirs is not a church in the conventional
manner, but a meeting house. In their early meetings there were no
ministers or priests—in fact all members of the Society of Friends are
placed upon an equal spiritual level.

Friends believe in the Fatherhood of God, the brotherhood of man,
and to that has sometimes jokingly been added: "the neighborhood of
Philadelphia." While we are prone to think of the City of Brotherly
Love as a great Quaker stronghold, actually there are more Quakers
living in other areas of the United States, notably Indiana, North
Carolina, Ohio, Iowa, California, Kansas, and Oregon, and it is
quite likely that each one of us has, somewhere in his background, a
Quaker ancestor. The Society of Friends is now a comparatively small

religious group compared to many others, as it constitutes less than
1/10 of 1 per cent of the population of the United States. But, two
hundred years ago the proportion of Friends was about six per cent of
the population, and to that six per cent many of us trace our ancestry.
The value of Quaker records cannot be overestimated. Upwards of
a half million persons have been registered as members of the Society
of Friends, over the past three hundred years. In some cases only the
names are mentioned in the Quaker records, and for others there are
complete vital statistics. Lineages covering twelve generations have
been compiled from Quaker records which go back to the time of
George Fox. Millions of Americans have from one to several hundred
Quaker ancestors.

Friends came to be called "Quakers" because of the physical and
emotional manifestations that accompanied their early gatherings
where it was asserted that those who did not know quaking and trem-
bling were strangers to the experiences of Moses, David, and other
saints.

Quaker migration was under way by 1653, and at the time of Mr.
Fox's death, in 1691, there were 40,000 Quakers. England persecuted
them as "Dissenters" and threw many of them in prison. This led
thousands to seek homes in other lands. Quaker missionaries arrived
in Virginia, Rhode Island, Massachusetts, and Maryland, between
1656 and 1658, where they made converts and set up meetings.
George Fox visited America in 1672 and this gave fresh impetus to
the movement. By 1700 Friends had acquired New Jersey and Delaware, and founded Pennsylvania. They were politically powerful
in Rhode Island, North Carolina, and Maryland, and had organized
meetings in all the colonies except Connecticut and South Carolina.
There were 971 Quaker ministers in the United States in 1884, of
whom 371 were women.

From 1725 to 1775 there was a heavy migration from Pennsylvania,
New Jersey and New England, south into Virginia, North and South
Carolina and Georgia. Around 1800 there was another great Quaker
migration from the south to the Northwest Territory. Quakers who
had always been strong advocates of the anti-slavery movement,
prison reform and the care of the insane, found life unpleasant in the
south, and lured by the virgin soil of the Northwest Territory, emi-

grated to Ohio, Indiana and Illinois. Many Quakers migrated from North Carolina to Indiana, stopping for a time in Ohio. Many of these people were aged, and like all Quakers, they kept meticulous records, so their birth dates often go back as far as the 1740's, and antedate Indiana Territorial records. Today there are 100,000 Quakers in the United States, and of these fully one-third reside in Indiana.

Throughout the years there have been several "splits" in the organization of Friends. In 1828 the Hicksites separated from the main body. This was brought about by the fact that a man named Elias Hicks made the statement that Jesus Christ was a mortal man and not a Divine Being. His followers were known as Hicksites, while those who remained loyal to the accepted doctrines were known as Orthodox Quakers. The Hicksites established their own meetings and were promptly "disowned" by their orthodox brethren. The Hicksites founded Swarthmore College.

The "Wilburites" split from the main society in 1845. They were followers of John Wilbur of Hopkinton, Rhode Island, who took a stand against an English Quaker named Gurney whom he believed to be antagonistic to the original doctrines of the Society. This is a comparatively small group which had about 4000 communicants in 1918.

Accuracy and thoroughness have always characterized the Quaker mind, and for that reason good records have been kept from their very beginnings in England. George Fox admonished the Friends to keep vital records and to make their wills. In 1656, in Yorkshire, England, it was directed that a record be kept in every meeting, of the births of the children of members, and of the burials of the dead. Had it not been for this provision, there would be no records of English Friends who, as Dissenters, were not permitted to be listed in the Parish Registers of the Church of England. Many certificates were brought from meetings in the British Isles and Europe, and most of these records have been preserved, and give valuable clues to pre-American ancestry. It was not until about 1850 that Quakers had their vital records recorded in civil offices, and it is in these unpublished record books that the ancestry of millions of present-day Americans lies buried.

Society of Friends—Their Meetings and Records

A knowledge of the various meetings, their purposes, and the records kept, is necessary in order to do comprehensive research.

FIRST DAY MEETINGS were purely for worship. Quakers always designated the days of the week, and the months of the year, by numbers, as they did not recognize the names of pagan Gods.

MONTHLY MEETINGS were the business meetings of the Society in which records of individual members were kept. In these are found the records of births, deaths, and marriages, certificates of removal, and disownments. The certificate of removal gives the member's name and occupation, the name of the meeting of which he is a member in good standing, and other statements such as "he received his education amongst us," indicating that he had been a member of the meeting for a long time. When a member is "received" into a new meeting, his former residence is made a part of the record. When a Friend decided to remove from one locality to another, he was required to obtain a Certificate of Removal from the clerk of his meeting, and this was directed to the clerk of the meeting where he proposed to settle. This record would then be entered in the monthly meetings of both places, and is a good way to trace migrations of a family.

THE QUAKER MARRIAGE RECORD is one of the most interesting and important documents from the genealogist's standpoint, as all of the wedding guests sign as witnesses. Members of the immediate families of the bride and groom sign at the lower right side of the document, in the order of the closeness of their relationship, and friends of the couple sign at the left side.

A RECORD OF DISOWNMENT is a termination of membership, and thereafter there will be no further record of this individual in Quaker archives. Many were disowned for reasons which to us would seem trivial, and some were even amusing, such as "departing from the truth," or "being seen on the streets during meeting." One wonders who saw him. One could be disowned for marrying a non-Friend, for being married by an outside minister, for gambling, or being seen at a horse race. Again, one wonders by whom?

SUFFERINGS. During the Revolution, Quakers were not Tories and they were not Patriots, and so they got it from both sides, and this resulted in their being subjected to terrible sufferings. They kept records of these sufferings, and also kept lists of things that were taken from them by both sides.

MEMORIALS. Quaker memorials are similar to obituaries and contain much genealogical information.

MANUMISSIONS. Quakers set their slaves free and kept records of this.

QUARTERLY MEETINGS. Several monthly meetings form a quarterly meeting which assembles four times a year and includes worship, a business period, and a period for the consideration of the concerns of the common interest, and often a public lecture.

YEARLY MEETINGS. Yearly meetings comprise a group of monthly and quarterly meetings, in an area. At these meetings reports are given upon the advancement of Friend's principles, such as those of the Committees for Peace, Social Justice, Race Relations, Temperance, Religious Education, and so forth.

FIVE YEAR MEETINGS. This is a national organization which includes fourteen yearly meetings, and has a membership of 49,000.

There are 110,000 Quakers in the United States, 20,000 in England, 20,000 in Africa, and 20,000 in the rest of the world. They are organized into about fifty yearly meetings. Friends maintain nearly one hundred current publications, mostly printed in English, German and French. They also maintain one hundred and ten schools, most of the students of which belong to other religious groups.

Relation of Quakerism to History

Quakerism was born at a time when there was great intolerance, and its founder was imprisoned for daring to say that man needs no mediator between God and himself. Another great figure in history who also suffered imprisonment was William Penn, who established the Colony of Pennsylvania upon a foundation of religious liberty, and whose agreement with the Indians was the only treaty never sworn to and never broken. This peace which endured for over sixty years established Pennsylvania as the symbol of liberty and friendship all over the world, and attracted persecuted people to come to America and help build this nation. Racial tolerance was a sacred tradition among Friends who, as early as 1688, raised their voices against slavery. Their influence has been widely felt in the abolition of slavery, in the education of the freedmen, and in prison and other reforms.

Quakers who have figured prominently in American history are John Greenleaf Whittier, John Woolman, Herbert Hoover, and Richard Nixon.

Where are Quaker Meeting Records Located?

Unfortunately, there is no central location. They are deposited in many different places. Some are in one hundred or more meeting houses across the country. Some are in bank vaults and others in the clerk's bureau drawer. So Quaker records are difficult of access, and when located are difficult to use, as most lack indexes. But Providence brought forth a man who recognized this problem and contributed the last twenty years of his life to its solution.

William Wade Hinshaw

Wiliam Wade Hinshaw was born in Iowa in 1867. He was an opera singer who traveled all over Europe giving concerts. At the age of sixty he became deaf. It was then that he started compiling genealogical records of Quaker meetings in all states. He hired teams of abstracters to go to Quaker record depositories and copy the information. At the time of his death in 1947, he had compiled five volumes and collected enough material for the sixth volume. These six massive volumes are titled *The Encyclopaedia of American Quaker Genealogy,* published by Friends Book and Supply House, Richmond, Indiana. The first five volumes were published from 1936 to 1946. Their contents are as follows:

Volume I contains the 33 oldest meetings in North Carolina.
Volume II contains the four oldest meetings in Pennsylvania and New Jersey.
Volume III contains four meetings in New York City and three meetings on Long Island.
Volumes IV
   and V contain fifty-one meetings in Ohio and Southwestern Pennsylvania.
Volume VI contains meetings in Virginia.

Friends Historical Library of Swarthmore College

Besides the six volumes of American Quaker Genealogy, there was left, at the time of Mr. Hinshaw's death, a large collection of unpublished material which had been abstracted from the records of 307 meetings, chiefly in the Middle West, but including some old and important meetings in eastern Pennsylvania and New Jersey. All this material, together with Mr. Hinshaw's fine library of Quaker family histories, was turned over by Mrs. Hinshaw to the Friends Historical Library of Swarthmore College at Swarthmore, Pennsylvania, together with a sufficient amount of money to have this material copied on 3×5 cards. This project was carried out by twelve persons under the direction of Mr. Lyman W. Riley. The information was typed on the cards, proofread for accuracy, alphabetized, and filed in drawers in five steel cabinets also provided by Mrs. Hinshaw. These 285,000 cards, taken collectively, are known as the William Wade Hinshaw Index to Quaker Meeting Records. A cross index covers 13,438 family names and is a valuable tool for genealogical research.

The arrangement of the cards follows, in general, that of the six published volumes of the Encyclopaedia. They are first indexed by states, then alphabetically by meetings, then alphabetically by family names, and finally, alphabetically by given names, with the cards under each given name arranged by date. In order to work systematically and intelligently with Mr. Hinshaw's encyclopaedias and index cards, it is necessary to understand his abbreviations which are printed in the front of each volume, some of which are: med (married contrary to discipline); mou (married out of unity); ltm (liberated to marry); roc (received on certificate); get (granted certificate to); recrq (received by request); umbc (unbecoming conduct), and so on. This collection of Quaker records at Swarthmore relates to the "Hicksite" division, while the collection of "Orthodox" meeting records is located at 302 Arch Street, Philadelphia, Pennsylvania.

Friends Historical Library of Swarthmore College, at Swarthmore, Pennsylvania, was founded in 1871 by Anson Lapham, and after one disastrous fire and several building changes, is now housed in a fire resistant building given by Clement and Grace Biddle. Among its holdings are the following:

(1) William Wade Hinshaw Index to Unpublished Quaker Records which covers the following states together with the number of meetings.

Arizona (1)	Michigan (6)
California (13)	Minnesota (3)
Colorado (3)	Missouri (3)
Idaho (3)	Nebraska (9)
Illinois (16)	New Jersey (4)
Indiana (86)	Oklahoma (5)
Iowa (84)	Pennsylvania (13)
Kansas (49)	South Dakota (5)
Maryland (2)	Wisconsin (3)

(2) 20,000 books, pamphlets, and periodicals.

(3) Over 1000 volumes of original meeting records, including the Philadelphia Yearly Meeting (General Conference); 143 Preparative Monthly and Quarterly Meetings; original records of Friends General Conference; Ohio Yearly Meeting and 19 of its subordinate meetings; nine meetings belonging to the Illinois Yearly Meeting; Pennsylvania Yearly Meeting of Progressive Friends; microfilm copies of records of the Pennsylvania General Meeting of Primitive Friends; New York and New England Yearly Meetings; Sufferings Meeting of London Yearly Meetings; Registers of the Dublin Yearly Meeting.

(4) *Manuscript Collection.* A few items are:
John Woolman Mss.
Lucretia Mott Mss. (approx. 400 items)
Elias Hicks Mss. (approx. 350 items)
Owen Biddle Mss. (approx. 250 items)
John Greenleaf Whittier Mss. (approx. 100 items)
Charles F. Jenkins Autograph Collection (approx. 450 items)
William I. Hull Collection (approx. 50 boxes)

(5) *Family Papers.* Among the larger collections are:
Elkinton Mss. (1815–1928) (approx. 1000 items)
Ferris Mss. (ca. 1669–1928) (approx. 4000 items)
Richardson Mss. (1732–1896) (approx. 1800 items)
Truman Mss. (1819–1885) (approx. 500 items)

(6) *Manuscript Journals of Quaker Ministers.* A few are:

Samuel Bownas (1676–1753)
Joshua Evans (1731–1798)
Job Scott (1751–1793)
Elias Hicks (1748–1830)
Miers Fisher (1748–1819)
Isaac Martin (1758–1828)
Edward Hicks (1780–1849)
Joseph Foulke (1786–1863)
Dr. Nathan Shoemaker (1788–1868)
Joseph S. Elkinton (1730–1905)

(7) *Photographs*—many thousand.

(8) *Manuscripts on Friends Social Concerns*—as Peace, Indian Affairs, and so forth.

(9) *Doctrinal Writings of Major Quaker Leaders; First Editions of the Quaker Poet, John Greenleaf Whittier; anti-Quaker Literature.*

(10) *Ninety Quaker Periodicals* current from all parts of the world as well as many rare old periodicals dealing with slavery.

(11) *Largest Collection of Quaker Meeting House Pictures* extant.

(12) *Photographs, silhouettes, and sketches* of hundreds of individual Friends are available, and arranged in alphabetical order.

(13) *Many paintings and drawings of Quaker subjects.*

(14) *Map collection* showing locations of Quaker meetings, many no longer in existence.

(15) Many *wedding certificates, deeds,* and *genealogical charts* are available for consultation.

If you cannot visit Friend's Historical Library personally, research may be arranged by writing to Mrs. Mary Patterson, 320 Maple Avenue, Swarthmore, Pennsylvania. She is a competent genealogist who will look up your records for a nominal fee.

Indiana Quaker Records

More Quakers hold residence in Indiana today than in any other state. Many of these people are descendants of the North Carolina Quakers who migrated to Ohio, and from Ohio to Indiana. Therefore, records of Indiana Quakers, although they have not been published, really supplement Hinshaw's Volume One. The Indiana Yearly Meeting was set up in 1821, and all Quaker meetings in

Indiana, prior to that time, were under the jurisdiction of Ohio. Owing to the westward movement of migration, there have been many changes in the organization of the meetings, some of which have been "laid down," or discontinued, divided or merged. Sometimes entire congregations migrated from one state to another.

When a meeting was divided, and a new meeting formed, records of members were automatically transferred without any certificates of removal being issued. While it was the function of the Monthly Meeting to perform marriages, disown members, issue certificates of removal, and deal with matters of disobedience, many marriages were performed in the Weekday Meetings, and merely reported in the minutes of the Monthly Meeting, but the marriage certificate was supposed to have been brought into the Monthly Meeting for recording. Weekday Meetings were often located in a county, or even a state adjoining the location of the Monthly Meeting. Children born out of wedlock have been completely omitted from Hinshaw's work.

In 1857 the Orthodox Indiana Yearly Meeting was divided to form the Western Yearly Meeting which comprised the following Quarterly Meetings: Blue River; White Lick; Western; Union; and Concord, which had a total of 19 monthly meetings, 18 of which were in Indiana and one in Illinois. They also had 55 Weekday Meetings. In 1884, Indiana Yearly Meeting had a membership of 19,534, and Western Yearly Meeting of 12,466. The Indiana Orthodox Yearly Meeting was again divided in 1863 to form the Iowa Yearly Meeting, and again in 1872 to form the Kansas Yearly Meeting. So, the early records of Iowa and Kansas Quakers may be found in Indiana, just as the earlier records of Indiana Quakers may be located in Ohio, and still earlier in North Carolina.

The Indiana Yearly Meeting (Orthodox) comprised 15 Quarterly Meetings:

1. MIAMI (Est. 1809) located in Warren County, Ohio, comprised five Monthly Meetings which embraced eight Weekday Meetings.

2. WEST BRANCH (Est. 1812), located at West Branch, Miami County, Ohio, numbered three Monthly Meetings which covered seven Weekday Meetings.

3. FAIRFIELD (Est. 1815), located in Green County, Ohio,

included three Monthly Meetings which comprised eight Weekday Meetings.

4. WHITE WATER (Est. 1817), located in Wayne County, Indiana, was composed of six Monthly Meetings which included 16 Weekday Meetings.

5. BLUE RIVER (Est. 1818), located in Washington County, Indiana, was composed of three Monthly Meetings which embraced seven Weekday Meetings.

6. NEW GARDEN (Est. 1823) located at New Garden, eight miles north of Richmond, Indiana, was composed of five Monthly Meetings which together numbered 10 Weekday Meetings.

7. WESTFIELD (Est. 1825), comprised two Monthly Meetings, one held at Elk in Preble County, Ohio, and the other at Salem, in Union County, Indiana. Together they numbered three Weekday Meetings.

8. CENTER (Est. 1826), located in Clinton County, Ohio, comprised three Monthly Meetings and 13 Weekday Meetings.

9. WHITE LICK (Est. 1831), located in Morgan County, Indiana, composed of four Monthly Meetings which together number 10 Weekday Meetings.

10. ALUM CREEK (Est. 1835), meetings held alternately at Goshen and Gilead, Ohio, composed of four Monthly Meetings which included 11 Weekday Meetings.

11. WESTERN (Est. 1836), located in Parke County, Indiana, composed of six Monthly Meetings which together comprise 14 Weekday Meetings.

12. SPICELAND (Est. 1840), located in Henry County, Indiana, composed of three Monthly Meetings which numbered ten Weekday Meetings.

13. NORTHERN (Est. 1841), located in Grant County, Indiana, composed of four Monthly Meetings which together numbered 11 Weekday Meetings.

14. SALEM (Est. 1848), located in Henry County, Iowa, composed of three Monthly Meetings which together comprised 11 Weekday Meetings.

15. UNION (Est. 1849), located in Hamilton County, Indiana, composed of three Monthly Meetings which included five Weekday Meetings.

The Indiana Yearly Meeting (Hicksite) established about 1828, comprised four Quarterly Meetings:

1. MIAMI, located in Waynesville, Ohio, composed of eight Monthly Meetings which numbered 17 Weekday Meetings.
2. WHITE WATER, held alternately at Milford and Richmond, Indiana, composed of two Monthly Meetings which comprised eight Weekday Meetings.
3. WESTFIELD, composed of two Monthly Meetings which included two Weekday Meetings.
4. BLUE RIVER, located near Salem, Washington County, Indiana, composed of two Monthly Meetings, comprising seven Weekday Meetings.

English Friends' Records

Americans who are able to trace their ancestry to Friends who were here during the Colonial period, may be able to trace this lineage even further, by making use of the Gilbert Cope Collection of English Quaker Records at the Genealogical Society of Pennsylvania, 1300 Locust Street, Philadelphia. In 1904, under the direction of Gilbert Cope of West Chester, Pennsylvania, transcripts of English Friends' records, from the time of George Fox to the year 1725, were made, brought to this country, and placed in this depository. They are in bound volumes and cover the following Quarterly Meetings:

(1) Bedfordshire and Hertfordshire
(2) Berkshire and Oxfordshire
(3) Bristol and Somersetshire
(4) Buckinghamshire
(5) Cambridgeshire and Huntingdonshire
(6) Cheshire and Staffordshire
(7) Cornwall
(8) Cumberland and Northumberland
(9) Derbyshire and Nottinghamshire
(10) Devonshire
(11) Essex
(12) Gloucestershire and Wiltshire
(13) Herefordshire
(14) Kent

(15) Lancashire
(16) Lincolnshire
(17) London and Middlesex
(18) Norfolk
(19) Northamptonshire
(20) Suffolk
(21) Sussex and Surrey
(22) Warwickshire, Leicestershire, and Rutlandshire
(23) Westmoreland
(24) Worcestershire and Wales
(25) Yorkshire
(26) Scotland

These transcripts also include the following Supplementary Registers:
Volume 1. Bristol and Somersetshire
Cheshire and Staffordshire
Gloucestershire and Wiltshire
Northamptonshire
Herefordshire
Worcestershire
Wales
Volume 2. Cornwall
Essex
Lancashire
Suffolk
Westmoreland
Volume 3. Durham
Warwickshire
Leicestershire
Rutlandshire
Volume 4. Yorkshire

Quaker Bibliography

BESSE, JOSEPH: *Collections of Sufferings of the People Called Quakers.* 2 v. n. d.
(He discusses Quaker sufferings in England in first volume; in second
volume he includes some American sufferings in Massachusetts, Bar-
bados, and Virginia. This is brought down to about 1700, and is indexed by counties).

BEST, M. A.: *Quaker Biographies*. 5 v. 1926.

BEST, M. A.: *Rebel Saints*. 1925.

BOWDEN, JAMES: *The History of the Society of Friends in America*. London 1850, 1854. 2 v.

BRAILSFORD, MABEL R.: *Cromwell's Quaker Soldiers*. Contemporary Review. New York. 1915.

BRAITHWAITE, W. C.: *The Beginnings of Quakerism*. 1912.

BRAITHWAITE, WILLIAM C.: *The Second Period of Quakerism*. 1919.

BRINTON, H. H.: *Children of the Light*. Macmillan. New York. 1939.

CLARKE, M. E.: *The Friends in France*. Cornhill Magazine. London. 1916.

COX, JOHN, JR.: *Quakerism in the City of New York, 1657–1930*. Indexed. 1930.

CUNNINGHAM, Y.: *The Quakers from their Origin to the Present Time*. London. 1897.

Early Quakerism in Ireland. Friends Historical Society Journal. London. 1910.

Exiles in Virginia: With observations on the Conduct of the Society of Friends during the Revolutionary War: Comprising the Official Papers of the Government during that Period, 1777–1778. 1848. (302 pp.)

FISKE, J.: *Dutch and Quaker Colonies in America*. 2 v. 1900.

FOX, GEORGE: *The American Journey of George Fox, 1671–1673*. Friends Historical Society Journal. London. 1912.

The Friend's Intelligencer. (Periodical). Has been published over 100 years. They published the minutes kept at Monthly Meetings but cancelled some unbecoming conduct records in the minutes. Published obituaries of people who died since 1850, but these obituaries are not indexed.

Friend's Library. 1837–1850. 14 v. A collection of historical and literary remains of Quaker writers.

HODGKINS, L. V.: *A Book of Quaker Saints*. 1922.

HOLDER, C. F.: *The Quakers in Great Britain and America*. New York. 1913.

HULL, WILLIAM T.: *William Penn and the Dutch Quaker Migration to Pennsylvania*. 1935. Indexed.

JANNEY, S. M.: *History of the Religious Society of Friends from Its Rise to the Year 1828*. 4 v. Philadelphia, 1859–1867.

JONES, LEWIS T.: *The Quakers of Iowa*. Iowa State Historical Society. 1914. (360 p.)

JONES, M. H.: *Swords into Ploughshares*. New York. 1937.

JONES, RUFUS M.: *The Faith and Practice of the Quakers*. n. d. London and New York.

JONES, RUFUS M.: *The Quakers in the American Colonies*. London. 1911.

LAUGHLIN, S. B., ed.: *Beyond Dilemmas*. Philadelphia. 1937.

MORDELL, ALBERT: *Quaker Militant; John Greenleaf Whittier*. 1933.

MYERS, ALBERT COOK: *Immigration of the Irish Quakers into Pennsylvania, 1662–1750*. 1902.

Myers, Albert Cook: *Quaker Arrivals at Philadelphia, 1682–1750.* Being a List of Certificates of Removal Received at Philadelphia Monthly Meeting of Friends. Reprinted 1957. Southern Book Co. Baltimore.

Orange County, Indiana Marriages Performed at Lick Creek Monthly Meeting. National Genealogical Society Quarterly. v. 31.

Penn, William: *A Brief Account of the Rise and Progress of the People Called Quakers.* London. 1695.

Penn, William: *The Select Works of William Penn.* London. 1825.

Rees, Rev. R. M.: *A History of the Quakers in Wales and Their Emigration to North America.* Carmarthen. 1925.

Russell, Elbert: *History of Quakerism in General and in America.* n. d.

Sewel, William: *History of the Rise, Increase, and Progress of the Christian People Called Quakers.* 1722.

Sharpless, Isaac: *History of Quaker Government in Pennsylvania.* 2 v. 1900.

Sharpless, Isaac, and Gummere, Amelia: *The Quakers in the American Colonies.* 1911.

Sickler, Joseph S.: *The Old Houses of Salem County.* Salem, N. J. Sunbeam Pub. Co., 2nd. ed. 1949. (110 p.) The Quaker settlers adopted here the Flemish-bond style of brickwork in which the owner's initials, numbers, and other designs were set in the wall in colored brick. Eighty such houses are still standing.

Sickler, Joseph S.: *Tea Burning Town, Being the Story of Ancient Greenwich on the Cohansey in West Jersey.* Abelard Press. New York. 1950.

Sweet, William W.: *Religion in the Development of American Culture, 1765–1840.*

Thomas, ——: *Pedigree and Notes.* Register of Births and Burials, Society of Friends, West River, 1665–1810.

Thomas, Allen C., and Richard H.: *The Friends in America.* John C. Winston Co. Philadelphia. 1905.

Watson, W. L.: *Early Quakers and Their Meeting Houses in Rhode Island.*

Weeks, S. B.: *Southern Quakers and Slavery.* 1896.

Woolman, John: *A Journal of the Life, Gospel, Labours and Christian Experiences of John Woolman.* 1774.

Wright, L. M.: *Literary Life of the Early Friends, 1650–1725.* 1932.

Geographical Finding List in Genealogical Periodicals

In General

Index to biographical sketches published in "The Friend," vols. 27–36: Pubs. of the Genealogical Soc. of Pa. (3–109); Utah Gen. & Hist. Mag.

(2–145)
Location of records: Pa. Mag. of Hist. & Biography (27–249)
Quakers who came in the Speedwell. 1456: N.Y. Gen. & Biog. Record (65–45)

ENGLAND
Records: Pubs. of the Gen. Soc. of Pa. (3–226); Utah Gen. & Hist. Mag. (24–61); Nat. Gen. Soc. Quart. (34–73)

INDIANA
Orange County
Records: Nat. Gen. Soc. Quart. (31–115)

MAINE
Berwick
Records: N.E. Hist. & Gen. Register (72–253; 73–43, 124; 75–5)
China
Records (Harlem): N.E. Hist. & Gen. Register (70–268, 318)
Kittery
Quakers, 1734: Maine Historical Recorder: (1–65)
Vassalborough
Records, 1787–1907: N.E. Hist. & Gen. Register (68–162, 242, 379; 69–70, 171, 267, 308)

MARYLAND
Early Records: Pubs. of the Gen. Soc. of Pa. (3–197)
Records: Maryland Hist. Mag. (2 –101)
Anne Arundel County
Records: Pubs. of the Gen. Soc. of Pa. (3–197)
Cecil County
Quakers in 1696: Md. Hist. Mag. (7–328)
Easton, Talbot County

Records: Nat. Gen. Soc. Quart. (11–9)
Kent County
List of surnames in Quaker records: Md. Gen. Bulletin (2–19)
Montgomery County
Records, 1883–1891: Nat. Gen. Soc. Quart. (7–58)
Talbot County
List of surnames in Quaker records: Md. Gen. Bulletin (2–30)

MASSACHUSETTS
Quaker persecutions: Dedham Hist. Register: (4–32–36)
East Hoosac (Adams)
Records: N.E. Hist. & Gen. Register (71–360; 72–16, 107)
Essex County
Quakers: Essex Institute Hist. Colls. (1–135; 13–145); Putnams Monthly Hist. Mag. (2–179)

MICHIGAN
Adrian, Lenawee County
Early Quakers: Det. Soc. Gen. Res. Mag. (20–131)

NEW HAMPSHIRE
Dover
Records: N.H. Genealogical Record: (1–49, 113, 161; 2–29, 73, 123, 145; 3–31; 4–38, 65, 119, 159; 5–23, 57, 121, 171; 6–17, 81, 121, 179)

NEW JERSEY
Diary of a Quaker, 1776:

171; 17–218)

Long Island
  Records: N.Y. Gen. & Biog.
  Record: (3–184; 4–32, 94,
  190; 5–38, 102, 186; 6–97,
  192; 7–39, 85)

Mosherville, Saratoga Co.
  Inscriptions: Michigana (2–
  2: 2)

New York City
  Records: N.Y. Gen. & Biog.
  Record: (3–51)

Quaker Hill, Dutchess Co.
  Records: Old N.W. Gen.
  Quart. (3–79, 117, 168);
  Conn. Quart. (4–114)

Washington County
  Records, 1739–1850: N.Y.
  Gen. & Biog. Rec. (46–122)

NORTH CAROLINA

Gulford County
  Marriages and witnesses;
  New Garden Monthly
  Meeting, 1752–1770: The
  North Carolinian (1–31–32,
  61–63, 75–76)

OHIO
  Quaker settlements; Ohio
  Gen. Quart. (2–145)

Franklin Township, Fulton Co.
  Inscriptions: Dt. Soc. Gen.
  Res. Mag. (17: 107–8)

Miami County
  Records: DAR Mag. (68–
  560, 628, 691)

Waynesville, Warren Co.
  Records: DAR Mag. (76–
  714)

Records, 1824–1827: Old
N.W. Gen. Quart. (8–52)

PENNSYLVANIA
  Quakers in Revolutionary
  War: DAR Mag. (76–145)

Bucks County
  Births, 1680–1684: Ancestral Notes (2–11)

Merion, Montgomery Co.
  Harriton Friends' Ceme-
  tery: Hist. Rec. Wyoming
  Valley: (1–63)

Philadelphia
  Marriages, 1682–1714: Proc.
  N.J. Hist. Soc. (1–9–19);
  Marriage certificates: Pa.
  Mag. Hist. & Biog. 18–
  256, 262, 511; 19–535, 536
  22–376; 29–115; 32–104,
  255); N.Y. Gen. & Biog.
  Rec. (49–391)
  Quaker residents, 1757–60:
  Pa. Mag. Hist. & Biog. 16–
  219)
  Records, 1682–1759: Pubs.
  Gen. Soc. Pa. (1–251; 2–
  93; 4–141; 6–64, 201, 295;
  7–70, 179, 251; 8–76, 174,
  261; 9–35, 164, 236; 10–56,
  123, 238; 11–9, 127, 230;
  12–30, 151; 13–24, 210; 14–
  34, 160, 267; 15–99)

RHODE ISLAND
  Records: Narragansett Hist.
  Reg. (7–65, 164)

Portsmouth
  Records: N.E. Hist. & Gen.
  Register (103–231)

South Kingston
  Records Monthly Meeting:
  Narragansett Hist. Reg. (7–
  65, 164)
SOUTH CAROLINA
  Charleston
  Records: S.C. Hist. & Gen.
  Mag. (28–22, 94, 176)
TENNESSEE
  Migration from Guilford,
  N.C.: East Tenn. Hist. Soc.
  Pubs. (18: 47–58)
VIRGINIA
  Freedmen's schools, 1862–69;

Va. Mag. Hist. & Biog.
  (61: 419–429)
Cedar Creek, Hanover Co.
  Meeting House: Wm. &
  Mary Quart. Hist. Mag.
  (19–293)
Frederick County
  Quakers: W. Va. Hist. Mag.
  (3–55)
Nansemond & Isle of Wight Cos.
  Records: Pubs. Southern
  Hist. Assn. (6–220, 304, 408,
  499; 7–17, 96, 207)

REFERENCES:

Bulletin of Friends' Historical Association, v. 40, Number 1.

Jacobus, Donald Lines: *Index to Genealogical Periodicals.* 3 v.

Johnson, William Perry: *The Quaker Records of Indiana;* reprinted from National Genealogical Society Quarterly in N.G.S. Special Publications, Number 16.

Rubincam, Milton: *English Friends' Meeting Records* in National Genealogical Society Quarterly, September 1946.

Tolles, Frederick B.: Lecture before American University's Sixth Institute of Genealogical Research.

Tolles, Frederick B.: *William Wade Hinshaw Index to Quaker Meeting Records.* National Genealogical Society Special Publications No. 14.

Williams, Ethel W.: *Index to Genealogical Periodicals* (1952–1957) In progress.

14. FAMILY HISTORY VERSUS FAMILY GENEALOGY

FAMILY HISTORY VERSUS FAMILY GENEALOGY—SUMMARY—
WRITING YOUR FAMILY HISTORY—WRITING YOUR FAMILY
GENEALOGY.

There are two methods of compiling ancestral history; one is by ascendants and the other is by descendants. The end results are quite different. A family history is a compilation of the ascendants of one individual. A family genealogy is a compilation of descendants of an immigrant ancestor or ancestors.

One should first undertake the preparation of his family history before attempting the more complicated task of doing a family genealogy. To do a family history, one starts with oneself and works back (by ascent), from generation to generation, to the immigrant ancestor, if possible. The end result is the complete lineage of one individual.

The family genealogy starts with the immigrant ancestor, or ancestors (often several brothers came to the United States, without their parents, and each established a "branch" of the family), and traces down, (by descent), generation to generation, all of their descendants, to the present generation. This is an arduous, complicated task, involving many individuals, which requires widespread research and voluminous correspondence, but when completed, it is a great achievement, if well done.

After you have defined your problem, study the angles of approach to its solution. Will this family be found in census records, in probate records, in land records? Were public vital records kept where this ancestor resided, during his lifetime? Have you checked the church records? Did he live at the right time to have served in any war, and if so, did he receive a pension or bounty land? In other words, what records are available for the region in which he lived, during his lifetime?

The foundation of genealogical research is based upon the exact identity of each individual ancestor. Ask yourself—*who* was he, and *when* and *where* did he live? There are many complications which make identity difficult. You may find several individuals having identical Christian and surnames, living contemporarily in a community. By determining the parents of each, the children of each, and the spouse of each individual, you may be able to positively identify him. In law, a vital record is not considered proof of identity; it only establishes proof of the fact that a birth, marriage, or death occurred. In bureaucratic countries where a close tab is kept on all citizens, positive identification of the individual is not so difficult as in democratic countries where the individual has more freedom of action.

In genealogical research the following sources are useful in establishing the identity of an ancestor: family histories and genealogies; Bible records; family letters and papers; diaries; vital and church records; probate and land records; school records which are accepted as proof of age in most states; town and county histories; directories and professional and trade histories; documents pertaining to civil and military service; obituaries and undertakers' records. The latter now give almost positive identification, some, for example, including the following information: name; race; residence; father's name and birthplace; mother's maiden name and birthplace; deceased's birthplace and date; age; cause of death; physician; name of husband or wife or nearest of kin; military record; social security number; occupation; employer; religion; clergyman; cemetery; date of burial; grave record.

As you collect material for a family history, it is a good idea to keep a record of the brothers and sisters of each ancestor; even though they are only collaterals, their ancestry is the same, and it may be on record. If you decide, later on, to compile a family genealogy, this information will be very valuable. The Family Group Sheets mentioned in Chapter 3 are very useful for this purpose. Be sure to document clearly each statement you make, so that any one may locate and check your sources of information.

Summary

I.   SOURCES

    1. Primary

       a) Original records

    2. Secondary

       a) Printed records

          1. Books

          2. Periodicals

          3. Manuscripts

II. WHERE TO SEARCH

    1. HOME (Primary and secondary)

       a) Family and Bible records

       b) Interviews with relatives

    2. LIBRARY (secondary)

       a) Family genealogies

       b) Town histories

       c) County histories

       d) Published census records

       e) Published vital records

       f) Published probate records (abstracts)

       g) Published State Archives

       h) Published State Papers

       i) Published Ships' Passenger Lists

       j) Published church records

       k) Atlases—maps—gazetteers

       l) Directories

       m) Muster rolls and military records

       n) Surname books

       o) Indexes and guides

       p) Biographies

       q) Newspapers

    3. ARCHIVES (Primary)

       a) Town or township records

       b) City or municipal records

       c) County records

    1. Vital records
    2. Land records
    3. Probate records
    4. Tax records
  d) Territorial and State Records
  e) Federal Records
    1. Census Population Schedules
    2. Mortality Schedules
    3. Military Service Records
    4. Pension Applications
    5. Bounty Land Warrants
    6. Homestead Applications
    7. Ships' Passenger Lists

III. RESEARCH MECHANICS

  1. METHODS
    a) Ascent—end result—family history
    b) Descent—end result—genealogy

  2. FACTORS
    a) Time
    b) Place
    c) Deductions from known facts
    d) Define problem—study angles of approach

  3. STRUCTURE
    a) Exact identity of each individual
      1. Who?
      2. When?
      3. Where?
      4. Occupation
        a) Directories
        b) Biographies
        c) Professional and Trade Histories
        d) Government appointments
        e) Government Commissions
      5. Military Service
      6. School Records

One of the most difficult decisions that faces the compiler of a family history is when to stop searching and start writing. There are always unexplored frontiers in family history research. There is always the chance that Uncle John may return the questionnaire you sent him so long ago, with added information about his branch of the family, or that an opportunity may come to visit the old cemetery in Ohio—but don't wait too long—the years are passing and it may be later than you think. You will never be wholly convinced that further search won't land you a Mayflower ancestor, but in such an event, a supplement could be written. Look over your material and if you have a fairly well rounded-out, well documented story of your family —start writing!

Writing Your Family History

ARRANGEMENT OF MATERIAL:
1. Frontispiece. (May be a family coat-of-arms, the ancestral home, or the portrait of a beloved ancestor).
2. Title Page. (Exact title; author; publisher; printer; date; copyright).
3. Preface or Foreword. (Explain arrangement, numbering system; sources; scope; acknowledgments; dedication).
4. Contents.
5. List of illustrations.
6. List of abbreviations used.
7. Ancestral chart.
8. Family lineages.
9. Index.

While it isn't necessary to do so, it simplifies the arrangement to break down the material into four lineages based upon the four grandparents of the individual whose family history is being set up. Then write up the families in each lineage according to the outline below. The numbers on the ancestral chart are used in parentheses after an ancestor's name wherever it appears in the family history, for ready reference to his position on the family chart. In recording the history of a family, each ancestor's biography is written once, and not repeated in subsequent pedigrees.

Start with the first known ancestor in each family. The immigrant's

family will be generation one. If you have found pre-American
ancestry, start with the first known ancestor. Pre-American ancestors
are lettered, not numbered. Let us say, for example, your IA (abbreviation for immigrant ancestor) is James Roberts; he is generation
one. You also have three known generations of Roberts in England.
James' father, William, who resided in Cambridge, England, will be
lettered A; William's father, James, is lettered B; James' father, John,
is lettered C. Arrangement:

> C.   John Roberts
> B.   James Roberts
> A.   William Roberts
> 1.   James Roberts, (IA)

ARRANGEMENT OF FAMILY HISTORY:
1.   Name of Family—(The Roberts Family)
2.   Illustration of Family Coat of Arms
3.   Heraldic Description of Coat of Arms
4.   Family Name—Its Origin and Meaning
5.   Résumé of Pre-American Ancestry, if found
6.   American ancestry

GENERATION:
1.   JAMES ROBERTS (1620–1688)
     Immigrant ancestor (or first known ancestor in America); name;
     dates of birth and death; place of burial; date and place of
     marriage; name; dates of birth and death of wife; names of her
     parents and their place of residence; state the name of ship upon
     which immigrant came and date and place of first settlement;
     write up the important and interesting events of his life, to
     include education, occupation, civil and military service,
     changes of residence and so forth. Then list his children in
     chronological order as:
     i   John b. (date and place); d.y. (date and place)
     ii Martha b. (date and place); d. (date and place, and
         place of burial); m. Abner Howe, son of John and Mary
         (Jones) Howe, (date and place)
     iii John b. (date and place); d. (date and place); m. (date
         and place); wife's name (date and place of birth and
         death, and names and place of residence of her parents)

       iv   Mary (record same information as for Martha)

2.   JOHN ROBERTS (dates of birth and death of iii above)
Record information as for generation one, above, and continue,
in this manner, generation by generation, to yourself.

ARRANGEMENT OF FAMILY GENEALOGY

      C.   JOHN ROBERTS

      B.   JAMES ROBERTS

      A.   WILLIAM ROBERTS

First Generation:

1.   JAMES ROBERTS (IA to America)
Biographical material as in preceding. Children:

          i   John, d. y.

    2 ÷ ii   Martha m. Abner Howe

    3 ÷iii   John

        iv   Mary d. unmarried

Second Generation:

2.   MARTHA-2-ROBERTS (James-1)
married Abner Howe. Biographies. Children, surnamed Howe:

    4 ÷ i   James

       ii   Jacob d.y.

     iii   Sarah d. unmarried

    5 ÷iv   Isaac

    6 ÷ v   Ebenezer

    7 ÷vi   Aaron

3.   JOHN-2-ROBERTS (James-1)
Children:

    8 ÷ i   James

    9 ÷ ii   Edward

   10 ÷iii   John

   11 ÷iv   Joseph

In the third generation James Howe will be number 4, Isaac Howe
number 5, Ebenezer Howe, number 6, and Aaron Howe number 7.
James-3-Roberts will be number 8, and his brothers, Edward, John,
and Joseph 9, 10, and 11, respectively. This numbering system may
be continued indefinitely. Small Roman numerals are used in numbering the children of each family, and when preceded by a plus sign the
line is carried down in subsequent generations. Arabic numerals are

assigned only to those individuals whose lines are continued. The above is only a skeleton outline which is to be filled out with biographical material.

In the family history, of the immigrant's four children only the descendants of John are traced, since the individual whose family history is being compiled descends from John, whereas in the family genealogy, the descendants of all four of the immigrant's children and all of their descendants are traced as far as possible. In this family only two of the immigrant's children left descendants.

15. DO'S AND DON'TS

Do   consider genealogy as a social science, and a vital branch of history.

Don't   interpret "social science" as a means of raising your social status on the basis of the achievements of your ancestors. *DO* make your own contribution to society.

Do   contact all members of your family and ask them for information regarding its history.

Don't   delay until they are gone.

Do   write down everything as it is told to you, always making sure that *dates* and *places* are included.

Don't   trust your memory, and do not use scraps of paper. Keep a note book for this purpose.

Do   devise a system to keep your notes orderly.

Don't   keep your notes higgledy-piggledy so that you have to hunt for them.

Do   use primary sources whenever possible.

Don't   use secondary sources (except as clues), when primary sources are available.

Do   make a record of family traditions.

Don't   write up traditions as facts unless you can prove them.

Do   get acquainted with your nearest genealogical library, and learn how to use its catalog and holdings.

Don't   expect the librarian in charge to do your research or your thinking for you; his function is only to provide you with material.

Do   have your work organized before going to the library.

Don't   browse. Know what you are looking for, then learn how and where to find it.

Do   treat library materials with the same care you would give your own.

Don't   underscore words, write in margins, turn down corners, or otherwise disfigure books that are not your own. Many genealogical books are long out of print, have become rare, and are fragile. They cannot be replaced and it is a privilege to use them. DON'T misuse that privilege.

Do   keep exact references on every item you copy; use your reference work sheet.

Don't   neglect this. Your work will be of little value if it cannot be verified.

Do   learn to evaluate library materials.

Don't   believe all that is printed.

Do   make a chart of your ancestors.

Don't   trust to memory as to where Nathaniel fits into the ancestral background.

Do   keep a record of the references you find to each family.

Don't   neglect to check them off after they have been exhausted.

Do   read over your bibliography frequently. What made no sense to you at the last reading, may, in the light of new discoveries, afford you the clue you seek.

Don't   neglect this.

Do   start compiling your own bibliography to fit your specific needs.

Don't   trust your memory as to the references you have consulted; keep a record of them.

Do   keep searching, even though you find nothing.

Don't   get discouraged and give up after a few set-backs. Use a new angle of approach—the try-angle.

Do   use whatever guides and indexes are available in the library in which you work.

Don't   neglect to learn how to use them; they have done a lot of your work for you.

Do   keep your biographical material organized and arranged by families.

Don't   wait until it gets out of hand before you start.

Do   ask each library that you visit what special collections they have.

Don't	expect the librarian to give you an inventory of their holdings unless you ask for it.
Do	form the habit of using maps, atlases, and gazetteers.
Don't	be misled into thinking that today's map looks anything like the one that was current at the time your ancestors occupied the land.
Do	remember that boundaries of states and counties have changed.
Don't	disregard this fact; it may lead you astray.
Do	learn to search and use public records.
Don't	forget that many public records are primary records, and a visit to the court house is as important as a visit to the library.
Do	learn how to interpret public records.
Don't	interpret records made a hundred or more years ago in the light of today's social customs. A century ago county clerks in Michigan were registering ear marks and log marks, and today they are registering machines that emanate radiation.
Do	make a practice of using land records, probate records, and census records.
Don't	depend upon the findings of others; make the search yourself. Mistakes have been made, copied and recopied by those who do not check original records.
Do	cultivate the acquaintance of your local abstracter. He is a good man to know.
Don't	forget that abstract office records are not public records.
Do	learn how to use the document division of your library. Find out where the government document depository for your state is located and get acquainted with its facilities.
Don't	pass up government documents because they look technical and uninteresting. They contain important and authentic facts that you should know.
Do	regard *time* and *place* as *prime factors* in solving your problems.
Don't	forget that a statement in a genealogy, without modification as to time and place, is meaningless.
Do	get interested in the personal lives of your ancestors, and study the part they played in the history of the times in which they lived.

Don't   fail to retrospect your thinking into the period of history in which your search is centered.

Do   write your family history and place it in some suitable depository.

Don't   wait until you have successfully traced every line, for that time may never come, and your work may be lost to posterity.

16. EMIGRATIONS—IMMIGRATIONS— MIGRATIONS

MIGRATION TRAILS — INTERNAL MIGRATIONS — MICHIGAN MIGRA-
TIONS—GEOGRAPHICAL PITFALLS.

Settlement of the United States began in the early 1600's, on
a narrow strip of land extending for a distance of about a thousand
miles along the Atlantic seacoast, from Virginia to Maine. Beyond
this narrow foothold, to the north, south, and west, lay the great un-
tamed American frontier. So dense did the wilderness extend in those
directions, that it has been said that a squirrel could have gone from
the Atlantic to the Pacific without ever touching the ground, had
there been no rivers to cross. But those rugged pioneers were not content to remain in the narrow confines of their first settlement, for the
spirit of exploration and adventure which brought them to America
bade them push ever onward in search of new and wider horizons.
This great American characteristic of exploring and conquering new
frontiers has brought about much more than mere geographic expansion; it has contributed a modern culture to the world. In every
one of the fifty states that now comprise the United States may be
found descendants of those intrepid souls who first brought civilization to our eastern shores.

Migration Trails

The first inland settlements were along the large navigable rivers.
The first trails in this country were narrow paths beaten down by
wild animals on their way to watercourses and openings abundant in
succulent forage. The Indians, also in search of food, widened these

trails on their hunting expeditions. Then followed the early settlers who expanded them into cart roads. As the population increased, a demand arose for improved transportation inland, and by the time of the American Revolution there was a need, also, for military roads. A century later, these early trails were further developed into routes traversed by the Conestoga Wagons and Prairie Schooners of those hardy pioneers who were destined to open up the great West.

The Old Connecticut Path was a colonial highway between Boston and Albany. The Iroquois Trail was another colonial road between the Hudson and Mohawk Valleys of New York. The Great Valley Road was the main road south from Western Pennsylvania to Knoxville, Tennessee, and Huntsville, Alabama. The Kittaning Path was an Indian Road between Philadelphia and the Allegheny and Ohio Rivers. The Old Walton Road was built in Tennessee, in 1795, between Knoxville and Nashville. The Old Northwestern Turnpike was a migration highway built about 1825 from Winchester, Virginia to Parkersburg, West Virginia (then Virginia). In 1765 Daniel Boone built the Wilderness Road through the Cumberland Gap, near the point where the states of Virginia, Tennessee, and Kentucky now meet. This became the emigrant trail over which the Virginians and Carolinians traveled to settle Kentucky. John L. McAdam, a Scottish engineer, built a gravel and crushed stone surface road (macadam) in 1792, from Philadelphia to Lancaster, in Pennsylvania. General Forbes built a military road from Philadelphia to Fort DuQuesne (Pittsburg) in 1780.

General Braddock opened a road from Pennsylvania to Fort Cumberland, Maryland, in 1755. This was also a military road. In 1802 there were stagecoach lines between Boston, Massachusetts, and Savannah, Georgia. In the early 1800's trails were opened through the Appalachian Mountains so that settlers could reach the Ohio country. In 1806 Congress made the first appropriation for federal road construction. The National Pike was built from Cumberland, Maryland, across the Appalachian Mountains to Wheeling, West Virginia (then Virginia), in 1817. By 1833 it extended to Columbus, Ohio, and later to Indianapolis, Indiana, Springfield, Illinois, and to St. Louis, Missouri. This is now U.S. 40, a transcontinental route from the Atlantic to the Pacific. In 1822 the Santa Fe Trail was opened to promote trade with Mexico. The Oregon Trail, which later

became U.S. Route 30, was opened in 1842 and carried settlers to
the Pacific Northwest. At a point just north of Salt Lake City, Utah,
the California Trail connected with the Oregon Trail and continued
to San Francisco. It was over this route that the "49ers" traveled in
search of gold.

The Virginia Colony, established in 1607, increased very slowly,
and by 1630 had a population of only about 3000. At that time the
Plymouth, Massachusetts Colony, numbered but 300. By 1640 the
population of New England was around 25,000. In 1634 a small
colony of English Catholics settled in Maryland. The English peasant-
ry began immigrating to Virginia, so that by 1640, its population
was estimated at 7,500, and was augmented later by the great Cavalier
migration at the close of the English Civil War.

Meanwhile the Dutch had taken possession of the Hudson Valley
and the western part of Long Island. The Swedes had gained a foothold on the Delaware, in the vicinity of Wilmington, and also in
Chester County, Pennsylvania. Descendants of these Swedes are
among the first families of Pennsylvania today, and among the old
landmarks is Old Swede's Church. At the time of the Revolution
Philadelphia was the second city in size in the British Empire, being
exceeded in population only by London. The Swedes lost their holdings in 1655 to their more prosperous Dutch neighbors. By 1664
New Netherlands had a population of 7000.

In 1700 the Carolinas were beginning to be colonized. East Jersey
was settled by an English emigration and a Puritan Colony from New
Haven, Connecticut, while West Jersey was settled by English
Quakers, and later settlers came from New York and New England.

English and Welsh Quakers and a few Germans came to Pennsylvania. The Welsh Quakers arrived in 1682 and settled on what is
known as the Welsh Tract, just west of Philadelphia, in Montgomery,
Delaware, and Chester Counties. Place names today indicate clearly
where they settled, for example, Bryn Mawr, Narbeth, Glen Ellyn,
Radnor, Glen Loch, Gwynedd—all are names well known on the
"Main Line" today. In 1700 the population of the English Colonies
in America was 262,000.

In the early 1700's small numbers of French Huguenots settled in
the American Colonies, the greatest number going to South Carolina
and New York State. Some of them, like John Jay, the first Chief

Justice, were prominent patriots during the Revolution. There were some Huguenot settlers in Pennsylvania.

Germans did not come in any considerable numbers until the founding of Pennsylvania. A small Mennonite migration trickled into Pennsylvania from 1683 to 1709. The great Palatine migration occurred from 1709 to 1727, when the Palatinate was so ravaged by war and economic and religious tyranny that many took refuge in England. Queen Anne's government helped some to gain access to America. Some were transported to New York, where they settled near Newburgh and Rhinebeck on the Hudson, and at Palatine Bridge and German Flats along the Mohawk. After a few years their settlements had fanned out into the Mohawk and Schoharie Valleys. A few were dissatisfied and found their way into southern Pennsylvania where they settled, and some went to Maryland and North Carolina. Among these families were the Weisers, Herkimers, Rockefellers, and Wanamakers. In 1710 Swiss Mennonites and Palatines came directly to Pennsylvania and were followed by Dunkers and other sects. By 1730 Pennsylvania numbered between 15,000 and 20,000 Germans in its population. Between 1727 and 1775 a few Germans and Swiss settled in Georgia and the Carolinas, but the majority came to Pennsylvania. Nearly 70,000 entered through the Port of Philadelphia during this period. In 1775 one third of the population of Pennsylvania was German (about 100,000). Religious persecution did not bring these later immigrants who were mostly of the peasant class and came to seek relief from the burdens of feudalism. They were a deeply religious people, honest and industrious. They lived within their own social settlements and did not mingle with other racial groups but clung tenaciously to their native language and customs, developing a dialect still in common usage, and known as "Pennsylvania Dutch."

The Scotch Presbyterians from Ulster, Ireland, came in great numbers during the eighteenth century to escape religious bigotry and economic oppression at home. There were many pure Irish who left Ireland during the famine of 1740, so that by 1773 fully one half of the Presbyterian population of Ulster had come to America. A small proportion went to New England where many settled in Londonderry, New Hampshire. Some went to Cherry Valley, New York, and several thousand others directly to Virginia and the

Carolinas, but by far the greater number took up life on the Pennsylvania frontier. As the frontier advanced they followed and settled in Maryland, Virginia, and the Carolinas, Georgia, Kentucky and Tennessee. It has been estimated that this racial group comprised 38 per cent of the American armies during the Revolution.

In 1718 a law was passed in England which provided asylum in the American Colonies for some types of criminals, in lieu of capital punishment, and many were transported here. Some were political offenders; these were chiefly Scotch prisoners of war. Most of these war prisoners were sent to New England, but a few were sent to Virginia, Maryland, and South Carolina. Records of Old Bailey Prison indicate that over 10,000 criminals were sent to penal colonies in Maryland and Virginia. There were many honest immigrants who bound themselves as indentured servants to pay their passage. Pennsylvania received the greatest number of indentured servants, mostly German and Irish.

African Negroes were brought to Virginia as slaves, as early as 1619. The slave trade so increased that by the time of the American Revolution, there were 500,000 slaves in the colonies, or approximately one-fifth of the total population.

Internal Migrations

In 1750 the population of colonial America numbered over a million people, and in 1790 when the first census was taken, the population was nearly four millions, and all east of the Mississippi. With this population increase more land had to be occupied and the frontier moved inland. Massachusetts sent settlers into New Hampshire and Maine which later became a dependent of Massachusetts. Massachusetts, Connecticut, and Rhode Island all contributed to the settlement of Vermont. Ethan Allen, with his brother Seth, and cousin Remember Baker, went to Vermont from Litchfield, Connecticut, in 1769. Connecticut claimed a strip of land across northern Pennsylvania, known as the Wyoming Valley, and began settlements there. The Dutch expanded in all directions in the Hudson and Mohawk Valleys, and in New Jersey. The Germans and Scotch-Irish expanded their settlements westward into Pennsylvania.

In 1726 Marylanders and Pennsylvanians went up the Shenandoah Valley of Virginia, and by 1751 were in northwest Carolina. Settlement started in West Virginia in 1729, and in eastern Tennessee in 1757. A Virginian named Samuel Houston, of Ulster-Scot ancestry, migrated to Tennessee where he learned military science from Andrew Jackson, and in 1829 he settled in Texas where he led the army to victory after the Alamo defeat. Another Irishman by the name of David Crockett went to Tennessee, became a congressman, and afterwards went to Texas where he fell at the Alamo, and his has become one of the most celebrated names in American folklore. Another Texan, Moses Austin who was born in Durham, Connecticut, in 1761, learned to reduce lead ore and made bullets for the American army during the Revolution. After the war he followed the lead mines to Virginia, then to Missouri, and was granted permission by the Spanish Government, in 1820, to settle 300 American families in Texas. All this helped to pave the way for the independence of Texas and its annexation to the United States in 1846. After Moses Austin's death, his son Stephen continued the work of colonizing Texas, the capitol of which bears his name. In 1770 General Phineas Lyman of Suffield, Connecticut, organized a company called the "Military Adventurers," and took 400 New England families to Natchez, Mississippi, which was then held by Spain. The grant did not materialize, but the New England settlers were allowed to remain there as squatters, and descendants are still there. James Harrod went from Pennsylvania to Kentucky in 1774, and founded Harrodsburg.

From 1785 to 1825 New Englanders poured into New York State. In 1788 settlements were made on the Ohio River at Marietta, by Connecticut colonies under the leadership of General Rufus Putnam and Reverend Manassah Cutler. In 1788 and 1789 families came from Pennsylvania and settled at Cincinnati and at North Bend under the leadership of Judge Symmes. Settlements were made in Minnesota in 1805, in Montana in 1809, and in Oregon and Washington in 1811. Thus, within a thirty-year span, after independence was secured, there were settlements across the continent, from the Atlantic to the Pacific. In 1819 Florida was purchased from Spain and that gave us the oldest city in the United States, Saint Augustine, which was established in 1565.

General John C. Fremont made an exploring trip to Sacramento in 1844 and found five hundred American families already settled there, and in 1846 they were fighting in the United States army against Mexico. This resulted in the cession of the Pacific Southwest to the United States in 1748. This territory then embraced the present state of Utah into which had come a great migration headed by Mormon leaders Joseph Smith and Brigham Young, both natives of Vermont, who had gone early to New York State, and because of continued persecution, had traveled westward through Ohio, Illinois and Missouri, and finally came to their journey's end at Salt Lake City.

While we were engaged in combat with Mexico, friction was also developing with Great Britain over the Oregon country. Interest in the far Northwest had been stimulated by reports brought back by New England sea captains, by John Jacob Astor's American Fur Company, by missionaries to the Indians, and by the Lewis and Clark expedition. The man who is regarded as having been instrumental in securing the Oregon Territory for the United States was Marcus Whitman who was born in 1802, at Rushville, New York, and went to Oregon as a missionary in 1835. It was he who opened a wagon road called "The Oregon Trail," in 1843, over which one thousand emigrants traveled to the end. Many of them came from the Ohio country. This was the one factor which placed Oregon indisputably under American rule, so that the United States reached from the Atlantic to the Pacific, and "Uncle Sam had land enough to give us all a farm."

Definite migration patterns developed over the years. For example the Western Reserve of Ohio was settled by Connecticut people—a look at place names on the map will tell you that, for there are such names as Norwalk, Fairfield, Ridgefield, Norwich, Lyme, Greenwich, New London, New Haven, and many more. But usually family migrations were taken by degrees. Many Yorkers came to Ohio and settled for some years, long enough to own land and to leave behind records, thence on to Michigan, Wisconsin, Iowa, and West.

Americans are not a stationary people. Few families have remained in the ancestral home through several generations. This makes genealogical research fascinating, interesting and challenging. Consider, for example, the migrations of a well known family—that of President

Lincoln. The immigrant was Samuel Lincoln who came from Hingham, England to Hingham, Massachusetts, in 1637. His son Mordecai lived out his years in Massachusetts, but Mordecai of the next generation moved to Berks County, Pennsylvania, and his son, John, settled in the Shenandoah Valley of Virginia. John's son Abraham, grandfather of the President, moved to Kentucky where the family remained for two more generations before going to Illinois. When families migrated usually some members remained behind in the native state, which accounts for the widespread distribution of members of a family.

At first transportation was by water, but rivers sometimes flowed the wrong way and poling upstream was hard and tedious. Some rivers contained falls or rapids which necessitated portage. The opening of the Erie Canal in 1825 served to make the Northwest Territory more accessible to New York and New England. Some waited for winter and drove sleighs when the ice was thick on the rivers, until a system of roads was developed. But, in the 1800's transportation by water was still the better mode of travel.

Michigan Migrations

Before the Pilgrims stepped foot on Plymouth Rock, French explorers had visited Michigan, in 1611 and 1612, and by 1670 there were forts and fur trading posts at St. Ignace and Michilmackinac. Records of the early French missionaries to northern Michigan have been translated and preserved under the title: "Jesuit Relations and Allied Documents; Travels and Explorations of the Jesuit Missionaries in New France, 1610 to 1791," edited by Reuben Gold Thwaites, in 73 volumes. In 1697 Fort St. Joseph (Niles) was established and in 1701 Sir Antoine Cadillac brought fifty French families to Detroit. Their descendants were the first woodsmen in the Michigan lumbering industry, and they were the people who introduced the Paul Bunyan legend to the Saginaw pineries. In 1750 Detroit had 650 inhabitants including 100 soldiers. By 1779 Michigan had 3000 inhabitants. In the year 1781 the Spanish flag was raised over Niles when Fort St. Joseph fell.

In 1795 the John Jay treaty was ratified by Congress, the British relinquished all claim to the Northwest Territory, and on July 11, 1796, the Stars and Stripes were raised for the first time on Michigan soil, at Detroit. On January 11, 1805, Michigan Territory was established, with Detroit as the capital. Just six months later Detroit was completely destroyed by fire—an event which precipitated the development of Michigan's great lumbering industry. Detroit had to be rebuilt and sawmills went up along the St. Clair River and lumbering operations were begun. In 1810 Michigan had a population of 4,762, but two years later the United States declared war against England, and both Mackinac and Detroit fell to the British. It was not until 1818 that public land sales began in Detroit, and by 1820 Michigan Territory had a population of 8,096, of which fewer than 2000 were inhabitants of Detroit. Detroit, Sault Ste. Marie and Mackinac were the largest cities.

Otober 26, 1825, saw the opening of the Erie Canal, and the intermingling of racial groups that characterized Michigan's 19th-century population pattern began. Settlers from New York and New England came pouring into southern Michigan, until, by 1837, two-thirds of Michigan's population were Yorkers and New Englanders. By 1830 the population had reached the figure of 31,639. The fur trade had reached its peak and there was a severe depression.

The first German immigration into Michigan was from 1830 to 1848. The State had published a pamphlet called "The Emigrant's Guide to the State of Michigan," which had been distributed in Germany, and which listed the price of land at $1.25 and less, per acre. The first sizable German group settled in Washtenaw County, in 1830, and the first German Church in Michigan, two miles west of Ann Arbor, was dedicated in 1833. The first German families to settle in Washtenaw County were the Schillings, Allmendingers, Manns, Muellers, Pauls, Becks, Laubengayers, Schmidts, Stollsteiners, Eberhardts, and Klingmanns. Immigrants from Ruthen in Westphalia came from 1837 to 1839 and established another German settlement twenty-five miles northwest of Lansing, in Clinton County, which they called Westphalia. In 1845 another German settlement was made at Frankenmuth in Saginaw County. In 1849 a group of Germans migrated from Washtenaw County to Saginaw County and established the town of Sebewaing. The greatest German immigration took place from 1880 to 1885 due to the severe depression in

Germany. Many of these people settled around Saline and Monroe.

In 1845 there was a potato famine in Ireland, and that sent large numbers of Irish to Michigan. Many went to the Upper Peninsula and worked as miners, and others took up farm land throughout southern Michigan. Beaver Island was populated entirely by Irish immigrants.

In 1846 a revival movement within the State Church in The Netherlands resulted in secession and the "Secessionists" were persecuted by the civil authorities; as a result a group of fifty-three families headed by their secessionist pastor, Dr. A.C. Van Raalte, left Rotterdam and landed in Detroit. After some prospecting they bought one thousand acres of government land, extending to Lake Michigan, between the Grand and the Kalamazoo Rivers. Here they established a town and named it Holland. Soon afterwards four hundred and fifty-seven more refugees from The Netherlands came and bought another section five miles east of Holland—and this settlement was named for their home province—Zeeland.

Finns settled in the Upper Peninsula in great numbers, in 1863, and because of their great physical endurance, became famed as miners and loggers. A distinctive Finnish contribution to the State is the development of cooperative stores. In 1913 a strike in the copper country occurred, and the merchants refused them credit, so they initiated their own cooperative stores, and by 1937, there were thirty-five cooperatives operating in the Northern Peninsula.

The Grand Rapids and Indiana Railroad, in 1870, sent an agent to Sweden and Norway, to offer inducements to immigrants to settle on their cut-over timberlands, and thousands responded. In Delta and Dickinson Counties they still retain their national customs, but in Kent, Muskegon, Mecosta, Osceola, and Leelanau Counties, they have become assimilated into their environment. The Scandinavian element—Swedes, Norwegians, and Danes, worked the copper and iron mines in the Upper Peninsula, where their mining directors were Cornishmen from County Cornwall, England, as the Cornishmen understood the technic of deep mining construction.

In 1872 a group of Polish people settled at Rogers City in Presque Isle County, and many others located in Detroit, Hamtramck, Lansing, Saginaw, Bay City, Grand Rapids, and Flint. In 1880 many Italians came to the Upper Peninsula mining districts, but in later

years, Italian immigrants went to the cities, especially to Detroit, to
work in the automobile plants.

Thus, Michigan's composite population picture portrays an inter-
mingling of many races. French families pioneered in southeastern
Michigan and all the southern tiers of counties were settled by New
Yorkers and New Englanders, followed later by Germans and Irish.
Then came the Scandinavians, the Finns, the Poles and Italians.
Many Negroes found homes in Michigan during and after the Civil
War. Michigan's great natural resources plus her diversified industries
are sufficient to provide a good way of life for them all.

When you have reached a stalemate in your research, after having
placed an ancestor in a certain county of a state, and you are wonder-
ing where do I go from here, or from whence did these people come,
the answer may be found in books on migrations. See Chapter 28—
Bibliography—Migrations Within the United States. Also consult
county and town histories to find where their settlers came from.

Geographical Pitfalls

Shifting boundary lines of counties and states present one of the
great pitfalls in genealogical research. Try to determine if an official
publication has been issued by the state, giving the laws regulating
these boundary changes. If you cannot locate such a publication,
turn to the general section of the county history; that will tell you
when the county was organized, from what parent county (if any) it
was set off, and the dates of organization of the townships. It is always
well to remember, if you cannot find records of people who lived
near the border of a county, or of a state, that they may have resided
in the adjacent county or state.

REFERENCES:

AMERICAN UNIVERSITY SIXTH INSTITUTE OF GENEALOGICAL RESEARCH;
notes taken on lectures, at Washington, D.C.

BILLINGTON, RAY A.: *Westward Expansion; A History of the American
Frontier.* New York. 1949.

BUTTERFIELD, ROY L.: *Migrations Within the United States.* Notes taken
from lecture given before the Tenth Annual Seminar on American
Culture at Cooperstown, New York.

BUTTERFIELD, LOY L.: *On the American Migrations*. New York History. 38: 368–386.

CLINE, LEONARD: *Godhead*. Viking Press. N.Y. 1925 (Finns).

FLORER, W. W.: *Early Michigan Settlements*. Pub. by author. 1941.

HOLBROOK, STEWART H.: *The Yankee Exodus; An Account of Migrations from New England*. New York. 1950.

HUDGINS, BURT: *Michigan Geographic Backgrounds in the Development of the Commonwealth*. Wayne Univ. Press. 1948.

LUCAS, HENRY S.: *Netherlanders in America*. Univ. of Michigan Press. 1955.

PIETERS, ALEIDA J.: *A Dutch Settlement in Michigan*. Eerdmans, Grand Rapids. 1923.

ROSENBERRY, LOIS (KIMBALL) MATHEWS: *The Expansion of New England;* the Spread of New England Settlements and Institutions to the Mississippi River, 1620–1865. Boston. 1909.

STILWELL, LEWIS D.: *Migration from Vermont*. Montpelier. 1948.

17. ANCESTRAL ROOTS IN NEW ENGLAND

When we speak of source states in connection with genealogy, we usually think of the first thirteen states. New England has been described as the place where a man got his spiritual sustenance from the Bible, and his physical sustenance from the sea. The initial migration to New England was religious. Later migrations were economic. At the time of the early migrations to New England, there were weaknesses in the English church, and opinion was divided as to how these weaknesses should be overcome. Some wanted to purify the church. These people were called Puritans, but they were intolerant and ruthless; they broke away from the church to purify it, and became more intolerant than it was.

The other faction wanted to leave the church, so they were called Separatists. They first went to Leyden, Holland, but left there in 1620 for Virginia, and landed instead, on Cape Cod. There were fifty persons on the Mayflower who left issue. The grandsons of the Pilgrims went into the shipping business and became wealthy. When Oliver Cromwell gained control, many Puritans returned to England as they thought happiness was at hand.

In New England there are more records that are useful in working out a family history than in other parts of the country, and they are better preserved. Since New Englanders were predominantly a land-owning class, they made wills and had courts of probate in which to record them, to guard the rights of minors and other dependents. When transferring land they often included "recitals of title" and they provided for public registry of their deeds, something which was almost unknown in the England of their day. Marriage was regarded, in the main, as a civil contract and not a sacrament. Thus marriages of the early days are more often found in town than in church records. Vital records were kept by the town clerks, and not by church officials.

Early New Englanders always chose an Old Testament name for child. It is said that they closed their eyes, opened the Bible to a page, placed a finger on a line, and whatever proper name was included in that line became the child's name.

In looking for county records in New England, it is well to remember there are not so many places to look. All the New England States combined do not have so many counties as Michigan. There is a total of sixty-seven counties in the New England States, whereas Michigan has eighty-three counties.

Massachusetts

The Commonwealth of Massachusetts comprises fourteen counties, 39 cities and 312 towns which are not only geographically but genealogically very important, because in them are found the earliest records of New England, including those of Plymouth Colony in 1620, and Massachusetts Bay Colony in 1628, which were consolidated in May, 1692, under the Provincial Charter of William and Mary. We speak of Massachusetts as a commonwealth, which it is. The United States comprises forty-six states and four commonwealths. The commonwealths are Massachusetts, Virginia, Pennsylvania and Kentucky.

It must be remembered that Massachusetts embraced New Hampshire until 1679, Maine until 1820, and the present Duke and Nantucket Counties were under the Province of New York until after 1691. Massachusetts Bay Colony comprised the counties of Essex, Middlesex, Suffolk and Norfolk. The colony of New Plymouth known as "Old Colony" included the present counties of Barnstable, Bristol, and Plymouth, except the town of Hingham and part of Rhode Island. In the 1746 settlement of the boundary line dispute, the Royal Commission took the towns of Barrington (with parts of Swansea and Rehoboth), Bristol, Tiverton, Little Compton and Cumberland from Massachusetts and awarded them to Rhode Island. There are a number of deeds relating to adjacent parts of Massachusetts in the Rhode Island Colony Deeds; also some wills in the Secretary of State's office in the State House at Providence, Rhode Island.

Printed Records on Plymouth Colony

When the two colonies were consolidated in May 1692, the Old Plymouth records remained in the hands of the last secretary of the colony, Mr. Samuel Sprague of Marshfield. At his death in 1710 the old records were taken over by Massachusetts and sent to Plymouth where the old books of deeds, wills, inventories, and probate records were deposited in the Plymouth Registry of Deeds Office where they now are. The remaining court papers and documents were deposited in the Plymouth County Court House where they were almost totally destroyed by fire, November 7, 1881.

All of the known extant loose papers in these ancient files were gathered together after the fire by an unknown recorder and placed in *The Plymouth Colony Scrap Book* (1636–1693) which is in the Plymouth Registry of Deeds Office where the documents have all been preserved between sheets of silk. The documents are mostly original wills and probates, many of which have wax seals attached. Charles Henry Pope transcribed the records from this scrap book and it was published by Goodspeed of Boston in 1918.

Other printed sources are: *Of Plymouth Plantation* by William Bradford which is the prime source for Plymouth history to 1646. This has been reprinted many times. The 1952 is the last and best edition which has modernized spelling and punctuation and was edited by Samuel Eliot Morison. This book, together with his latest history, *A Chronological Story of the Old Colony of New Plymouth*, 1620–1692, New York, 1956 are the best books for the study of this colony. *Mourt's Relation* consists of extracts from the journals of Bradford and Winslow and was printed in London in 1622. There have been several reprints but the best edition with notes, is that of H. M. Dexter published in 1865. Edward Winslow's *Good Newes from New England* (1624) and his *Briefe Narration* (1646), both important sources, are reprinted from *Young's Chronicles of the Pilgrim Fathers*. The Records of the Colony of New Plymouth in New England, in twelve large volumes (1620–1692) were edited by Nathaniel B. Shurtleff, M. D. (vols. 1–8) and David Pulsifer (vols. 9–12). At the Plymouth Registry of Deeds are found five early volumes of wills and inventories dating from 1633–1686. The Mayflower Descendant has printed volumes one and two and part of three.

Printed Records of the Massachusetts Bay Colony

The principal printed records of the Massachusetts Bay Colony are: *The History of New England* (1630–1649) by John Winthrop; *Records of the Governor and Company of the Massachusetts Bay in New England* (1628–1686), 5 volumes; *Records of the Court of Assistants of the Colony of the Massachusetts Bay* (1630–1692), 3 volumes; *the Acts and Resolves, Public and Private, of the Province of Massachusetts Bay* (1692–1780), 21 volumes; *Session Laws and Statutes; the Journals of the House of Representatives of Massachusetts (to 1755)*, 31 volumes published by The Massachusetts Historical Society; *Reports of the Record Commissioners of the City of Boston*, 39 volumes of verbatim transcripts of original records of which volume 32 contains the *Aspinwall Notarial Records* (1644–1651), published in 1903; *The Massachusetts Historical Society Publications*, consisting of 79 volumes of *Collections*; 68 volumes of *Proceedings*; and some fifty special publications, all of which are rich in source material. Other publications are *The Historical Collections of the Essex Institute, The Colonial Society of Massachusetts, The Prince Society of Boston. The Session Laws* were first printed in 1661, and are the laws passed at successive legislative sessions. *Statutes at Large* were first printed in 1648, and are the statutes in full as originally enacted, as distinguished from abridgements, compilations and revisions. They contain a wealth of genealogical information, such as acts of naturalization, change of name, divorces, and marriages made legitimate. Many genealogical problems have been solved by a methodical search of the Session Laws and Statutes. Copies of the *Session Laws and Statutes* are to be found in the Massachusetts State Archives, the State Law Library, and in the various county law libraries.

Massachusetts Archives

The Massachusetts State Archives in the State House, Boston, contain a wealth of source material in some 327 bound volumes of documents, part of which have been indexed. The first 242 volumes were arranged by subjects and dates by Joseph B. Felt. There is much unbound material dating to 1800. These contain much early Plymouth material, including deeds and probates, as well as many town records. *Massachusetts Soldiers and Sailors of the Revolutionary War*, a compilation from the Massachusetts Archives, was collected and published from 1896 to 1908 by the Secretary of the Commonwealth. *The Soldiers and Sailors of the War of 1812* has also been published.

Census Records

The first Massachusetts census was taken in 1764 and 1765. It contained totals only—there was no population schedule. The first Federal census taken in 1790 is in print. The second Federal census taken in 1800 is in the Library of Congress. Massachusetts State censuses are in the state archives at Boston, including 1855, 1865, and 1875 as well as copies of the Federal censuses of 1850, 1860, 1870, and 1880. The 1800 census of Rehoboth is the only town census of Massachusetts that has been published. This is in Early Rehoboth by Richard LeBaron Bowen, volume 4, chapter 6, published in 1950.

Maps

Maps of towns and other political divisions, beginning in 1649, are in the Massachusetts State Archives at Boston and are valuable in genealogical research. In 1794 the Commonwealth provided by law that "accurate plans be made of each town and district, to a scale of 200 rods to an inch, to be filed in the Secretary's office." These were duly filed, except for the town of Chelsea, and are to be found in the Secretary's Office, Division of Archives, and are titled: "Town Plans," 16 volumes, 1794. Later these plans were used as a basis for maps of Massachusetts proper and for the District of Maine, and were published in 1801.

In 1830 the Commonwealth again ordered "accurate plans to be made of each town and district, upon a scale of 100 rods to an inch, upon a minute and accurate survey, to be lodged in the Secretary's office." These plans, except for the towns of Carver, Chelsea, Littleton, Nantucket, New Bedford, and Plympton, are on file in the Secretary's office, Division of Archives, titled, "Town Plans," 15 volumes, 1830. Also there is a Rehoboth map on file, and one for Seekonk, dated 1831, which was the eastern part of the original town of Rehoboth, and also an 1827 map of Pawtucket, Massachusetts, (which is now in Rhode Island), but originally the northern part of Seekonk. A facsimile of this map is published in *Early Rehoboth*, vol. 4.

In recent years the Commonwealth of Massachusetts published two excellent maps showing the division of the state into counties and towns. One is $31\frac{1}{2}'' \times 21''$ and the other $13\frac{1}{2}'' \times 9\frac{1}{4}''$ and they may be obtained by applying to the Massachusetts Department of Agriculture at Boston.

Court Records

As mentioned before. Plymouth Colony Records, 1620–1697/8, in twelve volumes, have been published as have also the Records of the Massachusetts Bay Colony, 1628–1686, in six volumes. The court system of Massachusetts is extremely complicated, as many courts have been established, abolished and revived again since 1636. This is fully explained in *First Report, Massachusetts Commissioner of Public Records* published in 1885. Printed court records are *Records of the Superior Court of Judicature*, 1693–1788, for several counties. These are in the office of the Clerk of Supreme Judicial Court for the County of Suffolk at Boston where there are also one hundred and ten volumes of *Minute Books*.

In the old Boston Courthouse there are vice-admiralty court records, records of the collectors of customs of various ports and apprentice indenture papers. There are about three thousand indentures binding apprentices, filed with the town clerk from 1734 to 1805. These are in the custody of the Boston Record Commissioners. Naturalization papers begin about 1805 and are in the county courthouses. They contain the following information: name of town and country where born; names of parents; date of birth; place of residence in America. Some of these are indexed. For information on Massachusetts court records, see "*A Bibliography of Published Materials on Early New England Court Records*" by William Jeffrey, Jr., assistant law librarian at Yale. It was first published in the July, 1954, issue of the Boston Public Library Quarterly and reprinted in pamphlet form for the Ames Foundation, Harvard Law School.

Town Records

There were three principal types of town records for both Plymouth and Massachusetts Bay Colonies. These were Proprietors' Records, Town Meeting Records, and Tax or Town Rate Lists.

The colonies granted large tracts of common lands to groups of prospective settlers called Proprietors, for the establishment of towns. These records ante-date Town Meeting Records. They contain the metes and bounds of land assigned to individual settlers, and often show land which has come down by descent in families, although no title is shown by recorded deed. In these cases the Proprietors' Records are very important, for the courts have decided that these titles are valid as against the record in the registry.

The early Town Meeting Records contain everything that was made a matter of record in town meetings, and include land transactions, vital records, copies of court orders, rate lists, constables returns, warning out notices, overseer of the poor reports, ear marks and cattle brands, stray cattle, and soldier lists. These have not been published, are not arranged in chronological order and are not indexed. But a very few have been transcribed. The earliest birth, marriage, and death records are found in the Town Meeting Books and often in the County Court Records. Vital records were originally entered in the Town Meeting Books, with all of the children listed under the name of the father. This kept them in family units, but when they were transcribed for publication in the printed vital records, these family units were broken up and the names of the children listed in alphabetical order. This is another reason why access to the original records is the best source. Marriage intention records were started about 1700. Marriage records in towns which bordered on another state are often missing, as persons unable to obtain permits in their own towns, crossed the state line and were married in the adjoining state. Vital records for 214 Massachusetts towns have been transcribed and published.

The Town Rate Lists are really tax lists and are not in the Town Meeting Books, but were listed on separate sheets of paper, and given to the constables for collection. They are an important source of genealogical information. All assessments were made by districts and the names entered by home lots, not alphabetically. Also, it was customary to prefix to a man's name such titles as Mr., Esquire, Sergeant, Deacon, and so forth, all of which helps in establishing the identity of the man. These lists were folded and tied in bundles and are in the town clerk's offices.

The location of church records in Massachusetts is found in detail in "Reports of the Massachusetts Commissioner of Public Records." In the first report (1885), pages 9–79 and 80–132, will be found "Existing Churches by Towns, Existing Churches by Denominations, and Extinct Churches by Towns;" in the tenth report (1897) will be found, pages 1–189: "Historical Data of Massachusetts Churches, Parishes, Precincts, and Religious Societies, Past or Present;" Twelfth Report (1900) lists "Additional Church Records;" the Fifteenth Report (1902), pages 14–16, lists "Plymouth Church Records, 1620–1859" and "Publications of the Colonial Society," volumes 22 and 23.

Vital records in Massachusetts are found in the offices of the town clerks. From these the New England Historic and Genealogical Society has transcribed and published records of 214 towns to 1850. Church records cover a later period than the town records and the location of these is found in the various reports of the Massachusetts Commissioner of Public Records.

The counties have Registries of Deeds and these are sometimes in several places in a county, and are arranged by districts. Probate records are not all kept in the county seat but in probate districts of which there are several in most counties. For an inventory of Massachusetts county records, see "*Massachusetts Records,*" by Richard LeBaron Bowen. Rehoboth, Massachussetts. 1957.

The New England Historic and Genealogical Society of Boston was founded in 1844 and has published the New England Historical and Genealogical Register, a quarterly, since 1847. It contains a wealth of material on New England families and is found in most genealogical libraries. There is an index to the first fifty volumes as well as a volume index to all the volumes. Mr. Jacobus' Index to Genealogical Periodicals indexes volumes subsequent to volume 50 up through 1952 and this index is being continued. Membership in this Society is $15.00 a year, with the privilege of borrowing some books by mail.

The Federal Tax

In July, 1798, Congress levied a direct tax on the people of the United States which then comprised sixteen states. The returns for Massachusetts and Maine were deposited in the Old Boston Custom House where they were long buried in obscurity. In 1855 a janitor was caught tossing these papers into the furnace, and was stopped. They were then transferred to the New England Historical and Genealogical Society where they are preserved, bound in twenty volumes, some of which are indexed. The records of a few towns were lost in the fire. These records list the name of the owner, or tenant, of each house, in every town in Massachusetts and Maine. This is important information for there are always many tenant residents of a town whose names never get into the tax records. This was called "The Federal Dwelling House Tax."

Connecticut and Vermont

As source states, Connecticut and Vermont should properly be taken up together. Vermont may almost be called the child of Connecticut since it was largely settled by Connecticut people. A look at the maps of the two states will tell you that. You will find the Connecticut towns of Wethersfield, Norwich, Coventry, Fairfield, Hartford, Windham, Wallingford, Woodstock, and many others duplicated in Vermont. In both states the town is the important civil unit concerned with land and vital records. There are also probate districts which are independent of either towns or counties.

Vermont was settled by people from the Connecticut valley and western Massachusetts, especially from Berkshire county. Connecticut was settled by Massachusetts people by whom it was called "The Promised Land," and John Winthrop was called "Moses." The people who settled in Hartford came from Newtown (Cambridge); those who settled in Windsor came from Dorchester, and those who settled in Wethersfield came from Watertown. Since Vermont was settled largely by Connecticut people, it is natural that provisions for record keeping in the two states are similar. Connecticut has eight counties; Vermont has fourteen.

Vital records were kept by the towns in both states, and in both states there is a central depository. The Secretary of State of Vermont has files of vital records from the towns as well as copies of gravestone inscriptions from cemeteries. This collection was made mandatory by a law enacted about 1914. The Barbour Index of vital records in the State Library at Hartford serves the same purpose in Connecticut. These records cover the period of time from the very earliest settlement to about 1850. The Burton Historical Collection of the Detroit

Public Library, the State Library at Madison, Wisconsin, and the Western Reserve Library in Cleveland, all have microfilm copies of the Barbour Index. Vital records were not published in books very extensively in either state, as they were in Massachusetts. Bailey's *Early Connecticut Marriages* was published in seven volumes for various towns. See Chapter 28—Bibliography, Vital Records. Miss Abby Hemenway's *Vermont Historical Gazetteer*, five volumes, was published from 1868 to 1891, and is a collection of the town histories of Vermont. It was indexed in 1923.

Land records were also kept by the towns in both states. These have been microfilmed by the Mormons and copies placed in the state libraries at Montpelier and Hartford. Vermont Land Records are deposited in the Public Record Office in the Supreme Court and State Library Building at Montpelier.

Probate records are recorded in districts in both states and there are more districts than counties in each state. Vermont probate districts are listed in volume 27 of *The American Genealogist*. Probate districts and towns for Connecticut are listed in the front of volume one of Manwaring's Digest of Early Connecticut Probate Records, Hartford District, pages ix–xxx.

Federal census records are extant for both states. The 1790 census, although it was not taken until 1791 in Vermont, has been published for both states, and the 1800 census for Vermont was published by the State of Vermont.

LIBRARIES AND HISTORICAL SOCIETIES. The Connecticut State Library and the Connecticut Historical Society are both located in Hartford, but not together. Some of the collections in the Connecticut State Library which relate to genealogy are:

Lucius Barnes Barbour Collection of Connecticut Vital Records.

Sherman W. Adams Collection of Official Rolls and Lists Relating to the French and Indian War.

The Colonel Edwin D. Judd Collection of Civil War Military Rolls and papers.

The Sylvester Gilbert Collection of papers relating to the American Revolution.

The Captain John Pratt Collection of Military Papers, 1778–1824.

The Major E. V. Preston Collection of Civil War Military Rolls and Papers.

The Colonel Daniel Putnam Letters.

The Governor Trumbull Papers and Manuscripts.

The Robert C. Winthrop Collection of Manuscripts Relating to Early Connecticut.

The Samuel Wyllys Collection of Manuscripts Relating to Witchcraft and Crime in Early Connecticut.

The Enfield Shaker Collection.

The William F. J. Boardman Collection of Books and Manuscripts Relating to Genealogy.

The Sherwood Collection of Connecticut Newspapers.

The Welles Collection of American Newspapers from about 1820–1840.

The Daniel N. Morgan Collection, including the table upon which the Emancipation Proclamation was signed.

The 1662 Charter of Connecticut—of Charter Oak fame.

The Stuart Portrait of Washington.

The early manuscript probate records of many Connecticut towns are also in the State Library vaults, and may be examined upon application. The Office of the Secretary of State, in Connecticut, has a wealth of material, such as:

Land records, 1640–1673.

Patents of towns, 1671–1705.

Colony Records of Deeds and Patents, 1723–4.

State Records of Deeds and Patents of Land, 1795–1846.

Records of the Commissioners of the United Colonies, 3 volumes covering 1643–1702.

Western Reserve (Ohio) Deeds (1800–1807)

Connecticut Land Company's Certificates for Western Reserve Lands.

Connecticut Land Company's Mortgages of scrip in the Western Reserve, 1796–1807.

Some of the documents in the Connecticut State Library which relate to genealogy are:

Militia, 5 volumes, 1678–1757.

War with Indians, and French and Indians, 3 volumes, 1675–1725.

Wars with Spain and France, 7 volumes, 1740–1744.

Revolutionary War Muster Rolls and Soldiers' Accounts, 36 volumes.

Indians, 2 volumes, 1647–1789.

Susquehanna Settlers (Pennsylvania), 1755–1796.
Colonial Boundaries, 1662–1827. (Rhode Island; New York; Massachusetts).
Civil Officers.
Lotteries and Divorces.
Insolvent Debtors.

The Connecticut Historical Society

Among the holdings of the Connecticut Historical Society are the following items that are of especial interest in genealogical research:

Over 2000 Manuscript Genealogies compiled by early genealogists.

Many historical manuscripts.

Fine library of local histories of New England states.

Other printed material includes Historical Society's Publications and the most complete collection in existence of early Connecticut imprints, including sermons, laws, almanacs, and political controverisal pamphlets.

The extensive library of the Society of Mayflower Descendants of Connecticut is deposited here, and accompanying this is a manuscript list of the names of about 5000 descendants of Mayflower passengers.

The Connecticut Historical Society has published *The Hartford Land Papers, Revolutionary Rolls*, and *French and Indian War Rolls*.

The first librarian of the Connecticut Historical Society was Rev. Thomas Robbins who was also a teacher, and is noted for his "Century Sermon of Danbury," as this is the only account preserved of this town's first one hundred years, owing to the burning of the town records, April 27, 1777, when General Tryon invaded and burned the town. It was customary, in colonial times for some renowned minister to deliver a "Century Sermon" at the close of the first 100 years of a town's existence, and in these are usually found a great deal of family history.

The Connecticut Historical Society maintains a loan service to members. A letter received in 1955 from Miss Marjorie E. Waterman, Chief of the Reading Room, The Connecticut Historical Society, 1 Elizabeth Street, Hartford 3, Connecticut, reads, in part: "The Charles G. Woodward Memorial Genealogical Loan Collection comprises genealogies and town histories which are duplicates, or are given to the Society for the specific purpose of being placed in the loan collection. The collection is anything but in order and is unlisted. It is, however, good as far as it goes. Any of the books may be borrowed for a month at a time, at the cost of 50 cents per month which is to cover mailing and any possible damage. If, when making a request for a book, the person will state his problem at the same time, it would be to his advantage because if the request is not included in the loan collection, we would be able to look up the information in our regular genealogical collection." This loan service is open to members, and the cost of membership is the cost of the Admission Fee, $3.00, which takes the place of the first year's dues; thereafter annual associate dues are $2.00. There may also be obtained from the Connecticut Historical Society, a mimeographed list of genealogical and historical books which they have for sale, and members may purchase the books for 20 per cent discount."

The Middlesex County Historical Society is located at Middletown and has many books. The New London County Historical Society is housed in the Captain Nathaniel Shaw mansion which it owns, having purchased it from Nathaniel Shaw Perkins in 1905. The Fairfield County Historical Society holdings include vital, church and cemetery records. This library has much correspondence of Roger Sherman, nephew of Roger, the Signer, a noted lawyer who became associate judge of the Supreme Court of the State. He moved from Norwalk to Fairfield in 1807. His letters have both legal and genealogical value. A list of the houses burned by the British, July 7 and 8, 1779, and a copy of a letter from General Gold Selleck Silliman to Governor Trumbull describing the march to and the burning of Danbury by the British, April 27, 1777, are valued possessions. The copy was made that year. The landing of the enemy at Westport and how they made their way through Redding and back through Ridgefield and Wilton to Saugatuck, and their boats, is described. The town records are complete with the exception of one very early book said to have been carried away by Ludlow when he removed to Virginia in 1654.

The New Haven Colony Historical Society, 114 Whitney Avenue, New Haven, has manuscript genealogies of Guilford, Milford, and East Haven families, a collection of letters of the Huntington family of Norwich, during the Revolution, and correspondence of Jared Ingersoll prior to and during the Revolution.

The Sterling Memorial Library of Yale University must be mentioned. While its primary purpose is to serve research workers in the field of American History, in its genealogical material are about 2500 volumes relating to New England families, especially families of New Haven, and of Yale graduates, and of persons closely connected with the history of Yale University.

In Vermont, the State Library, the Supreme Court, and the Vermont Historical Society, are all housed in the same building in Montpelier. The Historical Society has a Graves Registration File, church records, the Colonial Dames Collection, and the Daughters of the American Revolution Collection.

Besides Hemenway, other printed records of value relating to Vermont are Vermont State Papers; Records of the Council of Safety and Governor and Council of the State of Vermont, 1775–1836. Grantees of townships set up by Governor Wentworth of New Hampshire may be found in volume 26, New Hampshire State Papers. Vermont records are to be found in volume 4 of O'Callaghan's Documentary History of the State of New York. New Hampshire claimed the territory which now comprises Vermont but it was held by New York State under the Duke of York's charters of 1664 and 1674. Other libraries in Vermont are at Bennington and Middlebury.

It should be mentioned that other important publications relating to Connecticut are anything authored by Donald Lines Jacobus, a native of New Haven who has dedicated his life to Connecticut genealogy; among his works are *The American Genealogist*, *Periodical Indexes*, *Families of Old Fairfield*, *New Haven Families*, and others.

Rhode Island

Rhode Island has but five counties. Land records are kept by the towns, the same as in Connecticut. There are no special probate districts. Probate records are kept by the towns. Court records are kept by counties. Vital records have been printed but contain many errors. See Chapter 28—Bibliography, Vital Records. Town histories are not numerous. The library of the Rhode Island Historical Society is in Providence and contains many manuscript genealogies, and some public records.

New Hampshire

New Hampshire has ten counties. Probate records in New Hampshire differ from those in the other New England States, in that all wills for the colonial period (up to 1775) were probated in one offiice, at Dover. Wills after 1775 are in the county offices.

In the New Hampshire Archives are printed a series of Town Papers which are very helpful in genealogical research. Vital records have been transcribed to cards and arranged in one alphabet at the State Library at Concord. The New Hampshire State Papers have been published and contain much important source material, such as abstracts of wills, Revolutionary muster rolls (4 volumes), and so forth.

The Granite Monthly, a periodical which at one time contained a wealth of genealogical material, is now chiefly devoted to history. It was indexed by Mr. Jacobus in his *Index to Genealogical Periodicals* up to the time it had no further genealogical value. *The Genealogical Dictionary of Maine and New Hampshire* by Davis and Libby is a valuable work. Numerous town histories have been published for New Hampshire towns. Some are better than others. *The New Hampshire Historical Society Proceedings* (5 volumes), published from 1872-1908, are very valuable. Another good source is the *New Hampshire Genealogical Record* of which only seven volumes were published from 1903 to 1910. Volumes 1–6 contain records of Dover, N. H., Quakers. It is well to remember that records concerning New Hampshire are sometimes found in Massachusetts or in Maine.

Maine

Maine has sixteen counties. Maine was a part of Massachusetts until 1820, but there are original records of great genealogical value at York which was the center of the permanent early settlement. York deeds have been published in about twenty volumes. York probate records have also been published, but not in their entirety. Early wills were published in the Maine State Papers. *The Maine Historical and Genealogical Recorder,* nine volumes, published from 1884 to 1898, contains much very useful genealogical material.

18. TRAILING ANCESTORS THROUGH NEW YORK STATE

PATTERN OF SETTLEMENT—COLONIAL BOUNDARY DISPUTES—
LAND RECORDS—THE PATROON SYSTEM—THE MANOR SYSTEM
—LIBRARIES—COUNTY RECORDS—VITAL RECORDS—CENSUS
RECORDS—BIBLE, CHURCH AND CEMETERY RECORDS—IMMIGRA-
TION AND NATURALIZATION—MILITARY RECORDS—LOCAL HIS-
TORIANS—SOCIAL HISTORY—"THE SPIRIT WAY."

Family historians of Michigan are deeply interested in New
York State sources, for there has always been a strong bond of kinship
between the people of these states. In fact, Michigan may well be
called the child of New York and the grandchild of New England, for
in 1837 two-thirds of Michigan's population were New Yorkers and
New Englanders, and 85 per cent of the pioneers of southwestern Michigan were "Yorkers." So, the family trees of their descendants are
rooted deep in the soil of New York State, and deeper yet in the soil of
New England which sent many settlers to New York State. The social
customs of Michigan people simulate more closely those of the people
of New York than of any other state.

A look at Michigan place names on the map indicates fairly well
from whence the first settlers came. For example, Michigan counties
of Clinton, Genesee, Livingston, Monroe, Otsego, and Wayne, all
have their counterparts in New York State, although, undoubtedly,
Wayne, in both instances, was named for General Anthony. Looking
at place names of towns in Michigan and New York, we find in both
such names as: Ithaca, Utica, Flint, Marshall, Lansing, Mount Pleasant, Ovid, Rochester, St. Johns, Trenton, Vassar, Yale, Monroe,
Lyons, Elmira, Baldwin, Albion, Charlotte, Brooklyn, Adrian, Cazeno-

via, and Fenton, to name but a few. Michigan village and township place names read like a gazetteer of New York, and often afford a clue to the region in New York State from whence the first settlers came.

Pattern of Settlement of New York State

The first Dutch settlement was made in 1614. New Rochelle was settled by the Huguenots in 1688. In the early 1700's many Rhode Island people settled in eastern Rensselaer County, and Pennsylvanians migrated to southwestern New York. In the late 1700's there was a heavy migration of New England people from Connecticut, Massachusetts, and Vermont, to Oneida County. Many Connecticut people went to Delaware County. Long Island was heavily populated by people from Connecticut, many of whom went later to New Jersey and central New York counties.

In 1710 the German Palatines arrived, and in 1718 the Scotch-Irish settled in Orange and Ulster Counties, and in 1738, more Scotch-Irish migrated from Londonderry, New Hampshire, to Orange County, under the leadership of John Lindsay. The greatest migration from New England to New York was between 1786 and 1805. At this time there were also migrations from New Jersey and from Ireland. The Erie Canal was opened in 1825 and a great exodus of "Yorkers" began pouring into Michigan, as water transportation was quicker, safer, and much cheaper.

Colonial Boundary Disputes

In colonial times New Hampshire claimed all of the territory now embraced by Vermont, and New York claimed the territory west of the Connecticut River, under the Duke of York's charters of 1664 and 1674. In July, 1674, the King's Council decreed New Hampshire's boundaries to be "the western banks of the River Connecticut from where it enters the Province of Massachusetts Bay to the 48th. degree of Northern Latitude" (the Canadian boundary). In spite of this ruling the controversy continued, but the line that was finally accepted still constitutes the boundary between Vermont and New Hampshire. In 1777 Vermont declared her independence from New

York. While the area that is now Vermont was part of New York State, it comprised four counties—Charlotte, Gloucester, Cumberland, and a small area in the southwest region was attached to Albany County. Along with independence, Vermont also claimed land west of Lake Champlain, from the source of the Hudson River (in Mt. Marcy in central Essex County) to the Canadian border. In 1814 the line between New York and Vermont was surveyed and marked by a joint commission, changed again in 1876, and ratified by Congress April 7, 1880, when Vermont ceded to New York a small tract comprising that part of Fairhaven, Rutland County, west of the Poultney River.

New York still claimed all the territory east to the Connecticut River, which took in the western part of the present states of Massachusetts and Connecticut. The New York-Connecticut boundary was established in 1787, by commissioners appointed by Congress, and the line was described: "Beginning at a monument erected in 1731 by Commissioners from Connecticut and New York, distant from the Hudson twenty miles, and running north fifteen degrees, twelve minutes and nine seconds, east fifty miles, forty-one chains and seventy-nine links, to a red or black oak tree marked by said commissioners, which said line was run as the magnetic needle pointed in 1787." In 1786 Massachusetts relinquished to New York the tract known as the "Boston Ten Towns" in the southwest corner of Massachusetts; and in 1853 a small tract of land known as "Boston Corner" was ceded to New York by Massachusetts, taken from Berkshire County, Massachusetts, and added to Columbia County, New York. One of the most confusing things for genealogists is the fact that during the New York-Massachusetts controversy, Massachusetts held the land rights and granted the titles to land, but the land was under the civil jurisdiction of New York State, so the search for land records in this region would be in Massachusetts, but the court actions in New York.

The New York-Connecticut controversy continued until 1880 when the present boundary was fixed. In effect, it is a line twenty miles east of the Hudson, starting on the Mamaroneck River.

The New York-New Jersey boundary was plainly defined under the Duke of York's grant to Sir George Carteret, in 1664, but was unsettled until 1679 when commissioners appointed by the King fixed it substantially where it is today.

The New York-Pennsylvania boundary was the least controversial of all, as it was on a line 43 degrees North Latitude where it was crossed by the Delaware, and from there a line was run westward. Both states appointed commissioners for this purpose in 1774; the work was finished in 1787 and ratified in 1789.

In 1781 New York surrendered all claim to land west of its present boundary, as did all of the original states; this was the land of the Public Domain. Pennsylvania purchased from the United States, a triangle of land on Lake Erie, in order to have an outlet to it. This is now Erie County, Pennsylvania.

For New York and New Jersey material, see *Stilwell's Historical and Genealogical Miscellany; Data Relating to the Settlement and Settlers of New York and New Jersey*," 5 volumes. New York, 1903–1932. The first two volumes contain records. See also Rosalie Fellows Bailey's book, *Old Houses of New York and New Jersey*. This not only describes and illustrates the houses, but gives a documented family history of the people who occupied them. For border disputes, see *Boundaries*, 2 volumes, published by the University of the State of New York. Albany. 1884.

Land Records—The Patroon System

In 1626 Peter Minuit, Director of the Dutch West Indies Company, bought Manhattan Island from the Indians for $24.00 worth of trinkets, and founded New Amsterdam. From this center, settlements were systematically organized in all directions.

In 1629 the Dutch West India Company granted special charters to Patroons, authorizing them to purchase land from the Indians, and plant colonies. For each colony of fifty persons older than fifteen years, the Patroon was given a tract of land 16 miles along one side of a river, or 8 miles along both sides, and "so far into the country as the situation of the occupiers will permit." Over the colonies thus established, the Patroon had almost political and judicial authority. Among the estates thus founded was Rensselaerwyck, opposite Fort Orange, or Albany, which endured from 1630 to 1838. By the Patroon system the land was leased and the tenants had no title to the land, but they could sell their lease rights. The thing that makes genealogical research so difficult is that these leases were not public records, but were the private records of the Van Rensselaer family. There is a state publication concerning these leases, called *The Van*

Rensselaer-Bowier Manuscripts. The State Library at Albany has indexes to these leases. They contain family papers and Bible records, land transfers, survey books, and plat maps. The rents on these leases had to be paid even though the amount was sometimes "two fat hens and a bushel of wheat each year." Another publication that refers to these leases is titled: *The Van Rensselaer Correspondence.*

There were between 60,000 and 100,000 tenant farmers on Rensselaerwyck when anti-rent troubles started in 1838. For a better understanding of the tenant's viewpoint, read Dorothy Canfield Fisher's *Vermont Tradition*, pages 55–133, published in 1953, and Henry Christman's *Tin Horns and Calico*, published in 1945.

The Goldsbrow-Banyar Patent was another similar tenant-lease plan. This collection is in the State Library at Albany, and consists of journals kept by the land agents, and contains an amazing fund of genealogical information, but has not been printed. The Dutch grants were confirmed by the English after they took over the land. England granted military patents after the colonial wars. These took in Oneida and Seneca Counties, and are also in the State Library.

The Manor System

The English set up a Manor System, similar to the Dutch Patroon System, along the Hudson, and on Long and Staten Islands. This was a system of tenants and leases also. The Livingston Manor was held by Robert Livingston, in Ulster County. Palatines settled there in the early 1800's. These are not public records but they are on deposit in the Franklin Delano Roosevelt Library at Hyde Park. The English granted patents, and the grants are in volume four of the Documentary History of New York. This system also makes genealogical research extremely difficult, as there were no deeds, and these leases were not recorded. At his death a man had little or no property to dispose of, so there were no probate records, and about all the sources of information were the meager tax lists, census and church records.

New York had but ten original counties when it was occupied by the Dutch. This arrangement remained unchanged for fifty years. In 1774, England, as a last gesture, made two more counties, Tryon and Princess Charlotte. The question then came up—how large should a county be? It was decided that it should be small enough so that a man could travel from his home, in any part of the county, to the county seat and return in one day.

The Land Bureau is in the Secretary of State's Office, at Albany. There are many deeds and mortgages, from very early to late times. One may write there for early miscellaneous land records.

Some other printed land records are: *Calendar of New York Colonial Manuscripts; Endorsed Land Papers, 1643–1803*, Albany. 1864. This covers the petition for surveys and copies of Indian deeds. These include the land that went from the province to the individual. There are three series:

(1) Calendar of Land Papers.

(2) Calendar of Council Minutes which gives the grant date.

(3) Calendar of Patents. The patent gives the title, and includes papers in connection with the grant, and sometimes considerable genealogical information is included. The book is out of print.

Another printed record is titled: *Eighteenth Century Records of the Portion of Dutchess Country, New York, that Was Included in Rombout Precinct and the Original Town of Fishkill*. This is in the Collections of the Dutchess County Historical Society, vol. 6, published in 1938. It contains tax lists and lists of deeds and mortgages. Another publication is *History of the Pioneer Settlement of Phelps and Gorham's Purchase, and Morris' Reserve*. Rochester, 1851. A name index was made in 1946 by LaVerne C. Cooley of Batavia. *The Pioneer History of thr Holland Purchase of Western New York*, published in Buffalo, in 1849, was also indexed in 1946, by Mr. Cooley.

Libraries

The New York State Library at Albany has considerable manuscript material. They have Dutch records, tax lists, non-resident wills, military service records, muster rolls, pay rolls of the Erie Canal workers, marriage bonds, and patents. Smaller libraries have a wealth of regional material.

The Grosvenor Library at Buffalo has fine collections of material covering the Niagara area. They answer requests within reason, and are very prompt. The Syracuse Public Library has a Pioneer Index for Onondaga County up to 1850, abstracts of wills from about 1786–

1842, completely indexed census records, and church and cemetery records for Onondaga, Oswego, Cayuga, and Chenango Counties. The Rochester Public Library has considerable material on Ontario, Wayne, and Monroe Counties. Cornell University Library at Ithaca has extensive holdings of manuscript records which include family papers, church and cemetery records.

The Flower Memorial Library at Watertown has extensive collections of material on Jefferson County families. These are not open to the public, but a request addressed to Mrs. Keith Stanton, 129 Haley Street, Watertown, New York, will be answered, if return postage is included. There is a fee for extended searches. The collections include: cemetery inscriptions (the DAR has copied every burial ground in the county and all are indexed); Bible records; lists of Revolutionary and War of 1812 soldiers; deeds from 1805; wills from 1828 (fire destroyed the earlier ones); state census from 1825; (have 1835 through 1875, except 1845 which is missing. They also have 1905, 1915 and 1925 which is the last state census taken by New York State) Federal census of 1850 through 1880; vital records for 1847, 1848, 1849 which are the only ones kept prior to 1883; also marriages and deaths from early newspapers; all these records have been copied and indexed.

In New York City there are three large libraries with extensive holdings. The New York Public Library has a fine genealogy department, as also has the library of the Long Island Historical Society in Brooklyn. The New York Genealogical and Biographical Society has a fine library. Their holdings contain much material on New York families. This organization is to New York State what the New England Historic and Genealogical Society is to New England. It was founded in 1869, and has published the New York Genealogical and Biographical Record since 1870.

Mention should also be made of the collection at Fonda, in Montgomery County, which is now called the Department of History and Archives. This was established in 1936 with a WPA appropriation. They have collected, transcribed and indexed town and village records, school and church records, highway records, cemetery records, census records, military and land records, and in fact everything of value, including family records and papers. Fonda is a very important place to do research, since Montgomery was a mother county in the early days, and included all the central part of the state, comprising thirty-seven present-day counties. In 1876 a history of every county in the state was compiled.

Country Records

Land records in New York State are found in the county clerk's office. These include deeds, mortgages, chattel mortgages, judgments, adoptions, incompetents, coroner's inquests, assumed business names, homestead exemptions, court papers (civil actions), soldier's discharges, infant's real estate, decedent's estates, certificates of conviction, habitual criminals, registry of physicians and nurses, firemen's discharges, licenses to peddle, farm names, collector's bonds, conditional sales, state census records for the county and towns within the county, marriage records from about 1908, and corporation records. Earlier records are filed with town clerks or with the Bureau of vital statistics at Albany.

Probate records. Wills begin with the organization of the county. Before the counties were organized probate records were colonial or state records, and during the Dutch regime they were under the jurisdiction of Notary Publics and were called Notarial papers. After the organization of the county a Court of Probate was established. So, in the state records there are wills. Maine and New Hampshire also published wills in their state papers. For published probate records of New York State, see Bibliography—*Published Probate Records*.

Other published material on New York State that should be checked includes:

Cemetery Records of Orange, Sullivan, Columbia, and Rockland Counties, compiled by Gertrude A. Barber; *Minutes of Orphanmaster's Court of New Amsterdam, 1663–5*; *Minutes of the Executive Boards of the Burgomasters of New Amsterdam, 1631–4*; *Records of Walewyn Vander Veen, Notary Public, 1662–4*, two volumes, published by the Colonial Dames of New York State, 1902–1907.

Guide to Genealogical and Biographical Sources for New York City, 1783–1898, By Rosalie Fellows Bailey, 1954; Bibliography of Syracuse History, by Franklin H. Chase, published by the Onondaga Historical Association, Syracuse, 1920; Check List of Books, Maps,

Pictures, and Other Printed Matter Relating to Westchester County and the Bronx, by Otto Hufeland, published in *Westchester County Historical Society Publications* Number 6, 1929; Bibliography of New York City Directories, 1626–1783, published *in Bulletin of the New York Public Library*, October 1942.

Obsolete New York Towns and Villages in *Civil List of the Colony and State of New York*, 1888, edited by Edgar A. Werner, Albany, 1889. (pp. 584–586; Existing Towns; pp. 567–578; Principal Villages, pp. 579–583); *Long Island Genealogical Source Material* by Herbert F. Seversmith, *Publications of the National Genealogical Society*, Number 9, 1948–9; *The Dutch Records of Kingston, Ulster County, New York*, 1658–1664, revised and translated by Samuel Oppenhein, in *Proceedings of the New York Historical Association*, vol. 11, 1912; *Tax Lists of the City of New York*, 1695–99, in *Collections of the New York Historical Society*, 1910–11; *Book of the Supervisors of Dutchess County, New York*, 1718–22, Vassar Brothers, Poughkeepsie 1908; Manuscript Collections in the Library of the National Society of the Daughters of the American Revolution, Washington, D.C. These comprise hundreds of volumes of cemetery, church, family, Bible, vital, probate, land, and military and pension records, all copied by New York State Chapters.

Vital Records

The Bureau of Vital Records was established in 1880. For printed vital records, see Chapter 28—Bibliography, *Published Vital Records*.

Census Records

New York State took a State Census in 1835, 1845, 1855, 1865, 1875, and 1915. The State Census of 1855 was published by Franklin B. Hough. It listed the names of each member of the family and is modeled after the 1850 Federal Census. The Federal Census of 1790 for New York State has been published, and the enumerations of 1800 through 1880 are on microfilm. Much of the 1800 Federal Census has been published by counties in the New York Genealogical and Biographical Record.

Town Census Records. In 1847 a law was enacted which authorized up-state towns to take a census. This was handled by the Superintendent of Schools. These returns are sometimes found in the offices of the county clerk.

In 1957 the New York State Library published a *Bulletin* edited by Edna L. Jacobsen, which lists an inventory of all New York State Census records. See Bibliography—*Census Records*. The early censuses and assessment rolls in colonial New York are in the *Documentary History of the State of New York*, by E. B. O'Callaghan, 4 volumes, Albany, 1849–1851.

Bible, Church and Cemetery Records

Church records are semi-official records in New York State. There were marriages by banns and by license which was a bond until 1784. Banns were published in church for two or three weeks, and sometimes the date of the bond was six months before the date of the marriage. Besides the printed sources listed in the Bibliography in Chapter 28, under the heading of Vital Records, other sources are: Marriages Published in the Christian Intelligencer of the Reformed Dutch Church, 1830–1871, by Ray C. Sawyer. 10 v. Typescript, 1931–3; Deaths, ibid., 7 v. Typescript; Notices of Marriages and Deaths Published in Newspapers Printed at Poughkeepsie, New York, 1778–1825, Helen Wilkinson Reynolds, editor, in *Collections of Dutchess County Historical Society*, Number 4, 1930.

Early Connecticut Marriages as Found in Ancient Church Records Prior to 1800, by F. W. Bailey, 7 v., New Haven, 1896–1906, contains also marriages of New York people; *The Manual of the Reformed Church of America*, 1628–1902, by Edward T. Corwin, lists the place of the church and gives the old name, and also the name of the clergyman. *French Gazetteer* is also helpful in locating the places.

The Encyclopaedia of American Quaker Genealogy by William Wade Hinshaw, volume 3, contains records of meetings in New York, including Long Island. Other Quaker records are at Friends Library at Swarthmore, Pennsylvania. For other New York Quaker records write Percy E. Clapp, Friend's Meeting House, 221 East 15th Street, New York City.

An Inventory of Church Archives of New York State, Exclusive of New York City, was made by the Works Projects Administration.

The Vosburgh Records are a series of typescripts of records of New York churches, edited by Roy Woodward Vosburgh, and transcribed by the New York Genealogical and Biographical Society. There are 101 volumes and they are in the State Library of New York. There is also a copy in the Library of Congress. Microfilm copies are found in some other libraries.

Early records of the First Presbyterian Church of Syracuse, New York, 1828–1850, were published by the Genealogical Society of Central New York, Syracuse, 1902.

Bergen County, New Jersey Marriage Records from the Entries as Originally Made at the Courthouse by the Ministers and Justices of the Peace of the County, 1795–1878, by Mrs. Frances A. Westervelt, 1929; (index by Nicholas G. Blauvelt, 1946), contain many New York entries.

Early Settlers of Western New York, Their Ancestors and Descendants, 9 v., by Janet Foley. (includes church and cemetery records).

The Holland Society of New York Year Books and Collections, 1886–1929 contains early church records of New York City, Albany, and New Jersey.

A Memorial Census for Duanesburgh. Cemetery Records published at Delanson, New York, 1935.

History of the First Presbyterian Church of Monroe, New York, edited by Mrs. C. Arthur Brooks, indexed by George Lewis. Mimeo. 1956.

Tombstone inscriptions from the Abandoned Cemeteries and Farm Burials of Genesee County, by LaVerne C. Cooley. Batavia, N.Y. 1952.

Genealogical Records from Family Bibles, 1581–1917, by Jeannie F. J. Robison and Henrietta C. Bartlett, published by the National Society of Colonial Dames of New York, 1917.

Daughters of the American Revolution Records for New York State: there are three series of typewritten compilations—(1) Unpublished Family Bible Records, Together with Genealogical Notes and Other Published Data. (92 v.); Unpublished Cemetery, Church, and Town Records (217 v.); Graves of Revolutionary War Soldiers Buried in New York State. (15 v.).

The Colonial, Revolutionary, and Post-Revolutionary History of the State of New Jersey. (New Jersey Archives). These include abstracts of wills, marriage licenses, and newspaper notices. Many are records of New York people.

Immigration and Naturalization

In New York State an alien applied to the Colonial Assembly for naturalization, and their minutes and journals contain discussions regarding naturalizations. The original naturalization records are at the State Library in Albany, and are indexed from 1825 to 1913. Printed sources:

Laws of the State of New York, 1777–1801. Pub. 1886–8. 5 v. Includes private claims, name changes and naturalizations.

Naturalization of Foreign Protestants in the American Colonies, Pursuant to Statute 13, George II. *Publications of the Huguenot Society of London*, 1921. v. 24.

The Burghers of New Amsterdam and the Freemen of New York, 1675–1866. In *Collections of the New York Historical Society*, 1885.

Indentures of Apprentices, 1694–1708, and 1718–1727. *In Collections of the New York Historical Society, 1885 and 1909.*

Genealogical Data Relating to the German Settlers of Pennsylvania and Adjacent Territory, from the Advertisements in German Newspapers Published in Philadelphia and Germantown, 1743–1800, compiled by Edward W. Hecker. Typescript. 300 pp. 1935.

Passenger Lists of ships bringing Dutch immigrants during provincial period are published in the Holland Society's *Year Books*, 1886–1929.

List of Passengers who arrived in the United States from 1 October, 1819, to 30 September, 1820, Letter from the Secretary of State, 1821. In *Senate Document 118*, Serial 45, 16th Congress, Second Session.

Passenger Lists of Ships Coming to North America, 1607–1825. A bibliography, compiled by A. Harold Lancour, New York. *New York Public Library Bulletin*. 1938.

Military Records

Printed sources:

Colonial New York Muster Rolls, 1664–1770. Printed in the second and third annual reports of the State Historian of New York, 1096–7.

Military Minutes of the Council of Appointment of the State of New York, 1783–1821, 4 v, 1901–2.

Revolutionary Soldiers Resident or Dying in Onondaga County, New York, by W. M. Beauchamp. In Annual Volume of Onondaga Historical Association, 1914, (pp. 188–214).

Index of Awards on Claims of Soldiers of the War of 1812, Albany, 1860. (Gives place of residence of veteran in 1860; the number of the Certificate; to whom issued; amount; and place of residence).

State pensioners of New York are listed in the Provincial papers of New York.

The Bureau of War Records published by the Adjutant General's Office, Albany, gives records of the War of 1812, Civil War and later wars.

New York in the Revolution, 2 v. 1898, compiled by James A. Roberts, Comptroller.

Local Historians

New York State has a unique system of local historians. The local historian is a public official and his appointment is provided for by law. Some are paid a small salary out of public funds. His duties are to collect and preserve material relating to the political subdivision to which he is appointed, to examine the condition, classification and safety from fire of the public records; to call the attention of the local authorities and state historian to any local material which should be acquired, and to make an annual report to the State Historian and to the authority by whom appointed.

According to law each county may have a county historian, and each city, town, and village is required to have one. If all appointments were made there would be about 1600 local historians in New York State; at present there are about 1000.

Local historians are regarded as public servants, and the service they are required to give is defined. If any one seeks information regarding the local history of the area served by the local historian, it is his or her duty to supply such information, if possible.

Local historians are asked by the state to copy church registers prior to 1880 when the vital record law first went into effect; to copy old gravestone records, and to keep or copy salient information from newspapers. They are expected to belong to their local historical society and assist in its collection of records. Many have their rooms in the quarters of the local historical society. They are expected to assist and cooperate with teachers in the school programs, by providing them with material for purposes of instruction, and to help organize historical trips and pageants. They are also encouraged to work with the libraries and museums in their districts, and to write up the material they collect, or to supply it to others who wish to write it.

A New York State Association of local historians was organized in 1944, and is attempting to improve the status of historians, and increase the value of their work.

Social History

Since the fields of genealogy and sociology are so closely allied, and since Michigan may almost be considered the offspring of New York, the social history of New York State at the time of the great western migration which sent the early pioneers into Michigan should be examined.

The Spirit Way

In the early 1800's there was a narrow strip across New York State called "the spirit way." This was a part of the social structure of this region, in the early nineteenth century, and the thinking of many of our Michigan pioneers, and some of our own ancestors, was undoubtedly influenced by the events that transpired there. A number of new religious cults either developed there, or their exponents came with the New England migration into the state, at a time when the emotional tension caused by the repression of New England theology ran high, and all this left its impact upon society.

Among the first of these groups were the Shakers who were followers of Mother Ann Lee who came from England and settled near Albany, in 1776. The first Shaker community was established at New Lebanon in 1792, and by the time of the Civil War, this sect had about 6000 members, but is now practically extinct, although it made lasting contributions to agriculture and handicraft.

Then came Jemima Wilkinson (1758–1819). She was born in Rhode Island and her followers were called Wilkinsonians. Aroused by the highly emotional revivals of the New Light Baptists, and recovering from a severe attack of fever, she asserted that she had arisen from the dead, her body had been reanimated by the Divine Spirit, and she had returned as the Public Universal Friend. She and her converts settled, in 1788, at Seneca Lake. Marriage was prohibited and this resulted in many broken families. After her death, in 1819, the sect rapidly disintegrated.

John Humphrey Noyes founded the Oneida Community after he and his followers had been driven from Vermont. They called themselves Perfectionists. In 1879 Noyes left Oneida and took up residence in Canada, reigning the community by remote control. In 1881 the property was distributed and shares apportioned, and The Oneida Company, Limited, was incorporated at $600,000. That was the beginning of one of the greatest silver plating industries in the United States.

Joseph Smith (1805–1844) migrated from Vermont to Palmyra where he lived from 1815 to 1836. Here he had the visitation by the angel Moroni, son of Mormon, who revealed to him where the golden plates were buried, together with a key for their translation. On Cumorah Hill, near Manchester, Joseph Smith unearthed the golden plates that were destined to be the source of the Book of Mormon. On the west side of the hill, not far from the top, under a large stone, lay the plates, deposited in a stone box. He first saw them on September 22, 1823, and he visited them on each succeeding anniversary of that date, and in 1827 he took them from their hiding place. From 1827 to 1829, with Oliver Cowdrey, a Palmyra school teacher, he translated them and then returned them to the earth, and the Book of Mormon was published in 1830. This book, a translation of the plates, purported to be an account of the prehistoric inhabitants of America, and of the establishment of primitive Christianity among them, which it was Smith's mission to reestablish. It was in April of that year that the Church of Jesus Christ of Latter Day Saints was organized at Fayette, New York. They were a much persecuted people and in 1831, they moved to Kirtland, Ohio, and from there to Nauvoo, Illinois, and then to Carthage, Missouri, where Joseph Smith and his brother were murdered. Then it was that Brigham Young became head of the church and led the flock west to Salt Lake City where this great organization has built up the State of Utah.

On the summit of Cumorah Hill stands a monument forty feet high, illuminated at night, bearing the figure of the Angel Moroni, and on each of the four sides of the pillar is a bronze plaque, representing, on the west, Joseph Smith receiving the golden plates; on the south, "The Three Witnesses," who asserted they had seen Moroni, the gold plates, and had heard the voice of God; on the east, "The Eight Witnesses" who asserted they had seen and hefted the gold plates; and on the north, the exhortation of the Angel Moroni.

Then came William Miller, in 1831, from Vermont to Washington county and began preaching the Second Advent. His followers were called "Millerites" and they assembled on the Pinnacle Hills, near Rochester, October 24, 1844, to witness the end of the world and be gathered up to Heaven. The survivors of this disillusionment met in Albany in 1845 and organized the parent Adventist Church.

Spiritualism also had its beginnings here in this "Spirit Way," with the Fox sisters who moved from Hydesville to Rochester in 1848, where the mother church was organized and its first theology formulated, in the 1860's by Andrew Jackson Davis, a Poughkeepsie tailor. Lily Dale in Chautauqua county is now their headquarters.

This is but a brief résumé of the social life of the times in Upper New York State. There were other groups, one of which was a temperance group called the Tee-Totalers. Anti-Masonic factions were strong and sometimes violent.

This is a picture of the society our early pioneers left to establish homes in the Michigan wilderness, so if the thinking of our ancestors seems to us to have been erratic, let us consider the emotional tensions and instability existing in the country they left.

In fiction there have been several historical novels dealing with The Spirit Way, or as Mr. Carl Carmer calls it, "The Psychic Highway," and as Whitney R. Cross calls it, "The Burned Over District." Some of these are: Rhoda Truax's, *Green is the Golden Tree*, Constance Noyes Robertson's *Seek No Further*, Worth Tuttle Hedden's *Wives of High Pasture*, and Carl Carmer's *Genesee Fever*.

19. RESEARCH IN NEW JERSEY

Dutch settlements were early established in northeastern New Jersey. The Swedes settled along the Delaware River in the vicinity of Philadelphia, but were so harassed by the Dutch that they finally submitted to Dutch rule which endured from 1655 to 1664. This gave the Dutch control of the Hudson and Delaware River Valleys which separated the New England and Southern Colonies. For this reason, Charles II, then King of England, granted to his brother James, Duke of York, a vast territory which included much of what is now New England, New York and New Jersey. He transferred the territory now known as New Jersey to Lord Berkeley and Sir George Carteret, and in recognition of Carteret's defense of the Island of Jersey against the forces of Oliver Cromwell, the Berkeley-Carteret grant was called New Jersey.

The English flocked into East Jersey, now known as North Jersey. One could tell by the name of the town from whence the settlers came. Elizabeth, Shrewsbury and Middleton were settled by people from New England and Long Island, Woodbridge by Massachusetts Bay people, Piscataway by people from Piscataqua, New Hampshire. Newark was settled by Congregationalists from Connecticut.

In 1676 New Jersey was divided into two provinces—East Jersey which is now called North Jersey, and West Jersey which is now called South Jersey, and proprietors were appointed. East Jersey was settled by New England people and West Jersey by Quakers. Beginning in 1677 and for a number of years, many English settled in Burlington, Gloucester, Newton, Lucas, Pyne Point—now Camden, Rancocus, and Willingbury. Early settlers in the 17th century all came directly from England and Ireland, and a few from Scotland, and almost all were Quakers. In 1702 New Jersey came into the hands of William Penn who surrendered the government to British administration. The two provinces were united into the Royal Province of New Jersey, and they shared a governor with New York. Early in the 18th century many migrated south and settled in Frederick County, Virginia. Another settlement was made in Mississippi by New Jersey people. After the Revolution migration began again, and the New Jersey land speculators, under Cleve Symmes, settled Cincinnati, in 1788. About the same time, New Madrid, Missouri, then in Spanish Louisiana, was founded by the New Jersey Company led by George Morgan.

A large migration of Loyalists to Canada began in 1783. (They were Loyalists in Canada but Tories in the United States.) Loyalists settled in Nova Scotia and New Brunswick and some in Ontario. By 1800 a large Quaker migration took place. Simcoe was governor of Upper Canada, and inducements were held out to Quakers whom they considered much more desirable than the low class of English colonists that had been settling there.

Historical Geography

In 1682 there were seven original counties in New Jersey. Of these, Bergen, Essex, Middlesex, and Monmouth comprised East Jersey. Burlington, Gloucester, and Salem made up West Jersey. By 1790 there were thirteen counties, and today there are twenty-one.

Seven Original Counties

BERGEN—formed 1682—county seat, Hackensack. Passaic county was set off in 1837 and Hudson county in 1840. A part of Harrison township, Hudson county was added as Union township, in 1852.

ESSEX—formed 1682—county seat, Newark. Boundaries were defined January 21, 1710. A portion was set off to Somerset county in 1741, and another to Passaic county in 1837, and to Union county in 1857. The boundary was changed in 1876 and 1892.

MIDDLESEX—formed 1682—county seat, New Brunswick. Boundaries defined by Act of January 21, 1710. Boundary between Middlesex and Somerset counties was changed November 24, 1790. Somerset county was set off in 1688; a part was set off to form Mercer county in 1838; part was added to Monmouth county in 1844 and restored in 1845; part of Somerset county was added in 1850; part was added to Somerset county in 1858, and part to Union county in 1858.

MONMOUTH—formed 1682—county seat, Freehold. Ocean county was set off in 1850.

BURLINGTON—formed 1694—county seat, Mt. Holly. Hunterdon county was set off in 1714. A portion of Burlington county went to Mercer county in 1838, and another portion to Ocean county in 1891. Portions of Atlantic and Camden counties were annexed in 1902.

GLOUCESTER—formed 1694—county seat, Woodbury. Incorporated as a county 1710. Portion set off to form Atlantic county 1837; Camden county, 1844. Boundary between Gloucester and Cumberland counties changed 1892; part of Camden county added 1871.

SALEM—formed 1694—county seat, Salem. Portion set off as Cumberland county, January 19, 1748.

Origin of Other Fourteen Counties

SOMERSET—formed 1688—county seat, Somerville. Set off from Middlesex in 1688 and incorporated January 21, 1710. Portion of Essex county annexed 1744; boundary between Somerset and Middlesex counties changed November 24, 1790; portion of Montgomery township was set off to Mercer county in 1838; Tewksbury township, Hunterdon county, added in 1844 and restored to Hunterdon in 1845; a portion of Middlesex county was added in 1858.

CAPE MAY—formed 1692—county seat, Cape May Court House. Boundaries established January 21, 1710. Part of Cumberland county was set off to Cape May county in 1844 and restored in 1845; portions of Maurice River township, Cumberland county, were set off to Cape May county, in 1878, 1880, and 1891.

HUNTERDON—formed 1714—county seat, Flemington. Formed from Burlington county; part was set off to Morris county, March 15, 1739; to Mercer county, 1838 and 1839. Hopewell township, Mercer county was added to Hunterdon county in 1844 and restored in 1845; Tewksbury township was set off to Somerset county in 1844 and reannexed in 1845.

MORRIS—formed March 15, 1739—county seat, Morristown. Formed from Hunterdon county. Sussex county was formed from Morris county June 8, 1753.

CUMBERLAND—formed January 19, 1748—county seat, Salem. Cumberland was set off from Salem county; boundary between Gloucester and Cumberland counties changed 1892 and restored 1897; portion of Maurice River township was annexed to Upper township, Cape May county in 1844 and restored in 1845; portion added to Upper township, Cape May county in 1878; to Dennis township, Cape May county in 1891.

SUSSEX—formed June 8, 1753—county seat, Newton. Created from Morris county. A portion of Sussex county was set off as Warren county, November 20, 1824.

WARREN—formed November 20, 1824—county seat, Belvedere. Created from Sussex county.

ATLANTIC—formed in 1837—county seat, Mays Landing. Formed from the townships of Galloway, Hamilton, Weymouth, and Egg Harbor, Gloucester county; a portion of Hammonton was annexed to Burlington county in 1902.

PASSAIC—formed in 1837—county seat, Paterson. Created from portions of Bergen and Essex counties, and consisted of townships of Acquackanonk, Manchester, Paterson, Pompton, and West Milford.

MERCER—formed February 22, 1838—county seat, Trenton. Erected from townships of Ewing, Hopewell, Lawrence, and Trenton, of Hunterdon county; Nottingham township of Burlington county; and townships of East and West Windsor, Middlesex county. A portion of Montgomery township, Somerset county, was annexed in 1838; Hopewell township, Hunterdon county was annexed in 1839.

HUDSON—formed February 22, 1840—county seat, Jersey City. Created from Bergen county and consisted of Bergen and Harrison townships and Jersey City. Part of Harrison township was made Union township and annexed to Bergen county in 1852.

CAMDEN—formed in 1844—county seat, Camden. Formed from Camden, Delaware, Gloucester, Newton, Union, Washington, and Waterford townships of Gloucester county. The townships of Monroe and Washington were annexed to Gloucester county in 1871; a portion of Waterford township was annexed to Burlington county in 1902.

OCEAN—formed February 15, 1850—county seat, Toms River.

Created from Monmouth county and consisted of Jackson, Plumstead, Stafford, Union, Dover, and Brick townships. Little Egg Harbor, Burlington county was added in 1891, and part of Jackson township was added to Monmouth county in 1851.

UNION—formed March 19, 1857—county seat, Elizabeth. Created from Essex county and consisted of Elizabeth and the townships of Rahway, Union, Westfield, Plainfield, New Providence, and Springfield; boundaries were changed in 1876 and 1892.

The New Jersey State Library

The New Jersey State Library is located on the ground floor of the east wing of the State House Annex, West State Street, Trenton 25, New Jersey. Roger H. McDonough is the Director of the Division of the State Library, Archives and History.

Collections

Include 1500 family histories, mainly of New Jersey families, and families associated with other northeastern states. It includes unpublished manuscript histories, family trees, Bible records, printed books and pamphlets, as well as lineage books of the Daughters of the American Revolution, Daughters of Founders and Patriots of America, Daughters of American Colonists, and Sons and Daughters of the Pilgrims. Also, county and town histories of New Jersey, New Jersey History and Biography and Periodicals.

The Family Name Index is an analytical index to significant material on a family in the genealogical and historical books in the State Library. This is an index to parts of books and individual chapters in books, but not of every name mentioned in the books. It does not include periodicals or large sets of books which have their own indexes.

Heraldry. The library maintains a family name card index to reproductions of coats-of-arms in books in the library's collections. Both of these indexes are kept up to date as new books are added to the library.

The library has a fine collection of maps and atlases of New Jersey and its various subdivisions. It has genealogical and historical encyclopaedias and genealogical and historical periodicals. The library has large collections of newspapers of Trenton, Newark, and Freehold. Some of these date back to 1778. The index to vital statistics in Trenton newspapers covers the period from 1776 to 1900. Death notices and marriage notices (with a card for both bride and groom) are indexed on 3 ×5 cards. There are 120 drawers of these cards. There are other indexes which are given in the following paragraphs under the type of record.

Any one is welcome to go to the library to do his own research, but because of limited staff the library cannot comply with requests for information that involve extensive genealogical research. It will furnish names of competent persons who may be engaged to do this work. The library does not loan books.

New Jersey Archives

Archival materials are located in the Bureau of Archives and History, New Jersey State Library, Trenton 25, New Jersey.

A subject index, on cards, to archival materials which are in the Bureau, and in other locations in the state, such as local historical associations, is maintained. The Bureau also has various indexes to other groups of archival materials located in the State Library. Some examples of archives in the New Jersey State Library are:

Burlington county—Loan Office Mortgages, 1724–1750. 3 v.
Claims for damages by the British in New Jersey, 1776–1782.
Inquisitions on the dead, 1688–1798. 2 v.
Naturalizations in Chancery, 1834–1842. 4 v.
Petitions for Naturalization, 1749–1810.
Township Minute Books—various townships.

Published Archives of New Jersey

The first series consists of forty-two volumes and covers the history of the state from 1631 to 1817.

VOLUMES 1–10 relate to the colonial history of the state, and cover the period, 1631–1776.

VOLUMES 11 AND 12 contain newspaper extracts covering the period 1704–1750.

VOLUMES 13 TO 18 contain the Journals of the Councils and Governors, and cover the period 1682–1775.

VOLUMES 19 AND 20 contain newspaper extracts covering the period 1751–1761.

VOLUME 21 contains a calendar of New Jersey records, 1664–1703. (This is for East and West Jersey, locates land, and for the Quakers, identifies their homes in England).

VOLUME 22 contains marriage records from 1665–1800. (Not entirely accurate, and not complete, but useful for clues).

VOLUME 23 contains an abstract of wills from 1670–1730.

VOLUMES 24 TO 29 contain newspaper abstracts from 1762–1850.

VOLUME 30 contains an abstract of wills from 1730–1750.

VOLUME 31 contains newspaper extracts for 1775.

VOLUMES 32 TO 42 contain abstracts of wills from 1751–1817.

The second series consists of five volumes which contain newspaper extracts covering the period from 1776 to 1782.

Vital Records

In 1671 a law was passed requiring the registration of births, marriages and deaths, but it was not enforced until 1887. The New Jersey Department of Health, Bureau of Vital Statistics, State House, Trenton 25, New Jersey, has custody of records of births, deaths, and marriages, from May 1, 1848 to date.

BIRTHS

May 1, 1848–December 31, 1900 are indexed—complete alphabetical index for entire state.

January 1, 1901 to date are indexed—entire state is alphabetically indexed by individual years. (There are special indexes for some years by counties and cities, and surnames are arranged alphabetically.)

Suggestions for locating birth records before 1848: census records; baptismal records; family histories; periodicals; miscellaneous file at the New Jersey State Library.

DEATHS

May 1, 1848–May 31, 1878—complete alphabetical index for the period. June 1, 1878–December 31, 1900—not indexed but arranged by years, by counties and cities, and first letters of surnames.

January 1, 1901—to date—entire state strictly alphabetical by individual years with special indexes for some years, 1916 to 1929, inclusive.

Suggestions for locating death records before 1848: census records; church and cemetery records; family and local histories; miscellaneous file State Library; newspaper index in archives; periodicals; war records; wills and inventories.

For birth and death records, when the year is known no charge is made. when the year is not known, a charge of 50 cents is made for a search through the first three years, plus 25 cents for each additional year. A photostatic copy is $1.00 additional. No special application form is needed.

MARRIAGES

Before 1800 are located at the Office of the New Jersey Secretary of State, State House, Trenton 25, New Jersey.

1665–1800—Marriage bonds. (Very incomplete). These bonds represent approximately 25 per cent of the marriages which took place in this period. There is one alphabetical index for the whole period by bride's or groom's name. Printed index is in the New Jersey Archives, First Series, vol. 22. There is no charge for search of these. Photostatic copies are about 50 cents each. No special application form is needed.

1800–1848. During this period no statewide records of marriages were kept. Card index in the Bureau of Archives, State Library, covers some marriages in this period. They also have some county marriage record books.

Suggestions for searching this period: some county historical associations have made county-wide indexes for the 1800–1848 period; census records; church records; family histories; miscellaneous file in New Jersey State Library; newspapers; index to vital statistics in archives; periodicals; war records; wills.

1848–*to date*—marriage records are located at New Jersey Department of Health, Bureau of Vital Statistics, State House, Trenton 25, New Jersey. To send for a marriage record, the same regulations apply as for births and deaths.

Census Records

The following are in the New Jersey State Library:
The original New Jersey Census Returns for 1790, 1800, 1810, and 1820 are missing and presumed destroyed.

1830 FEDERAL—complete set on microfilm; 14 counties in 1830; gives name; sex; age; under various age groups for white and colored; slave and free.

1840 FEDERAL—complete set on microfilm; 18 counties; same information as 1830.

1850 FEDERAL—complete set in 16 volumes; 20 counties in 1850; gives name; sex; age; birthplace; occupation; value of real estate.

1855 NEW JERSEY STATE; 13 counties in three volumes; 7 counties missing; gives name; sex; race.

1860 FEDERAL—21 counties in 23 volumes—complete; gives name; age; sex; birthplace; occupation; value of real and personal property.

1865 NEW JERSEY STATE—13 counties in 4 volumes; 8 missing; gives name; sex; race.

1870 FEDERAL—21 counties in 25 volumes—complete; gives name; sex; race and same information as 1860.

1880 FEDERAL—21 counties on microfilm—complete; gives name; age; sex; birthplace; marital status; occupation; parent's birthplace.

1885 NEW JERSEY STATE—21 counties in 44 volumes and summary volumes— complete; gives name; age; sex; race; (age groups—5 yrs.; 5–20 yrs; 20–60 yrs; over 60 yrs)

1895 NEW JERSEY STATE—21 counties in 54 volumes—complete—same information as 1885.

Census Records in the New Jersey Department of Health, Bureau of Vital Statistics, State House, Trenton 25, New Jersey.

1905 NEW JERSEY STATE—21 counties in 74 volumes—complete on microfilm.

1915 NEW JERSEY STATE—21 counties in 99 volumes—complete on
microfilm.
The 1905 and 1915 State Censuses give the same information as the
1880 Federal Census.

Any request for information from the 1905 or 1915 New Jersey State
census records, must give the person's name, municipality and county
in which he lived at the time of the census; street name, house number,
and ward number, if any. In stating the municipality or township, do
not use the name of any unincorporated village or community since
these do not appear in the census records. Without this information
it is impossible to search the records. All requests must be in writing
or on a special form provided by the department.

Wills

The Secretary of State's Office at Trenton has original wills from the
earliest period to the present time, in bound volumes, and some are
arranged loosely in envelopes, and all are arranged by counties.
The Secretary of State has custody of these records but application
has to be made to the Clerk of the Superior Court, Probate Section,
State House Annex, Trenton 25, New Jersey.

From 1663 to 1900 there is an alphabetical list for each county.

From 1901 to date the entire state is in one alphabet.

All the wills and inventories are thoroughly indexed by the name of
the testator; it is not necessary to know the year of the will or the
date of death. No charge for searching is made unless no date is supplied or name of county is not supplied for wills prior to 1901. A
charge of $1.00 is then made regardless of whether the search reveals
the requested information. When the above information is known,
however, the documents may be requested for examination free of
charge. There is a short wait (up to half an hour) for older documents
which are stored elsewhere. Photostats are supplied at a charge of
$1.00 a sheet, payable in advance. Most of the wills consist of two
or three sheets and may have as many as five or six.

There is also a partial record, before 1953, and a complete record
after that date, for all estates for which letters of administration were
granted. This is merely a record, however. The actual documents are
retained in the various counties and must be consulted there.

Indexes and Abstracts of Wills are located in the New Jersey State Library, State House Annex, Trenton 25, New Jersey.

1670–1817—abstracts of wills in the New Jersey Archives in 13 volumes. Each volume covers approximately five years; abstracts are arranged alphabetically by testator.

1705–1830—index to wills in two volumes (v. 1—1705–1804); (v. 2 1804–1830). Each volume arranged alphabetically by testator.

1705–1900—index to wills in three volumes. (v. 1, Atlantic to Essex counties); (v. 2 Gloucester to Monmouth counties); (v. 3 Morris to Warren counties). Each county alphabetical by name of testator.

The early abstracts of wills in the archives are not always complete, and not always accurate, so it is well to check the original will. From 1750 to 1817, the abstracts are better as they mention the property, while the early ones only mention the individuals. In addition to the recorded wills, the Secretary of State's Office has twelve volumes of unrecorded wills. At the end of the third volume there is an alphabetical list of the names in the wills.

Deeds

Deeds before 1800 are located at the Office of the New Jersey Secretary of State, State House, Trenton 25, New Jersey. Deeds covering 1670 to 1800 are very incomplete; there are deeds for approximately only 25% of land transactions made during that period. There is one alphabetical index for the entire period, under both grantee and grantor. When applying, please give variant spellings of names. There is no charge for search and no special form of application is needed. Photostats are from 50 cents to $1.00 per page, according to size. The average deed is two to three pages long.

Some deeds before 1800 are located in the Office of the East Jersey Proprietors, Perth Amboy, and in the Office of the West Jersey Proprietors, Burlington, New Jersey. Deeds after 1800 are kept in the county clerk's offices of the respective counties. However, some are on file at the office of the New Jersey Secretary of State who has custody of the ancient deed books of East and West Jersey. There is a card index of the deeds started in 1703. The Secretary of State's Office has a book—Liber AAA of Commissions, 1703–4 which, gives important biographical details. Abstracts from this book, which gives much genealogical information covering the period 1703–1769, are found in the *Publications of the Genealogical Society of Pennsylvania*, vols. 6 to 10, inclusive. Other land records in the Secretary of States Office are abstracted in vol. 21 of the *New Jersey Archives*. The Secretary of State also has marriage records from 1711 to 1797, in bound volumes, arranged chronologically, and there is a card index so these may be found quickly, arranged by both bride and groom.

Other probable sources for material on property ownership: Archives; census; local history; maps; ratables.

Ratables

In the New Jersey State Library is a set of record books for towns and townships. These list the land owners for purposes of taxation. Some information on holdings of livestock is given. These are on microfilm. The period covered is roughly 1773 to 1822, and is incomplete. If there is a tax ratable book for a town covering this early period it somewhat replaces the 1790 Federal Census of which the New Jersey volume was destroyed. There is no name index. Therefore, searches must be made in each town book. Guides to towns and years covered for each place are located on cards in the Reference Library Catalog under "Ratables."

Military Records

All New Jersey Military Records are located in the New Jersey Department of Defense, War Records Office, Armory, Trenton, New Jersey. All extant military records of New Jersey men and women who served in all wars are kept in this office. Records before the Revolution are very sketchy, but from the Revolution on they are fairly complete. Records include those of service in the New Jersey Militia and National Guard as well as in the United States Military Forces. Fifty cents is charged for each search and $1.00 for each certified copy of a military record, payable in advance. Some charges are made whether the applicant visits the office or applies by mail.

The New Jersey State Library has the following military indexes: STRYKER, W. S.: Official Register of the Officers and Men of New Jersey in the Revolutionary War. 1872.

HISTORICAL RECORDS SURVEY, NEW JERSEY: Index of the Official Register of the Officers and Men of New Jersey in the Revolutionary War. 1941.

NEW JERSEY OFFICE OF THE ADJUTANT GENERAL: Records of Officers and Men of New Jersey in Wars, 1791–1815. 1909.

STRYKER, W. S.: Record of the Officers and Men of New Jersey in the Civil War, 1861–1865. 2 v. 1876.

The New Jersey Historical Society at Newark is an important depository of records. They have a large manuscript collection which includes numerous private collections of papers. The Charles Carroll Gardner Collection was established in 1933 and contains close to 100,000 items. These include original documents, originals of wills and deeds, also transcripts of church registers of what was East Jersey in colonial times but is now known as North Jersey. There is a good card catalog to this.

In Philadelphia, the Genealogical Society of Pennsylvania has much information on thirteen of the twenty-one counties of New Jersey, and has the most information on Burlington county because of the Quakers, including photostats of the 1709 census of Northampton township. It is often cited without reference but they were probably kept in Burlington county.

20. KEYS TO THE KEYSTONE STATE

The Commonwealth of Pennsylvania is much more than the Keystone State—deep within its archives are the keys to many genealogical problems, for in no other section of the country was there a greater mingling of races, creeds, and nationalities, each contributing to the general culture.

Most of the English colonies in the United States were founded by people of pure Anglo-Saxon stock. The history of the New England and the Virginia colonies is a simple story of a people having one language and one religion—and always acting in a unit. But in Pennsylvania it was different, for no other colony had such a mixture of languages, nationalities, and religions. There were Dutch, Swedes, English, Germans, Welsh, Scotch-Irish, Irish, and French. They were Quakers, Presbyterians, Episcopalians, Lutherans, Reformed, both Dutch and German, Mennonites, Tunkers, and Moravians—and all had a share in Pennsylvania origins.

The first settlers were Dutch (Netherlands) who came up the Delaware Bay, and settled upon the shores of the Delaware River in 1623, and held control for fifteen years (1623–1638). The Dutch occupied this land through rights acquired in Pennsylvania and New York by the discoveries of Henry Hudson, an Englishman in the employ of the Dutch East India Company. Pennsylvania, New York, New Jersey, and Delaware together comprised New Netherlands.

Then came the Swedes who wrested control from the Dutch and held the territory along the Delaware River for the next seventeen years (1638–1655). They were always at war with the Dutch, and in 1655 the Dutch reconquered the Swedes, regaining control of the land along the Delaware River which they held for another nine years

(1655–1664). This time they lost control of it to the English under the Duke of York who held it until the arrival of William Penn and the Quakers in 1682. For a good account of this period read, *The Swedish Settlements on the Delaware, 1638–1664*, by Amandus Johnson, published by the University of Pennsylvania, 1911, 2 volumes.

The men who founded Pennsylvania were intensely religious. For several centuries the people of Europe had been persecuting each other over differences in religion, and they brought these hatreds and intolerances to colonial North America with them. The Puritan was opposed to high living and the pleasures of the table, but was devoted to learning and literature. The Quaker despised learning, music, poetry, and the fine arts, which he considered frivolous amusements, but his beliefs did not prohibit good living and generous hospitality. Perhaps it was this balance that has kept our country on an even keel.

The English crown owed a great debt to William Penn whose deceased father had been an admiral in the English navy and had rendered great assistance in restoring Charles II and the whole Stuart line to the English throne. Inasmuch as they had given New Jersey to Lords Carteret and Berkeley, and Maryland to Lord Baltimore for the same service, it seemed only logical that they should give a greater tract to Penn's son since the father had never pressed his claim. William Penn, while a student at Oxford, had embraced the Quaker faith, became a preacher and was thrown into prison where he learned that there was a movement to plant a colony of English Quakers on the Delaware River in America. So, in 1681, the English crown gave Penn and his followers 55,000 square miles of valuable, fertile territory in Pennsylvania, a tract almost as large as England and Wales, and Penn owned the land, and the colonists were his tenants, but with free government. He sold land to the colonists on the basis of 5000 acres for 100 pounds plus an annual quitrent of one shilling for every one hundred acres. This arrangement remained in effect for the next ninety-four years until the American Revolution. Many Church of England people settled in and around Philadelphia, in 1682, in Bucks, Philadelphia, and Chester counties. They established Old Christ Church, and although hostile to the Quakers, after Penn's death his sons joined this church.

Penn and other Quakers made missionary tours into Germany where the people were in a state of religious turmoil, disunion and depression from the results of the Reformation and the Thirty Year's War, and as a result many sects had sprung up, all seeking greater liberty and prosperity. When Penn asked them to come to Pennsylvania they responded almost immediately, for they were unaccustomed to either religious or political liberty. Some of these newly formed religious sects were the Schwenkfelders (a small group—only six migrations from 1731 to 1737, but they kept good records which are in Schwenkfelder Library at Pennsburg, Pennsylvania), Tunkers, Labadists, New Born, New Mooners, Separatists, Zion's Brueder, Ronsdorfer, Inspired Quietists, Gichtelians, Depellians, Mountain Men, River Brethren, Brinser Brethren, The Society of the Woman in the Wilderness, and the Amish. Many of them believed in mysticism and were inclined to hermit life, and some even lived in caves or solitary huts in the woods. While they were not Quakers, some of their doctrines resembled those of the Quakers, and one of the larger sects—the Mennonites—were often called "German Quakers." They settled in the territory bordered on the north by Easton, west across the Susquehanna, and south to the Maryland border. This migration of these many German sects was from 1682 to 1702.

In 1683 the first German settlers led by Pastorious came to Germantown which is now a part of Philadelphia. After this there was a steady stream of Germans, and by 1727, they had settled in seven counties—Northampton, Bucks, Lancaster, Lehigh, Dauphin, Lebanon and York. There were sprinklings in other counties but these were the so-called German counties. Strassburger and Hinke wrote three volumes on the Pennsylvania German pioneers. These are ships passenger lists and refer to Palatines including Hessians, Bavarians, Moravians, Swiss, and others. These lists are found in the Division of Public Records at Harrisburg.

The later German migrations (after 1702) were made up of more Orthodox church people, mostly Lutherans and the German Reformed, or Calvinists. Large numbers of these German immigrants were "Redemptioners," that is, persons who had been obliged to sell themselves to the shipping agents to pay for their passage, and upon their arrival, the captain sold them to the colonists, and the redemptioner had to work for his owner for a period of five to ten years. They were also called "indentured servants." This was regarded as an ordinary and necessary business transaction and no stigma or disgrace was attached to it.

From 1682 to 1700 there was a great Welsh migration to Pennsylvania where they chose 40,000 acres between the Schuylkill and Delaware Rivers, because it so closely resembled the topography of their native country. This was located in Chester, Philadelphia, and Bucks counties, and later spread to Montgomery county. They were mostly Quakers but a few were Baptists and English churchmen. They insisted that this 40,000 acres constituted a "Barony" and it was known as the "Welsh Barony" until modern times when the name was changed to the Welsh Tract. The now famous Philadelphia "Main Line" is a part of this settlement, and the Welsh names are still in evidence as Haverford, Radnor, Narbeth, Bryn Mawr, Merion, Glen Ellyn, and many more.

The Scotch-Irish were an important factor after 1728. They were mostly descendants of Scotch and English Presbyterians who had gone to Ireland to take up the estates of the Irish rebels confiscated under Queen Elizabeth and James I. Towards the middle of the 17th century the confiscation of more Irish land under Cromwell increased the migration to Ulster where they were joined by many English and Scotch Lowlanders. These Ulstermen were the ones who defended Londonderry against James II, and who, in modern times, have resisted Home Rule. They had no sympathy for the Quakers except on the point of religious liberty, and that feeling was mutual. They were Presbyterians and Calvinists, and not opposed to war, as were the Quakers. As for the Indians, they held that the Old Testament commands the destruction of all the heathen. They liked to be by themselves so they pushed on to the frontiers, took the Indians' land, and exterminated them, so they were always in trouble with the Indians as well as with the government of Pennsylvania. They settled principally in five counties of western Pennsylvania—Westmoreland, Fayette, Greene, Washington, and Allegheny. (Read: *Pennsylvania Genealogies—Chiefly Scotch-Irish and German*, by Dr. William H. Egle.)

There were also other minority groups, among which were the French Huguenots. They came about 1750, and were French Protestants who had fled to Germany and the French-speaking area of Switzerland, to Holland and to Northern Ireland. They settled in small groups throughout Pennsylvania, and were patriots of note during the Revolution. (Read: *Memorials of the Huguenots*, by Rev. Ammon Stapleton.)

At the close of the colonial period in Pennsylvania, the Quakers, the Church of England people, and the miscellaneous denominations occupied Philadelphia and the region around it in a half circle from the Delaware River, as did also the Dutch and Swedes who were largely a remnant of the colony of New Sweden. Outside of this area lay another half circle containing the Germans, and beyond that were the Scotch-Irish whose principal stronghold was the Cumberland Valley of southern Pennsylvania, west of the Susquehanna, a region now containing Chambersburg, Gettysburg, Carlisle, and York.

There were three important early boundary controversies—one with Connecticut, another with Maryland, and still another with Virginia, and many Pennsylvania families can be traced back to one of these three states. The colony of Connecticut claimed the whole northern half of Pennsylvania. This dispute lasted for nearly fifty years, and at times assumed the proportions of actual warfare, known as the Pennamite Wars. Connecticut sent settlers to this region and the controversy was not settled until after the close of the Revolution. Documents pertaining to these settlers are called the Susquehanna Papers and are in the Connecticut State Library at Hartford.

Virginia claimed jurisdiction over a strip fifty-four miles inland from the southwestern Pennsylvania border, which included the counties of Westmoreland, Allegheny, Fayette, Washington, and Greene. Virginia called this the District of West Augusta, and divided it into three counties—Yohogania, Monongalia, and Ohio. Virginians held court in these three counties, while Pennsylvania held court at Hannahstown in Westmoreland county (near the present town of Greensburg). This conflict was more or less of a "cold war" but undoubtedly would have become a "shooting war" had it not been for the fact that both sides suddenly found themselves involved in the American Revolution, and those settlers who were loyal to Pennsylvania joined the Pennsylvania militia, and those loyal to Virginia, enlisted in the ninth and thirteenth Virginia regiments. Hannahstown was burned by the Indians in 1782, but all the records except some early assessment lists are intact at Greensburg. Most of the Virginia records have been preserved at Morgantown, West Virginia, and have been published under the title *Virginia Minutes,* by Crumrine. This episode in history is well described in *The Annals of Southwestern Pennsylvania,* by Lewis C. Walkinshaw.

The dispute with Maryland lasted over seventy years and sometimes resulted in bloodshed, until the close of the Revolutionary War when the surveying of the Mason-Dixon line was completed. There were two large manors claimed by Maryland in the present Adams county, called "Carroll's Delight," and "Manor of the Maske," where early tracts were granted. Adams was set off from York county in 1800, and includes within its limits Gettysburg, site of the famous Civil War battle. Adams county lies directly north of Carroll County, Maryland, but was part of Baltimore county at the time of the controversy. Some Pennsylvania records will be found in Maryland counties.

Maps showing these claims are found in the Pennsylvania Archives. The Connecticut claim is in Series 2, volume 18; the Maryland claim is in Series 1, volume 1 and volume 4; and Series 2, volume 16; the Virginia claim is in Series 3, volume 3. See Guide to the Published Archives.

Changes in political divisions make genealogical research difficult. For example, how many are aware of the fact that there was once a state named Franklin which existed for only four years during which time a state government was maintained, from 1784–1788, in the region now belonging to western North Carolina and Eastern Tennessee.

Pennsylvania research is difficult because of the shifting of the county boundary lines. At the beginning of the Revolution there were but eleven counties in the Commonwealth; now there are sixty-seven where all county records are now found. However, all records pertaining to the Revolutionary period are located in one of the eleven county seats in existence in 1775. The Bureau of Land Records of Pennsylvania compiled a Genealogical Map of the Commonwealth which is distributed by the Department of Internal Affairs, without which genealogical research in the state is almost impossible. This shows the evolution of the counties as well as the lands acquired by purchase and Indian treaties (1682–1792). Records of a family which resided on one farm through several generations are often found in as many as three or four different county seats, due to these changes in boundaries.

Land Records

The original land patents are in the State Land Office in the Capitol Building at Harrisburg. Under the Proprietary Government of Pennsylvania, when a man wanted to settle on a certain piece of land, he went to Harrisburg and made application in writing to the land office. This application was duly entered in a book, and a warrant, or order, was issued by the Secretary of the Land Office directing the Surveyor-General to make a survey for the warrantee. Two copies of this survey were made. One was recorded in the State Land Office and the other was delivered to the warrantee who, upon payment of the price of the land, was granted a patent. The warrantee was required to settle upon this land within two years, to clear five acres, and "to build a house fit for the habitation of man"; these were the words of the Act of Assembly, "and raise grain each year for five years." After he did these things and proved his settlement, the state would give him a patent for the land. When a patent was granted, the new land owner was required to name his property. These names are recorded, and often supply a clue as to the place from whence the settler came. The same regulation held also in Maryland. Records of the "Susquehanna Settlers" in the Connecticut Claim are in the State Library at Hartford.

Another way to obtain land was by "Squatter's Rights." The Assembly provided that any man could choose his four hundred acres to suit himself, take possession if it was not already occupied, build his house, live there for five years, clear five acres, then go to the Commonwealth, pay $150.00 and get a deed for the four hundred acres. The effect of this was that the settler who chose the first plan would pay the state $150.00 and get a warrant for four hundred acres, build a house, stay five years, and then apply for a patent. This resulted in ejectment suits, and some even went to higher courts. These cases were usually settled by giving the "squatter" one hundred and fifty acres, and the "warrantee" two hundred and fifty.

Deeds and mortgages have been recorded in Pennsylvania since 1676 when they were recorded by the clerk of the Court of Sessions, under the Duke of York's laws. Under William Penn's government was created an office called the Master of the Rolls. He recorded all deeds, mortgages and similar papers. In 1706 a law was passed which provided that an Enrollment Officer be kept in each county "to record or enroll deeds or conveyances, in a fair, legible hand, on rolls or paper, or in a good, large, well covered book of royal or other large paper." The recorder received one penny for each line he wrote.

Even after the office of county recorder was established, the office of Master of the Rolls was still maintained until abolished by the Act of 1809, but he only recorded original deeds and patents, while the county recorders registered deeds to property in their respective counties, taken from the original grants. By the Act of 1809, the records of the Master of the Rolls were turned over to the State Land Office in Harrisburg.

Documents in County Recorder's offices begin with the organization of the county, and include, besides Unclaimed Instruments (any recorded paper for which the owner did not return either to pay the fee or to pick up the document); Deed Books; Grantee and Grantor Indexes; Sheriff's and Tax Deed Index Books; Patent Book (from 1818 which contains the recorded patents to land granted by the Commonwealth, and gives the date the patent was granted, location and description of property, name of grantee, amount paid, and volume and page upon which it is recorded in the State Land Office); Mortgage Book and Index; Chattel Mortgage Book and Index; Corporation Records; Contracts; Names of Foreigners Who Took the Oath of Allegiance, from 1777.

Vital Records

Vital records have been registered by the Commonwealth of Pennsylvania since January 1, 1906. Some earlier records may be found in the counties, under the following laws or regulations: The Duke of York's laws provided that the minister or town clerk record births, marriages, and burials; the Acts of 1683 and 1684 required certificates of marriage to be registered, and another Act passed in 1690 required religious societies to keep a register of births, marriages, and burials. From 1852 to 1855 it was the duty of the Register of Wills to keep separate books and indexes for recording marriages, births, and deaths occurring within the county. These give the following information:

MARRIAGE REGISTER (1852–1855)

Names of parties and their parents: occupation, birthplace and

residence of husband; date of marriage; name and location of
district in which marriage ceremony was performed; name of
person performing the ceremony and of the witnesses to it; dates
of certificate and registration; signature of register or deputy.

BIRTH REGISTER (1852–1855)

Name; sex; color; birthdate and birthplace of child; parent's
names and place of residence; father's occupation; date recorded.

DEATH REGISTER (1852–1855)

Name; color; sex; age; occupation and marital status of the deceased; dates and places of birth, death, and interment; if deceased was a minor, his father's and mother's names; duration of
last illness; cause of death; date recorded.

In 1885 this responsibility was shifted to the State Board of Health
which was authorized to receive communications of Vital Statistics
from local health officers. These records are kept in the office of the
Clerk of the Orphan's Court of the county, and include these records
which give the following information:

Original Marriage License Applications from 1885

Full name; color; occupation; birthplace; age and residence
of each party; statement that neither party has a transmissable
disease; that the husband is physically able to support a family
and has not, within the previous five years, been an inmate of
a home for the indigent.

Marriage License Returns from 1885

The marriage license is divided into three sections—the first
known as the license, gives authority for the marriage to be performed—the second section is the original marriage certificate
which is filled out by the official who performed the ceremony,
and is given to the married couple—the third section is filled in
by the official who performs the ceremony, and is returned to the
Clerk of the Orphan's Court, who files it. The information includes the date of marriage; license number; names and addresses
of parties; and the signature of the official who performed the
ceremony.

The Clerk of the Orphan's Court also keeps a Marriage License
Docket Book and an Index to same which contains a record of all the

marriage licenses issued, together with the papers pertaining to it, as petitions for the appointment of guardians to give consent for the marriage of minors, and so forth.

BIRTH REGISTER (1893–1905)

This is a register of births prepared from information sent in by the assessors, and gives the same information as the birth register from 1852 to 1855.

DEATH REGISTER (1893–1905)

This is also a register of deaths prepared from information sent in by the county assessors, and gives the same information as the death register of 1852 to 1855.

For vital records previous to January 1, 1906, write to the Clerk of the Orphan's Court in the county seat, except for Philadelphia and Pittsburgh. Philadelphia records begin July 1, 1860, and Pittsburgh records start in 1870. For these records write the respective City Boards of Health. For nearly all of the vital records of early Pennsylvania, it is necessary to rely upon church records, many of which have been published, or are among the holdings of the various historical societies. Also, consider the fact that the ministers, in early times, were itinerant, holding services on succeeding Sundays in different churches; therefore a family might have their children baptized in a number of different churches, although their residence never changed. Marriage licenses were not required in Pennsylvania until 1884.

STATUS OF CITIZENSHIP IN PENNSYLVANIA:

INMATES were persons who did not own property, were married, and were probably mechanics or laborers.

FREEMEN were men 21 years of age, or older, and were unmarried, thus free of family obligations, but they were taxed as "freemen"; after marriage a man appeared upon the regular tax lists. Thus, a search of the tax records, year by year, enables one to determine when a man became 21 and when he was married. Another indication of his age is the age of his children which may be determined through family or tax records.

INDENTURED SERVANTS were bound out for life or for a term of years, usually the latter. A minor could be indentured by his parents, or when he was 21 years old he could indenture himself. The father sometimes indentured the son until free work equaled the debt the son owed the father, or he was indentured to another to pay for a piece of land.

Probate Records

Probate records, in Pennsylvania, are handled by the Register of Wills and the Clerk of the Orphan's Court. Under English law, the statute of 1683 prescribed the duties of the "Register" as "registering births, deaths, marriages, bond servants, wills and letters of administration, and writing marriage certificates on parchment." After 1684 this official was also required to keep a record of all freemen as well as all servants in the county. In 1706 a Register General was commissioned "for the probate of wills and granting of letters of administration." This remained in effect until 1776 when the constitution provided that a register's office be kept in each county and city. The Register of Wills has jurisdiction over wills and estate administrations, inventories and appraisements, inheritance taxes, and vital records from 1852 to 1855.

The Clerk of the Orphan's Court issues marriage licenses, keeps records and indexes of probate and orphan's court records, has jurisdiction over partition papers (proceedings in estates which are divided); bonds in connection with the settlement of estates; records of distribution of estates and releases by heirs; sale of real estate in probate; adoption records; records of soldiers who from 1783 to 1785 received a pension from the State of Pennsylvania.

The office of Prothonotary in Pennsylvania, is very similar to that of county clerk in Michigan. He acts as clerk of the county courts keeps records of the assets and estates of incompetent persons, habitual drunkards, and insolvents, handles the divorce docket, keeps records of executions, treasurer's deed books compiled from delinquent tax sales, conditional sales, fictitious names in business, election papers, and registers of professional and trades people.

Naturalization records are also kept in the prothonotary's office. The index gives the date of declaration of intention to become a citizen, the country from which he came, date the certificate was granted, and the names of the persons who vouched for him. The original papers sometimes give additional information such as age on arrival and the port in which the ship docked.

The Soldiers' Grave Register is in the office of Veteran's Affairs in each county. This register gives the soldier's name, cemetery in which buried, military attachment, dates, and the source of information. Soldiers of all wars are recorded as far as they were known. The location of graves of Revolutionary and War of 1812 soldiers are recorded as far as known, but many are not known, but the records of the soldiers of the Civil War, Spanish-American and World Wars are practically complete.

The Soldier's Discharge Book is kept in the County Recorder's Office and dates from 1868. It contains copies of military discharges of soldiers, sailors, and marines. It gives the veteran's name, places of birth and enlistment, physical description, military record, occupation, names of commanding officers, date of discharge or death, and date recorded.

The Pennsylvania Archives

One of the most important sources for genealogical research in Pennsylvania is to be found in the published archives. Most libraries with any Pennsylvania collection of any moment have these volumes. Published in ten series from 1838 to 1935, they comprise 138 volumes.

Preceding the publication of the Archives, there were two valuable works, the first of which is in six volums. and is entitled: *Votes and Proceedings of the House of Representatives of the Province of Pennsylvania*, begun by Benjamin Franklin in 1754, and terminated in 1776; the second work was Samuel Hazard's *"Pennsylvania Archives,"* in twelve vols. The Archives proper consist of the following:

COLONIAL RECORDS	16 volumes, 1838–1853, contain Provincial Minutes.
FIRST SERIES	12 volumes, 1852–1856, reproduce papers from the Secretary of the Commonwealth.
SECOND SERIES	19 volumes, 1874–1890, contains militia rolls; church records; Minutes of the Board of War and of the Navy Board, both of 1777; Wyoming Controversy with Connecticut; Whiskey Insurrection.
THIRD SERIES	30 volumes, 1894–1899, first 26 volumes contain militia rolls; lists of land warrantees and taxables; Virginia claim to western Pennsyl-

vania; an account of the donation lands. The last four volumes are an index to the preceding sixteen.

FOURTH SERIES 12 volumes, 1900–1902, contains mostly the Governor's Papers.

FIFTH SERIES 8 volumes, 1905, contains muster rolls and military lists mostly of the Provincial and Revolutionary period.

SIXTH SERIES 15 volumes, 1905–1907, first 14 volumes contain military rolls, covering chiefly the period from the Revolution to the War of 1812, with some material on the Mexican War; some orderly books and military accounts for the 1812 period; church records of marriages and baptisms; inventories of estates confiscated during the Revolution; some 18th century election returns. Volume 15 is an index to the Fifth Series.

SEVENTH SERIES 5 volumes, 1914, consist exclusively of an index to the more than one million names in the first 14 volumes of the Sixth Series.

EIGHTH SERIES 8 volumes, 1931–1935, reprint of the 18th century edition of "Votes and Proceedings of the House of Representatives of the Province of Pennsylvania."

NINTH SERIES 10 volumes, 1931–1935, contains 15 minuscript volumes in the Division of Public Records.

The principal places to do research are at the State Library and State Archives at Harrisburg. The State Library is a depository for DAR typescripts, has a considerable collection of county histories and family genealogies, atlases and plat books for most of the counties, an excellent collection of New England material. The Archives is housed in the same building and has much unpublished material. The State Land Office is in the Capitol Building. In Philadelphia, the Genealogical Society of Pennsylvania has fine collections of church records, Quaker records, abstracts of probate records, English Quaker records; descendants of Signers of the Declaration of Independence, etc. The Historical Society of Pennsylvania which has an excellent library, is housed in the same building at 1300 Locust Street. The

Huguenot Society of Pennsylvania has also moved their library to this building, from Norristown.

Most of the counties of Pennsylvania have historical societies, many of which have excellent libraries and collections. Among then:

The Lancaster County Historical Society has many cemetery records and manuscripts and their own papers are indexed. The Fackenthal Library of Franklin and Marshall College in Lancaster houses the Historical Society of the Reformed Church. This is one of the finest collections of Reformed and Lutheran Church Records in the country. Other Lutheran Church records are deposited in the Lutheran Theological Seminary at Mount Airy, Philadelphia.

The York County Historical Society has records of over 5000 families; 40,000 cemetery records have been copied in York and Adams counties; wills have been abstracted and filed alphabetically; early church records; obituaries; and practically all of the early records have been abstracted from the courthouse. They also have a fine genealogical library.

The Northampton County Historical and Genealogical Society at Easton has 1500 volumes and much manuscript material, maps and surveys of Easton and Northampton county. Published a magazine at one time. The Public Library at Easton also has a genealogical section containing typed copies of vital records taken from early newspapers. (Read: *The Forks of the Delaware*, by Herman Kiefer).

Carnegie Library in Pittsburgh has a genealogical collection. The Historical Society of Western Pennsylvania, 4338 Bigelow Blvd., Pittsburgh, has printed volumes, manuscripts, and newspaper collections on the history of Pittsburgh and western Pennsylvania. The Lehigh University Library at Bethlehem, and the Bethlehem Public Library both have genealogical collections. Schwenkfelder's Historical Library at Pennsburg, in Montgomery county has a genealogical collection in addition to church records. The Historical Society of Montgomery County, at Norristown, has manuscripts, church records, scrap books, family records, and local newspaper files. Hamilton Library and Historical Association of Cumberland County, Carlisle, has imprints, newspapers, and genealogical materials on Carlisle. Bucks County Historical Society at Doylestown has 11,116 volumes, 25,000 manuscripts, 10,119 pamphlets, on state and local history and genealogy. There are eight volumes of publications.

The Chester County Historical Society, 225 North High Street, West Chester, has church, school and county records, minute and account books, and newspapers from 1809, on Chester county. The Lebanon County Historical Society at Lebanon has manuscript family histories and newspapers on Lebanon County. They published several volumes of Society Papers. Wyoming Historical and Geological Society, 69 South Franklin Street. Wilkes-Barre, has 5,000 volumes on genealogy, 50,000 volumes on local history, 30,000 pamphlets, newspapers, manuscripts, account books, maps, photographs, and genealogical data on Luzerne County. The Swedish Colonial Society at Merion has a genealogical collection.

The Erie Public Library has a genealogical section, and the Erie County Historical Society, Old Custom House, Erie, has 300 volumes on the history of the region. Tioga Point Museum and Historical Society, Spaulding Museum, Library Building, 724 S. Main Street, Athens (Bradford county), has newspaper and Indian materials; French Asylum Manuscript Collection; many items pertaining to Sullivan's Expedition; French Refugees of 1793; and early canal history. The Northumberland County Historical Society at Sunbury has manuscripts and local newspaper files. The Moravian Historical Society, Whitefield House, Nazareth, has church materials on Moravian history, and publishes, irregularly, *The Moravian Historical Society Transactions*. The Mifflin County Historical Society, Lewistown, has colonial records, newspapers from 1822, and historical publications on Pennsylvania. Published *The Genesis of Mifflin County, Pennsylvania*, 1939, and *The Pioneers of Mifflin County*, 1942. The collections of Friends Historical Library at Swarthmore, were described in the chapter on Quaker Records.

Bibliography

BROWNING, CHARLES: The Welsh Settlement of Pennsylvania.

BUCK, SOLON AND ELIZABETH: The Planting of Civilization in Western Pennsylvania. Bibliographical Essay. Univ. of Pittsburgh Press. 1937.

FAUST, A. B., AND BRUMBAUGH, GAIUS M.: Swiss Emigrants to the American Colonies in the Eighteenth Century. 1920. 2 v.

HINSHAW, WADE W.: The Encyclopaedia of American Quaker Genealogy.

MEYNEN, EMIL: Bibliography on German Settlements in Colonial North

America, Especially on the Pennsylvania Germans and Their Descendants, 1683–1933. Leipzig. 1937. (Contains 7858 references).

RUPP, I. D.: Collections of Upwards of 30,000 Names of German, Swiss, Dutch, French, and Other Immigrants to Pennsylvania, from 1727 to 1776, With Statement of Names of Ships Whence They Sailed and Date of Their Arrival at Philadelphia. 1927. Index by M. V. Koger, 1935.

SIMMENDINGER, ULRICK: True and Authentic Register of Persons Still Living, By God's Grace, Who, In the Year 1709, Journeyed From Germany to America.

21. "ANSEARCHIN'" THROUGH OHIO

"ANSEARCHIN' " THROUGH OHIO—GATEWAY TO THE WEST.

Many families coming from New York and New England settled for a time in Ohio before continuing on into Michigan, Wisconsin and further west. Many who did not remain permanently in Ohio, stayed there long enough to leave records—land, census, vital, and probate.

Settlement

In 1783 the Treaty of Paris established the Northwest Territory. In 1786 the Seven Ranges was set off and was the first land ever surveyed by the Federal Government west of the Ohio River. This land did not sell at the price asked of $2.00 per acre, as the virgin soil of other parts of Ohio and Kentucky was to be had for a much lower price. So, in 1820, Congress reduced the price and sold this land for $1.25 per acre.

In 1788, twenty-six families, under the leadership of Major Benjamin Stites, came from Pennsylvania and settled on a 10,000 acre grant, at Columbia, at the mouth of the Little Miami River, and founded Cincinnati. In 1789, Judge John Cleves Symmes brought a group of settlers to North Bend, where they secured the Symmes Purchase, patented in 1794, at 37 cents per acre. In 1790, Fort Washington was constructed at Cincinnati for the protection of these three settlements against the Indians.

In 1790, four hundred French immigrants settled at Gallipolis in Gallia county. They were people unfitted for the hardships of pioneer life, and just couldn't make a go of it. And, besides that, their land title was defective, so the settlement was soon dissolved. They had really been defrauded by the government, so, in 1795, Congress granted a tract of 24,000 acres in eastern Sciota county (on the Ohio River) to them to repay them for their loss. This was called The French Grant. Many of these French people had wandered on into Indiana and Illinois and descendants are living there today.

In 1791 the first Virginia Settlement was made at Manchester on the Ohio River, under the leadership of Colonel Isaac Massie. This included the land between the Sciota and Little Miami Rivers, and was bounty land which had been granted by the State of Virginia for service in the American Revolution.

In 1792 the Donation Tract was established in Washington and Morgan counties. The Ohio Company donated to each settler one hundred acres, providing he would bear arms for the next five years against the Indians, and at the end of five years he was to receive a deed to the land.

In 1796 the Second Virginia Settlement was made at Chillicothe, under the leadership of Colonel Massie and Duncan McArthur. This was also bounty land which the State of Virginia had obtained very cheaply and paid for with Continental Certificates—and that is where the saying "not worth a Continental" originated.

In 1796, fifty-two families came from Connecticut, under the leadership of General Moses Cleaveland, and settled at the mouth of the Cuyhoga River, and founded Cleveland. The State of Connecticut had sold this land to the Connecticut Company, and it was known as the Connecticut Western Reserve. The money was set aside to be used as a school fund, the interest from which is used, to this day, to support Connecticut schools. The Western Reserve then comprised Huron, Erie, and Ottawa counties, from which thirteen present-day counties in northeastern Ohio, have been set off. The westernmost portion of this grant which now comprises Huron and Erie counties, was known as "The Firelands." The Federal Government granted this land to the State of Connecticut, to compensate them for a number of Connecticut towns that were burned by the British during the Revolution. This explains the reason for the township names of Huron county, which are: Fairfield; Ridgefield; Norwich; Lyme; Greenwich; New London; New Haven; and Norwalk. The price of the land in the Western Reserve was from 40 to 50 cents per acre, and sometimes as low as 35 cents.

In 1798, The Refugee Tract was set aside for citizens of the British Provinces of Canada, including Nova Scotia, who, because of their sympathy for the colonists during the Revolution, had their property confiscated by the British Government, so they fled to the colonies for safety. This tract was in Licking and Franklin counties, and included Columbus at the western end.

Other lands listed as Congress Lands were lands that were sold by the United States Government to individuals. The United States Military Lands were lands appropriated by the Government for officers and men who had served in the Revolution.

There is no state in the Union which has so honored the Revolutionary fathers in the names of its counties as Ohio. First, there are counties named for the Revolutionary Presidents, Washington, Adams, Jefferson, Madison, and Monroe. Second, the Revolutionary Generals have been honored in the county names of Warren, Greene, Montgomery, Putnam, Mercer, Hamilton, Knox, Wayne, Stark, Clinton, Fayette, Marion, Morgan, and Shelby. Then there are counties named for the three capturers of Major André, the colleague of Arnold, namely: Paulding, Williams, and Van Wert. Names of civilians of Revolutionary fame are also honored in the names of counties, Hancock, Franklin, Carroll, and Harrison. There is also Jackson, and although Andrew was but a boy at the time of the Revolution, he received a wound from a British officer which he carried to his grave.

In 1825 the Erie Canal was opened and emigrants swarmed into Ohio from New York and New England. In 1836 a cold war was brewing between Ohio and Michigan, over a strip of land five miles wide at the west end and eight miles wide at the east end, on the northern boundary of Ohio. This included Toledo. The Ohio militia started marching from Toledo towards Detroit, and somewhere along the way, they met the Michigan militia headed by Governor Mason, marching from Detroit to Toledo. Just as the twain were about to meet in a hot war, the president sent Peace Commissioners from Washington to suppress the quarrel, and Congress finally granted this land to Ohio which was then a state, while Michigan was still a territory, having been refused statehood, up to then. But, to appease Michigan, and leave no hard feelings, Michigan was given the Upper Peninsula. At the time it looked like a poor compromise for Michigan, but, as it turned out, it was a pretty good deal as Michigan's Northern Peninsula contains some of the richest ore mines in the world. Michigan had applied for statehood, and as some of the top brass of those territorial days had become over-anxious to have a state seal, they had one drawn up and already adopted in the Territorial legislature, bearing the motto, "Si quaeris peninsulam amoenam circumspice." But, by the time Michigan really became a state, on January 26, 1837, the motto was incorrect, because then there were two peninsulas, and the Latin endings should have been changed. This has never been done, by an Act of the Legislature, and the Northern Peninsula residents still feel that they are not included in the state seal.

Ohio County Records

Birth and death records from 1856 to 1867 are with the clerk of the courts, but are incomplete, Birth and death records from 1867 to December 20, 1908, may be obtained from the Clerk of Probate. These are also incomplete. Birth and death records after December 20, 1908, may be obtained from the Division of Vital Statistics, State Department of Health, Columbus 15, Ohio. Exceptions: if the birth or death occurred in Cleveland, Columbus, Toledo, Akron, Cincinnati, Dayton, Canton, or Youngstown, copies may be secured from the Municipal Bureau of Vital Statistics. Marriage records may be obtained from the Clerk of the Probate Court of the county. The Works Projects Administration Historical Records Survey made inventories for some of Ohio's counties.

Probate Records

For wills, administrations, and other probate matters, write the Clerk of the Probate Court at the county seat. Some of the probate records have been published:

Abstracts of Lucas County Wills to 1874. 6 v. 1954.
Abstracts of Washington County Wills and Administrations, 1788–1850.

Abstracts of Law Suits for Genealogical Material, 1828–1875, in
Fayette County. 1956.

Cemetery Records for Highland County. McBride. 1954.

The 1810 Tax Lists were published in the Ohio Genealogical
Quarterly, 1937–1942; also in the National Genealogical Society
Quarterly.

Land Records

Land records are found in the office of the county recorder except
Federal Land records which are in the Bureau of Land Management,
Department of the Interior, Washington, D.C. Bounty land warrants
are in the pension files of the National Archives. Western Reserve
deeds (1800–1807); The Connecticut Land Company's Certificates
of Western Reserve Lands, and the Connecticut Land Company's
Mortgages of Scrip for the Western Reserve (1796–1807) are all to
be found in the Connecticut State Library at Hartford.

In a book by Marcus Gaius Brumbaugh titled "Revolutionary War
Records of Virginia," published in 1936, are given the bounty land
warrants for the Virginia Military District of Ohio. All his information
was taken from the federal and state archives. It is possible that
information concerning the 10,000 acre grant to Pennsylvania people,
at Cincinnati, in 1788, may be found at the State Land Office in
Harrisburg, Pennsylvania.

Census Records

Ohio never had a state census enumeration. The first Federal
Census of 1810 was destroyed during the War of 1812. The 1820
Federal Census is all intact except Franklin and Wood counties. The
State Library at Columbus, and the Western Reserve Historical Socie-
ty Library at Cleveland, have census records on microfilm.

The Mortality Schedules of Ohio, for 1850, 1860, 1870, and 1880
are in the custody of the Ohio State Library at Columbus.

Libraries and Historical Societies

OHIO STATE LIBRARY, Columbus 15, Ohio.

This has a large collection of Ohio county histories, early marriage records, and cemetery records, and also of Ohio soldiers in the War of 1812. They have duplicating service.

OHIO STATE HISTORICAL SOCIETY

This was formerly called the Ohio State Archaeological and Historical Society and is located at the entrance to Ohio State University at Columbus. Their address is Ohio State Museum, Columbus 10, Ohio. They have the largest collection of Ohio newspapers to be found anywhere, also manuscripts, maps, and genealogical material. They have a biographical index of Ohio County Histories which was compiled by the Ohio Daughters of the American Revolution. They also have a duplicating service.

THE WESTERN RESERVE HISTORICAL SOCIETY, 10825 East Boulevard, Cleveland, is one of the best genealogical libraries in the country, and the fifth largest. Specific queries will be answered free of charge if the search does not take over an hour. They have much material on Ohio, especially the Western Reserve counties. They have the best collection of books on New Hampshire, extant. They also have the Barbour Index of vital records of Connecticut, on microfilm. Their collection of the records of all Shaker communities in the United States, is indexed. They have a twenty-drawer card index to the Genealogical Manuscripts of the Misses Curry. These manuscripts are deposited in the Library of the University of North Carolina, but newspaper clippings, obituaries, and other items have been added to the index file at Western Reserve. Their newspaper collection is extensive and they have large collections of material on the Civil War period. Their holdings include the original records of the Connecticut Land Company, and vital and cemetery records for Western Reserve counties. The library sponsored a valuable publication, *Women of the Western Reserve*, compiled by Gertrude Wickham, and they have also typescripts, by counties, of "Women Who Came to the Western Reserve Before 1850." These give the woman's married and maiden name, year and place of birth, and last residence before migrating to the Western Reserve.

THE CINCINNATI PUBLIC LIBRARY

has over one million volumes and an annex which houses public documents. In the genealogy card catalog there is a card for every family name that appears five or more times in a book in the library.

There is another local card catalog in which is listed any name found in any books, newspapers, magazines, scrapbooks, or pictures relating to Hamilton county. They have a complete set of directories from the first which was published in 1819. Records are preserved of the First Baptist Church in the Northwest Territory, founded in 1790, as well as Catholic and pioneer German cemeteries scattered throughout the Cincinnati area. The staff cannot undertake extensive research but will answer reasonable requests if an addressed, stamped envelope is enclosed. The address is Eighth and Vine Streets, Cincinnati 2, Ohio.

THE CINCINNATI HISTORICAL SOCIETY, Cincinnati, Ohio 45202.

has much manuscript material and a vital statistics card catalog covering cemetery and church records. There are maps and atlases showing ownership of land. The holdings include all Ohio county histories and many from Kentucky, Indiana, and Virginia. There is much information on the eastern states, and Cincinnati newspapers from 1793, and directories from the beginning, 1819. There are calendars for the Draper Manuscript Collections in the Wisconsin State Historical Library, and rosters of Revolutionary soldiers buried in Ohio and Indiana. Brief queries will be answered if an addressed, stamped envelope is included.

THE FIRELANDS HISTORICAL SOCIETY, Norwalk, Ohio.

has newspapers and materials on the Firelands. They published *The Firelands Pioneer*, in two series (1858–1878) (1882–1937).

22. ANCESTRAL TRAILS ACROSS THE BORDER

ANCESTRAL TRAILS ACROSS THE BORDER—RESEARCH IN CANADA —HISTORICAL GEOGRAPHY—THE PUBLIC ARCHIVES—PROVINCIAL RECORDS—PRE-REVOLUTIONARY SETTLEMENT IN NOVA SCOTIA.

Historical Geography

The Dominion of Canada consists of ten provinces and two territories. The Colony of Quebec was settled by the French in 1608. Quebec was ceded to Great Britain in 1763. In 1791 Canada was divided into two parts, Upper Canada which is now Ontario, and Lower Canada which is now Quebec. The French Colony of Acadia was early captured by the British, and from its territory the provinces of Nova Scotia and New Brunswick were later formed. As western Canada was settled, it was organized into the Northwest Territories from which have been formed the provinces of Manitoba, British Columbia, Alberta, Saskatchewan, and the territories of Yukon, and the Northwest Territory.

The Dominion of Canada was formed by the Confederation Act of 1867, to comprise the Provinces of Quebec, Ontario, Nova Scotia, and New Brunswick. Manitoba entered the Confederation in 1870, British Columbia in 1871, Prince Edward Island in 1873, Alberta and Saskatchewan in 1905, and Newfoundland in 1950.

Genealogical Sources

THE PUBLIC ARCHIVES OF CANADA, Ottawa, Ontario.
The Public Archives of Canada operates under the authority of the

Public Archives Act of 1912, and is under the administration of the
Department of the Secretary of State of the Dominion Government.
Holdings:

MAPS: there are 30,000 on file, dating from 1500.

PHOTOGRAPHS, PRINTS, ENGRAVINGS, AND PAINTINGS: approximately
70,000 are catalogued and indexed.

REFERENCE LIBRARY—50,000 volumes.

MANUSCRIPTS:

Old records transferred from various government departments.

Transcripts of records made in Europe and America.

Collections of items acquired by gift or purchase.

Official correspondence to and from Canada during both the
English and French regimes constitutes the State Papers. These
are supplemented by collections of private papers of families who
were closely associated with government matters. There are also
manuscripts which include the Minutes of the Executive Councils
of Upper and Lower Canada from 1764 to 1867, and minutes of
the Land Boards dealing with the granting of land in Upper and
Lower Canada, and general correspondence dealing with the
laying out of lands, building of roads and bridges and local
administration of government.

CENSUS RECORDS:

The first census was taken in 1666 of what was then the French
Colony of France. It listed every person by name, age, sex, place
of residence, occupation, and marital status. There are 3,215
persons listed. The original document of 154 pages is in the Archives of Paris, and there is a transcript in the Public Archives at
Ottawa, Ontario. After that census, enumerations were taken
at irregular intervals. The Act of Union which united the
provinces of Upper and Lower Canada, in 1841, provided for
a census in 1842, and every fifth year, thereafter. That was taken
for Upper Canada (Ontario), in 1842, but the census for Lower
Canada (Quebec) was not taken until 1844. In 1852 and 1861,
census enumerations were taken for Upper and Lower Canada,
Nova Scotia and New Brunswick.

By provision of the British North American Act, under which
Canada became a self-governing Dominion, July 1, 1867, and

subsequent legislation, a census enumeration was taken in 1871, and every ten years since. The last was in 1951. These records are in the Dominion Bureau of Statistics, Ottawa, Ontario. Census records previous to 1841 are kept in the Provincial Archives.

CHURCH RECORDS

Church records are generally found in the Parish Church. The registration of baptisms, marriages, and burials has been kept by the priests of the Roman Catholic Church in Quebec since the first settlements were made, and some date back to 1610. Ministers of other faiths kept similar records.

The Public Archives of Canada acquired the originals of some of the older church records from the Provinces of Quebec, Nova Scotia, and New Brunswick. The Provincial Archivists also have some Parish Registers in their custody. If you are seeking church records it would be best to write the Public Archives at Ottawa or the Provincial Archivist of the Province in which your search is located.

IMMIGRATION AND NATURALIZATION RECORDS

For information write to the Department of Mines and Resources, Citizenship Registration Branch, Ottawa, Canada.

VITAL RECORDS

Following the Confederation Act of 1867, each Province enacted its own legislation. The registration of births is not universally carried out, due to the vast extent of the country and the isolated residences of many inhabitants. The status of vital records, by Provinces, is as follows: The usual fee is $1.00 for a birth, marriage, or death certificate.

ALBERTA:

Province established 1905 when a Provincial Bureau of Vital Statistics was formed, and continued the records of the Government of the Northwest Territories. Births, Marriages and Deaths have been registered since 1886; there were a few in 1885. From 1886 to 1905 records are estimated to be 50 per cent complete. From 1905 to 1915, records are reasonably complete and are indexed. Address, The Deputy Registrar General, Department of Public Health, Edmonton, Alberta, Canada.

Probate records—address Courthouse, Edmonton, Alberta.

Land records—address Land Titles Office, Edmonton, or Inspector of Land Titles, Calgary, Alberta, Canada.

Provincial Archivist—address, Provincial Archivist, Provincial Library, Edmonton, Alberta, Canada.

BRITISH COLUMBIA

Birth, marriage, and death records since September 1, 1872. Records may be obtained from the Registrar of Births, Marriages, and Deaths, Parliament Buildings, Victoria, British Columbia. The custodian also has incomplete records of church registers for the Province, from 1836. Copies of all adoption orders are entered in the various Supreme Court Registries, are filed in Victoria, and have been integrated with the birth records where the birth occurred in the Province.

Probate records date from 1858. Address Registrar of Supreme Court, Victoria, British Columbia.

Land records—deeds date from 1861. Address Land Registry Office, Victoria, British Columbia.

Provincial Archivist—address Provincial Library, Victoria, British Columbia.

MANITOBA

Births, marriages and deaths have been recorded from 1812 but are incomplete to 1874. Address Registrar General, Vital Statistics Division, Department of Health and Public Welfare, 331 Legislative Building, Winnipeg, Manitoba.

Probate records date from 1891. There is no central registry. Address Surrogate Court of the district in which your search is centered.

Land records—no central registry. Address District Registrar of Land Titles Office in district concerned.

Provincial Archivist—address the Provincial Librarian, Winnipeg, Manitoba, Canada. —

NEW BRUNSWICK

Births, marriages, and deaths, subsequent to January 1, 1920 are in the custody of the Registrar General of New Brunswick, Frederickton. Early marriages were recorded in Registers of Civil Status kept by ministers and priests of the various denominations in the Province. These registers were kept in duplicate and one copy was filed with the Prothonotary of the Superior Court in the district. Some of these records date back to 1887. These registers covering the period from 1887 to 1919 were transferred to the Secretary of Sub-District Board of Health, at the county seat of each county. The original certificates are still unfiled and unindexed in the Legislative Buildings.

Records of the City of St. John which were not destroyed by the great fire of 1877, are in the custody of B. L. Gerow, Attorney, St. John, New Brunswick.

Probate records—address Register of Probates for each county. For older records, write the New Brunswick Museum, St. John.

Land records—address Register of Deeds in each county. Older records are at New Brunswick Museum, St. John, N. B.

Provincial Archivist—The Provincial Librarian, Department of Education, Frederickton, New Brunswick, Canada.

NEWFOUNDLAND

Vital records—Prior to 1891 vital records are in the custody of the various local clergymen of their respective denominations. Since 1891 vital records are in the custody of the Registrar General of Vital Statistics, Department of Health and Welfare, St. Johns, Newfoundland. All clergymen are registrars, and keep complete church records of births, deaths, and marriages, copies of which are furnished the Registrar General at St. Johns, quarterly for districts outside of St. Johns, and monthly for the City of St. Johns.

Registration of birth records began on March 15, 1891; they are complete and fully indexed. Registration of marriage records began June 2, 1891, and are also complete and fully indexed, as are the death records which began on May 1, 1891.

Probate records—write the Registrar of the Supreme Court, St. Johns, Newfoundland.

Land records—write the Registry of Deeds and Companies, St. Johns, Newfoundland.

Libraries and Historical Societies—Gosling Memorial Library, and the Newfoundland Historical Society, both at St. Johns.

NOVA SCOTIA

Vital records—write to Provincial Custodian, Registrar General, Bureau of Vital Statistics, Halifax, Nova Scotia. Birth and death records commence in 1864, but were discontinued from 1876 to 1908. It is necessary to know the approximate date and name of the county. Marriage records start in 1763 but are incomplete until 1864. Marriage licenses are granted by the Deputy Issuers of Marriage Licenses in the district where the marriage was performed.

Probate records—write Registrar of Probates in the probate district, of which there are twenty.

Land records—write Registrar of Deeds in each of the twenty probate districts.

Provincial Archivist—Provincial Archivist, Halifax, Nova Scotia.

· ONTARIO

Vital records. The Provincial custodian is the Registrar General, Parliaments Building, Toronto. Vital records were first registered in 1869, but there are incomplete records of marriages from 1812 to 1869. These are indexed. Municipal clerks collect records of births, marriages, and deaths, and transmit them monthly to the Registrar General.

Probate records—write Registrar of the Surrogate Court of the county.

Land records—write Register of Deeds of the county.

Provincial Archivist—Provincial Archivist, Parliament Buildings, Toronto, Ontario, Canada.

PRINCE EDWARD ISLAND

Vital records—write the Provincial Custodian, Registrar General, Provincial Building, Charlottetown, P.E.I. Birth and death records were first registered in 1906 and were incomplete until 1920 since when they are more complete and indexed. Prior to 1906 births and deaths were partially recorded by the churches. Registration of marriage records commenced in 1831. Records are complete in the Surrogate's office at Charlottetown, to June 1906 when they were transferred to the office of the Registrar General. They are fully indexed in both offices by grooms' names, only. Ministers are required to make a return on any marriage performed, within 48 hours of the ceremony.

Probate records—write Office of Judge of Probate, Charlottetown, P.E.I.

Land records—write Register of Deeds, Summerside, Prince Edward Island, Canada.

Provincial Archivist—The Librarian, Legislative Library, Charlottetown, P.E.I., Canada.

QUEBEC

Vital records—The Provincial custodian is the Registrar, Parliament Building, Quebec, or the Director of the Department of Health, City of Quebec, or the Prothonotary of the town. Certificates of marriages, births, and deaths, are made out in duplicate by the priests, rabbis, and clergymen. The certificate of marriage is the copy or the extract of the entry thereof in a registry of civil status. The registers in which the entries are made are always kept in duplicate and one copy is deposited with the prothonotary of the district. In requesting records one must state if it is for a Catholic or non-Catholic, and if for a citizen of Canada or an alien. Marriage records date back to 1642, and an index for Catholics is available from that time; for non-Catholics from 1760 to date. Birth records began in 1894. Records of death are handled not by civil but by religious authorities. If no clergyman is present at the death or burial of a non-Catholic, the record may be obtained from the doctor's certificate filed with the Provincial Bureau of Health. Otherwise it may be obtained from the private records of the Mount Royal Cemetery Company, 1207 Drummond Street, Montreal.

Probate records are deposited in the various Districts of Notaries, of which there are twenty.

Land records—are deposited in the various Districts of Notaries.

The Genealogical Institute Drouin of Montreal, Canada, located at 4184 St. Denis Street, Montreal, published a 40-page brochure which describes the Institute's history, its documentary evidence, professional personnel, diverse works, and testimonials. In its files are microfilms of 61 million documents, representing authentic records of every birth, marriage, and death, in French Canada, between 1621 and 1943. Under work of the Institute Master, Gabriel Drouin (son of the founder) is a new *Genealogical Dictionary of French-Canadian Families*, in three volumes, covering 1600 to 1700, to be followed by regional dictionaries, 1700 to

1850, and eventually one for each county, 1850 to 1950. Gaston Gervais, Director of Researches, explains that the Institute does not specialize in partial researches, but only in complete ascending genealogies. Moreover, they handle mostly genealogies of French-Canadian families, owing to the fact that the details in the English records are very scarce.

Provincial Archivist—Provincial Archivist, Quebec, P. Q., Can.

SASKATCHEWAN

Vital records—Provincial Custodian, Director of Vital Statistics, Parliament Buildings, Regina, Saskatchewan. Birth records commence in 1854, marriage records in 1878, and death records in 1882. All are completely indexed.

Probate records—write Clerk of the Surrogate Court of the proper district, or write the Registrar of Surrogates Courts, Courthouse, Regina.

Land records—write Land Titles Office, Regina.

Provincial Archivist—University of Saskatchewan, Saskatchewan, Canada.

NORTHWEST TERRITORIES

Vital records begin in 1899 but are sketchy prior to 1927. Address Registrar General of Vital Statistics for Northwest Territories, Department of Resources and Development, Ottawa, Ontario, Canada.

Probate and land records—there is no central repository. The Royal Canadian Mounted Police and other government officials accept, on occasion, wills and deeds for safekeeping.

YUKON TERRITORY

Vital records date from 1897 but are sketchy until 1900. Address Registrar of Vital Statistics, Yukon Territorial Government, Dawson, Yukon Territory, Canada.

Probate records—Address Registrar, Territorial Court, Dawson, Yukon Territory, Canada.

Land records—address Registrar, Land Titles Office, Dawson, Yukon Territory, Canada. Fee $2.00 for land or probate records.

Pre-Revolutionary Settlement in Nova Scotia

In studying Canadian sources one should not overlook the pre-

Revolutionary migration from the New England Colonies to Nova Scotia, which occurred between 1755 and 1764. These people were not Tories, as they did not go there at the time of the conflict. Some of this migration returned to the colonies at the onset of the Revolution, or shortly afterward. Descendants of those who remained, in many instances, migrated to the United States between 1800 and 1838, and even later, from 1850 to 1860, and some even went to the west coast, so many families, throughout the country, will find missing links in Nova Scotia. Suggested reading—*The Neutral Yankees of Nova Scotia*, by John Bartlett Brebner. This contains many footnotes and a comprehensive bibliography of Nova Scotia source material, both published and unpublished.

In 1749 after the exodus of the Acadians, Halifax was settled by the English. Men from Massachusetts, Rhode Island, and Connecticut who had served at the Siege of Louisburg, together with some fishermen from Maine, located there. Then it was proposed that vacant French lands be offered New England settlers. The following were the terms of settlement announced by the Council of Nova Scotia, in 1759:

Townships were to be twelve square miles, or about 100,000 acres.

100 acres of wild woodland was to be allowed each settler, with 50 additional acres for each member of his family.

Grantee agreed to cultivate or enclose one-third of the land within ten years, one-third more in twenty years, and the remainder in thirty years.

No one could be granted more than 1000 acres, but on fulfillment of the terms, he could receive another grant under the same conditions, Quit rent of one shilling for each fifty acres was to begin ten years after date of grant.

Each township of fifty or more families could send two representatives to the legislature.

Courts of Justice were the same as in Massachusetts and Connecticut, and freedom of religion to all except Catholics.

The terms were so generous that the response was immediate. There was a Massachusetts migration to Annapolis Royal about 1760. Lists of these settlers are given in detail in *The History of the County of Annapolis*, by W. A. Calneck, and also in the Supplement to this work. Granville, Annapolis County, was settled by people from Lunenburg, Massachusetts, and some from New Hampshire.

Rhode Island sent many settlers to Nova Scotia. A list is given in *The Narragansett Historical Register*, volume 7, pages 89–135, in an article by R. G. Huling titled, "The Rhode Island Emigration to Nova Scotia." Another account is found in *Americana*, volume 10, pages 1, 83, 179, in an article by A.W.H. Eaton, titled, "Rhode Island Settlers on the French Lands in Nova Scotia, in 1760 and 1761."

Connecticut settlers came as a colony, having secured the grant of two townships, Horton and Cornwallis.

From the Nova Scotia census of 1770 it is found that Amherst and Sackville were settled by people from Rhode Island, supplemented, in 1768, by the entire Baptist congregation from Swansea, Massachusetts, who, however, returned to Massachusetts, in 1776. Cumberland, Onslow, and Truro, were settled by Connecticut people. Liverpool was settled by Massachusetts and Connecticut people. Barrington, Yarmouth, Annapolis and Granville were settled by Massachusetts people. Horton and Falmouth were settled by people from Londonderry, New Hampshire.

In 1770 eighty-nine per cent of the population of Nova Scotia was either native born or American colonists. An account of this migration is found in the *Pennsylvania Magazine of History and Biography*, volume 51, page 244, titled, "Acadia—The Pre-Loyalist Migration And the Philadelphia Plantation " by W. O. Sawtelle. This gives a good account of Rev. James Lyon.

Settlement began in 1760 and the bulk of the settlers were from New London, Lebanon, Norwich, Windham, Windsor, Killingsworth, Lyme, Colchester, Hebron, Saybrook, Stonington, and Tolland, Connecticut. There is a complete record of the names of those to whom grants of land were made in Eaton's "History of Kings County, Nova Scotia." Among the most predominant names are: Horton, Bishop, Harris, Lathrop, Dickson, Reid, Miner, Fuller, Avery, Comstock, Crane, Denison, Godfrey, Jordon, Scovel, Southworth, Wickware, Bill, Newcomb, Parker, Porter, Tupper, Woodworth, Bartlett, Best, Caulkin, Huntington, Kinsman, Bigelow, Curtis, Congden.

23. ANCESTRAL TRAILS ACROSS THE SEA

RESEARCH IN THE BRITISH ISLES.

The first step in doing research in the British Isles is to get all the facts that are available regarding the immigrant on the American side of the Atlantic, first. Determine, if possible, his place of residence in Britain, his occupation and his religion. In his Declaration of Intention, a man often stated his exact place of residence in the mother country. Early Notarial Records of New England sometimes tell a great deal about the immigrant's place of origin abroad. Some religious faiths give Certificates of Removal, or Dismissals from one church to another. Ships passenger lists give the port of embarkation which may be far removed from the immigrant's former residence. In colonial times, if a man made an application for land, in Pennsylvania or Maryland, at least, he had to register a name for it. The most natural thing was to call it after his old home, and this very often affords a clue.

Before going to the British Isles to do research it is advisable to study the various styles of 17th century handwriting. Here are some references to this subject:

Penmanship of the Sixteenth, Seventeenth, and Eighteenth Centuries. By Lewis F. Day. Published by B. T. Batsford, London. n.d.

Some Examples of English Handwriting, Twelfth to Seventeenth Centuries. By Hilda E. P. Grieve. Chelmsford, England. Essex Record Office Publication Number 6. 1949.

More Examples of English Handwriting From Essex Parish Registers, Thirteenth to Eighteenth Centuries. Chelmsford, England. Essex Record Office Publication Number 9. 1950.

The Capital Letters in Elizabethan Handwriting. By R. B. McKerron. London. Sedgewick & Jackson, Ltd. 1927.

Sources for Research in England and Wales

The Society of Genealogists, 37 Harrington Gardens, London S. W. 7, is the first place one should visit for British research. Their library contains more than 30,000 books, many of which are on open shelves. Their collection of over 10,000 manuscripts is valuable and important. It includes Boyd's *Marriage Index* which contains over six million names. The period covered by the index is from about 1550 to 1840. It is a typescript index of transcripts of parish registers in various counties, either printed or existing in typescript or manuscript. The index does not cover all of the counties of England, and in the counties not covered it only contains registers which have *been copied and* which the compiler was able to obtain. A copy of the *Marriage Index Key* (price $1.00 post free) which may be obtained from the Society, gives detailed information about each county, and specifies which parishes are covered. The only other copy of Boyd's *Marriage Index* is in the Library of the Genealogical Society of Utah, at Salt Lake City.

The Society of Genealogists also has a card index of three million names, and over 4000 Parish Register transcripts. Their manuscript collections cover England, Ireland, Scotland, and Wales.

The British Museum

The British Museum, Bloomsbury, London, W. C. 1, has many rare books, a manuscript department, visitation records, catalogs and indexes. Here also are found valuable documents called "Ancient Charters" which contain 25,777 listings. Also housed here are the Domesday Books which contain the most ancient surveys in England. A few in the North are missing for 1085–86. They are written in Latin and give the name and title of every person of importance in the kingdom, and sometimes the fathers, wives, and children are mentioned. Here, too, are Parliamentary Records which are the records of settlements of family estates, and give long family pedigrees, naturalization of foreigners, licenses to change names and arms, authorization for individuals to remarry, and so forth.

Guildhall Library

The City of London Guild has many printed genealogical books. Their holdings include many of the original records of the 102 parishes in London. A bomb destroyed their index during World War II, but it is being redone.

Public Records Office

Public Record Office, 120 Chancery Lane, London W. C. 2, England, has many records but it is necessary to employ a professional researcher in order to interpret the records correctly. They have many researchers. It holds many tax records called subsidy lists. Its records date from medieval times and include: Chancery Proceedings; Inquisitions Post Mortem; Patent Rolls; Hearth Taxes; Manor Court Rolls; and Feet of Fines. They also have 1841 and 1851 census returns of England and Wales.

The British Record Society, 120 Chancery Lane, London, W. C. 2, England, since its founding in 1888, has published seventy-six volumes of classified indexes and over two million references to national records of Britain. The indexes are of wills and administrations, chancery proceedings, inquisitions post mortem, coram rege rolls, royalist composition papers, signet bills, Canterbury Archbishop's Act Books, and marriage licenses. Membership in this organization consists of Associate, $3.00, or Full Membership, $7.50. Full members receive the publications.

Somerset House

At the General Registry, Somerset House, London W. C. 2, England, are kept certificates of births, marriages, and deaths, in England and Wales, from July 31, 1837. Write either Somerset House or the Society of Genealogists for non-parochial registers and records, mainly prior to 1837. Some of these go back to 1642. Somerset House also has

the Marine Register Book which gives births and deaths at sea since
July 1, 1837, and Army Returns which are births, marriages, and
deaths, recorded in Army Registers; some of these go back to 1761.
In the Consular returns are births, marriages, and deaths of British
subjects in foreign countries. There are also many miscellaneous vital
records dating back to 1627. For a "general search" in the indexes,
requiring up to six hours time, the charge is one pound, and 1/- for
a "particular search," covering a period of five years for any given
entry. Non-parochial register search is 1/- per volume. A certified
copy costs 2/6.

There are also deposits of wills between 1653 and 1660. In 1662
Charles II did away with wills, but since 1858 all wills are filed there.
They also have records of non-conformist churches, including Friends'
from 1642 to 1837. There was a published index about one hundred
years ago, but it is seldom found in this country.

Friends' House

Friends' House is a depository for many Quaker records. Abstracts of
these records, to 1725, are in the Gilbert Cope Collection in the Genealogical Society of Pennsylvania, at Philadelphia. (See Chapter 13)

The Huguenot Society of London

For the Huguenot Society of London, address the Assistant Secretary,
56 Westbury Court, Nightingale Lane, London S. W. 4. This library
has recently been entirely recatalogued, and a new complete card
index is kept up to date. They have many rare old volumes and
manuscripts, and their greatest collection is Huguenot Pedigrees. The
work of the Society is of great interest to Ulster, where the town of
Lisburn was the important city of refuge for Huguenots in Ireland.
The publications of the Huguenot Society of London are to be found
in several libraries in the United States: New York State Library
(since 1895); The Library of Congress (since 1899); Cornell University
Library (since 1901); and Newberry Library, Chicago (since 1903).

County Libraries

County Records Offices, or County Libraries, are located in the various county seats, and compare to our state archives, not to our county records.

Types of records

WILLS: These are most important. They were filed as early as the thirteenth century, almost from the time of the Magna Charta, but then only from prominent families. The lower classes began filing wills about 1500. There is no rule as to time—the important thing to remember is that the ecclesiastical profession handled wills until 1858. The ecclesiastical jurisdiction was abolished in 1858, and before that time, wills were proved in the Archdeaconry, diocesan, or "Peculiar" Court having jurisdiction over the place where the testator died or held property. If he owned property in more than one such jurisdiction, the will was generally proved in the Prerogative Court of Canterbury, or in that of York. The Prerogative Court for the North of England was at York, and for the South of England, at Canterbury. They were indexed by twenty-year periods. During Cromwell's time, all wills were filed in London. It is difficult to find wills because they came under different church jurisdictions. There are no published calendars for many areas so it is necessary to know the county from whence the ancestor came. Many of the Prerogative Court records of Canterbury have been published, and photostats may be obtained by writing to Somerset House. Suggested reading: *Wills and Their Whereabouts*, by B. J. Bouwens. London. 1951.

PARISH REGISTERS: In 1538 Henry VIII set up a register of births, marriages, and deaths, so, from that time there were records in some 1400 or more parishes in England and Wales. Non-conformist's records were not included. There are many parish record transcripts in the library of the Society of Genealogists, but for those that have not been transcribed it is necessary to visit the church in question, or correspond with the Incumbent, enclosing an addressed envelope and an international postal money order. Copies of data recorded in parish registers may be obtained by paying a small fee. Where there are no parish registers, transcripts may be located at the Diocesan Registry. Before attempting English research it is important to know the county in which your search is centered, and for that information, there are three books that are most useful:

Keys to the Ancient Parish Registers of England and Wales. By Arthur M. Burke. London. 1908.

National Index of Parish Registers. By the Society of Genealogists of London. Copied by Katherine Blomfield and H. K. Percy Smith. London. 1939.

The Genealogist's Handbook; Being an Introduction to the Pursuit of Genealogy. The Society of Genealogists of London. London. 1937.

MARRIAGE BY LICENSE: Before 1837 not all marriages were by license, but most well-to-do people were married by license which was obtained from the Bishop of the Diocese, the Archbishop of the Province, the Dean of the Peculiar, or from the Archdeacon. The allegations upon which these licenses were granted, and which give valuable information, are still on file in the Bishop's Diocesan Registries, or in the Vicar General's Office and Faculty Office of the Archbishop of Canterbury, and may be inspected upon payment of a small fee. All of the above registries are located at Number 1, The Sanctuary, London, W. C. 1.

In Wales, the great libraries of Cardiff, Swansea, the University College of North Wales, and the National Library of Wales at Aberystwyth, should be consulted, as well as the Honourable Society of the Cymmrodorion, 20 Bedford Square, London, W.C. 1.

These are very important records as they give the places of residence of both the bride and groom, the trade of the groom, the parents of the bride, and the ages of the couple. These records have to be located through guides. See *A Select Bibliography of English Genealogy,* with Brief Lists for Wales, Scotland, and Ireland. By Howard Guy Harrison. London. 1937.

HERALD'S VISITATIONS, AND PEDIGREES OF NOBILITY are printed and in most libraries. The right of certain claimants to bear coats of arms was inquired into by officials known as Heralds, who made regular visitations, the earliest in 1412. From 1529 until the close of the seventeenth century, regular visits were made every twenty-five or thirty years, the last in 1686. The Heralds kept registers which frequently show connected pedigrees for a number of generations. They were taken to the College of Arms for registration, and are authentic for three generations. Pedigrees of nobility started when it was required that peers produce their pedigrees before the House of Lords.

CENSUS RECORDS: There are census returns for 1861, 1871, 1881, and each decade thereafter. These are at the General Register Office in Somerset House and are not available for inspection by the public but will be searched by the staff on payment of $1.50 for each address, but the exact address must be given. The application must be accompanied by a statement that the information sought is for genealogical purposes only, and will not be used for litigation.

LAND RECORDS: After the Norman invasion of England, in 1066, William the Conqueror divided England into seven hundred baronies and bestowed these upon his friends and followers. These were subdivided into 60,215 so-called "Knight's Fees," each allotment of land being possessed by a Knight, usually about one hundred acres. An account of these fees was taken from time to time. They commenced earlier than the national records. From them can be traced succession of families. The most ancient is called *The Black Book of the Exchequer*, which contains a list of the Knight's Fees during the time of Henry II (1154–1189). Pipe Rolls are annual financial accounts returned by the sheriff of each county, of all fines, fees, and expenditures handled by him, and are the most important series of documents after Domesday. They start in 1155 and continue to the present. Names of most men of families of property appear upon them, and nearly every ancient pedigree is indebted to them for assistance. Write Public Record Office, 120 Chancery Lane, London, W.C. 2, England.

TAX RECORDS: These began in 1524 when they began taxing yeomen, and were records of every man and every shire in England. From these much can be learned about the origin of surnames. In the 1630's the Ship's Money Lists were established. Charles I and Archbishop Laud would not allow any one to leave England unless he could prove he had paid his tax, and he had to pay a subsidy if he got away before the next year. Many did get away and the rolls are filled with the notations: "gone to New England." Bank's manuscripts in the Library of Congress contain many of these records of subsidies and others.

HEARTH TAX: This was levied from 1660–1674 upon any one who owned a house of any sort, even if in debt, if he was out of jail, on the basis of the number of hearths maintained in the house. These were arranged by counties, and are in the public record office, but are not indexed.

FEET OF FINES (1190–1853): Land records in the Public Record Office were arranged by county and date, and contain records of conveyances of title to property, which afford a clue as to when the ancestor left England, for after he sold his property, he is usually found in New England the following year. They also contain records of suits to extinguish dormant titles to property, and constitute deeds of settlement.

MANORIAL COURT ROLLS contain the names, residences, and descriptions of tenants, and show their marriages, wills, and so forth. These are in the Public Record Office, London, but many have been destroyed. A check list was published in 1923.

CHANCERY PROCEEDINGS are arranged by surnames. A family with any property at all is sure to have been involved in a suit at one time or another.

INQUISITIONS POST MORTEM. In the days of the Feudal System, on the death of each tenant in Chief, a tax called the relief tax was due the King by the heirs. This was started in 1219 and there are none after 1649. These records give the identity of the deceased, date of death, the land of which he died seized, his heirs and their ages.

PATENT ROLLS AND CLOSE ROLLS are written in Latin, on parchment, and contain records of the more prominent people, and are rolled into long rolls. Patent Rolls contain all kinds of Letters Patent, including those granting land; Close Rolls contain records of private deeds of sale.

APPRENTICE ROLLS. People from all over England went to London to learn a trade in one of the guilds. After serving seven year's apprenticeship, one could become a citizen or cutler of London, and usually about a year after a man left the guild, there will be a record of his marriage, and piecing it all together, the family story begins to take shape. These records include the date, place of residence of the parents, and the date appointed, and the master's name and trade. The Guildhall Library published a guide for London. This is *Harrison's Book* (q. v.). These Rolls have been indexed by the Society of Genealogists.

WELSH RECORDS are very difficult to use and require a great deal of study to interpret. Probably the best book on the subject is *An*

Approach to Welsh Genealogy by Major Francis Jones. The book is also very difficult to read with understanding. A copy is in the Library of Congress. Welsh records are in the great library at Aberystwyth, the capital of Wales.

Scotland

Scottish records are similar to those of England but more complex. Compulsory registration of births, marriages and deaths did not begin until 1855. Extracts may be obtained from the Registrar General's Office, New Register House, Edinburgh 2, Scotland, which also houses all of the ancient Parish Registers from which certified extracts may be obtained for a small fee. At the Old Register House, Calendars of Wills, Justiciary Records, Sasines, Deeds, and other legal documents may be consulted.

The Scots Ancestry Research Society, 4a North Saint David Street, Edinburgh, a non-profit organization, will assist overseas inquirers. There is a registration fee of $2.00, or $3.00 if the latest known date is prior to 1855. Investigation and report costs are additional. The maximum fee charged for tracing one ancestral line is $30.00, but the average search costs about half this amount.

There are census returns for 1841, 1851, 1861, and 1871 available for genealogical purposes. Write the Registrar General for information.

BIBLIOGRAPHY: *The Surnames of Scotland,* by George F. Black. New York. 1946. There are editions for England and Wales, also.

The Scot's Peerage, by Sir James Balfour Paul. Edinburgh. 1904–1914. 9 volumes.

Detailed List of the Old Parochial Registers of Scotland. Published by the General Register House, Edinburgh. 1872 (OP)

For books on the British Isles, write to Walford Brothers Book Store, 69 S. Hampton Road, London W.C. 1.

Ireland

As in English research, the first step in tracing Irish ancestry is to get all available information in this country before you attempt to extend your research across the sea. If your family records are meager consult town and county histories of the region where your ancestor settled, and you may find from whence he came. Look for his naturalization and immigration papers. If he served in the American Revolution, and lived long enough to apply for a pension, he had to take an oath as to where he was born. Check land records in the county where he bought land, and they may tell from whence he came. Check his will for any clues it may offer.

American libraries with good genealogical collections of Irish records are:

American-Irish Historical Society, 999 Fifth Avenue, New York City. They have large collections.

The Genealogical Society of Utah, Salt Lake City, has microfilms of all available records in Ireland.

The Library of Congress, Washington, D.C., has a great deal of Irish material.

Newberry Library, Chicago, Illinois, has a large collection.

The Historical Society of Pennsylvania has a check list.

The Huntington Library at Pasadena, California, has a fine collection.

The Los Angeles Public Library has an Index to Wills, an eight-volume collection of Parish Records for Dublin, and one volume for Londonderry, which begin about 1620. They also have Irish county histories.

The New England Historic and Genealogical Society, Boston, also has will indexes.

Start with the library or historical society nearest to the place where settlement was first made in America, and work back from there.

In Northern Ireland registration of Protestant marriages commenced on April 1, 1845, and of births, deaths, and Roman Catholic marriages, on January 1, 1864. The original records are in the custody of the Superintendent Registrars and District Registrars of the area in which the events occurred, and certified copies may be obtained from these officers. The central records since 1922 are kept at the General Register Office, Fermanagh House, Ormeau Avenue, Belfast, where an index covering the whole of Northern Ireland is maintained. The central records prior to 1922 are in the General Register Office, Custom House, Dublin, but if information is requested on any birth, death, or marriage which occurred in Northern Ireland prior to 1922, the Registrar General in Belfast will arrange for searches to be made on payment of the prescribed fee.

Many old wills were destroyed by a fire in Dublin, in 1922, but several thousands of copies, notes, and extracts from Ulster wills and other documents taken prior to their destruction are preserved in the Public Record Office for Northern Ireland, Law Courts Building, May Street, Belfast. This office also has lists of early rent rolls. These refer mainly to country dwellers of moderate substance. Information about persons in possession of land other than small tenants, may be obtained by a search in the Registry of Deeds, Henrietta Street, Dublin. Its records go back to the early eighteenth century. The Office of Arms, Dublin Castle, is another useful source of information.

Although many Irish Church Registers were destroyed by fire in 1922, about two hundred of those of Northern Ireland are still in the custody of the parish clergymen. A list of them is found on page 12 of the 1924 report of the Record Office of Northern Ireland, and the dates they cover may be ascertained from a list for all Ireland, in Appendix II, to the twenty-eighth Report of the Deputy Keeper of the Records of Ireland, published in Dublin, in 1896. This report is available in many public libraries. Only in a few instances do the parish registers of the Church of Ireland go back to the seventeenth century.

Principal Depositories in Ireland

OFFICE OF REGISTRATION, General Customs House, Dublin.
They have ship's manifests and immigration records. The records have been abstracted. They have about fifteen lists and these give the parishes from which the emigrants came. For this you should send $5.00.
THE SOCIETY OF FRIENDS, Eustace Street, Dublin.
If you have a problem in Quaker ancestry, write there. They have a fine collection. A fee of $5.00 should be enclosed.
NATIONAL LIBRARY OF IRELAND, Dublin.
The genealogical office is in Dublin Castle.
THE PUBLIC RECORD OFFICE OF IRELAND—THE FOUR COURTS.
The Registry of Deeds, Henry Street, Dublin. This is the public record office of Northern Ireland.

Historical Geography

The first important thing to do is to locate your ancestor by county, and some other clue in the county where the ancestor lived. Write over and have them located first. These are the locations to look for— the province, the county, the barony, the diocese, the parish, and the town or town land. It is just like finding an address in America where you locate a person by the state, the county, the town, or city, the street, and the number on the street.

The Episcopal Church division is the diocese; the Methodist Church division is the conference. The Barony is a division of the county where the voting takes place. The church is the parish.

Land records go by province, county, barony, town or townland, sometimes all or any part of these. Church records are known by diocese and parish. Probate records are known by county, diocese, town and townland. Marriage licenses are found in the parish diocese, as are marriage settlements. There are only four provinces. There were five originally. These are Ulster in the north; Linster; Midland in the southeast part; Munster in the south; and formerly Connaught.

Counties

There are thirty-two counties. In 1920 Northern Ireland remained under Great Britain, and the Republic of Ireland took twenty-six counties out of Ireland. Ulster had nine counties but six were taken out, so only three remained. After the separation in 1920, the counties still under English rule were: Antrim, Down, Tyrone, Londonderry, Fermanagh, Armagh. The remaining counties in Ulster stayed under the Republic of Ireland. They are: Donegal, Cavan, Monahan.

The most important thing to know in order to find church records is the diocese. The diocese goes back to the time Ireland was all Catholic, and it was not changed during the time of Henry VIII. The church of Ireland put the Catholic priest out but left the diocese the same, and placed the Archbishop of Armagh over all other bishops as Armagh was the most important.

Ireland was divided into twenty-eight dioceses, and then it was divided into thirty-two counties. The counties were superimposed over the dioceses. It is just like placing one crazy quilt over another one, for there may be four dioceses in one county, and there may be four counties in one diocese.

A barony is a subdivision of a county, which was once owned by a Baron. The parish was set up in 1659. Cromwell wanted to send the Irish and English whom he suspected of disloyalty, out of England, and at that time, there were adventurers who were going to Ireland to buy cheap land. So Cromwell paid his soldiers with land warrants in Ireland, the same as we paid our Revolutionary soldiers with Bounty Land Warrants, so he made a survey of Ireland to determine what land was available. This was called the first census of Ireland and was taken in 1659.

Sir William Petty made maps of the 216 Baronies and of the 2000 parishes. The land of every man was outlined, and every public house, and the names of cities and towns. He changed almost none, and upon this map he listed 25,000 townlands (a townland was the name of a farm). This map provides a wonderful clue to finding where your people lived. If you know the county and the place name, write to the Public Record Office of Northern Ireland, Mr. Kenneth Darwin, Law Courts Building, May Street, Belfast, Ireland. Ask him to search the following books for information if they are not available to you in this country.

BIBLIOGRAPHY:

Philips *Handy Atlas of the Counties of Ireland.* 1885.

Lewis' *Atlas of the Counties of Ireland.* 1837.

Typographical Index of Parishes and Townlands of Ireland, by Y.M. Goblet. Dublin. 1932.

These men took the maps of Sir William Petty and made lists with a cross index, so if you know only the townland, it will tell the county, parish, and so forth, and vice versa. These books are available in the Library of Congress, New England Historic & Genealogical Society Library, Boston, Newberry Library, Chicago, Library of the Genealogical Society of Utah, Salt Lake City, and the Huntington Library in Pasadena, California.

The General Alphabetical Index of Townlands and Towns, Parishes and Baronies was published, with a census of Ireland, by Alexander

Thom, in Dublin, in 1861. It will locate a family from a Townland, and is cross referenced. *The Parliamentary Gazetter of Ireland*, in three volumes, was published in 1841.

Land Records

These consist of wills, marriage records, tax records, leases, family manuscripts, and others. The Registry of Deeds, Henrietta Street, Dublin, has complete land records, from 1708. These cover deeds, leases of over three years, mortgage foreclosures, marriage settlements, partition of estates and some memorials of wills. These are indexed by names of Grantors and Grantees, alphabetically, for periods of 10 and 20 years. Locations are not listed until after 1833, then the places are listed by dates and geographic locations. The Genealogical Society of Salt Lake City sent two men to Ireland to microfilm these records, and it took them two years to do it. The only reason they were allowed to microfilm these records is the danger of war; if another war should destroy the records, there would be a copy in the United States.

The land records contain some marriage settlements, as these often involved land, some wills, and many leases. The favorite period for a lease to run in Ireland is sixty-one years, or three lifetimes. Some times lands were leased forever, with a minimum of sixty-one years.

Public Record Offices have many land records. The Public Record Office burned in 1922, but in Dublin, beginning in 1869, they published a catalog called "Reports of the Deputy Keeper of Public Records." These contained volume after volume of fiants. A fiant is the same as a warrant which began when Henry VIII established the Church of England in England, and took property in Ireland and granted it to loyal people. These grants were made to people of importance. He issued 508 fiants and they contained much genealogy, often two or three generations. Edward VI issued 476 fiants all of which are in the Reports of the Deputy Keeper. Then followed Philip and Mary who gave these back to the monasteries—276 fiants. Elizabeth took them from the monasteries and returned them to the people. She colonized Ireland and issued 6782 fiants, and there is an index to all of them. These go through Charles II, but are published only through Elizabeth.

The Earls of Ireland and the Great Chieftains, in the last year of

the reign of Queen Elizabeth, sent men into Ulster in a bloody revolution. James I colonized further and took lands from the Earls
of Antrim, first, as they had contributed to the Revolution, and land
went back to the state in Antrim, Down, Armagh, Londonderry,
Tyrone, Donegal, and Fermanagh. The first Scotch went about 1585,
in the McDonald Clan, with a thousand men and attacked the northeast corner of county Antrim, took the land, and settled their people
there. Elizabeth died in 1603 and James granted the property to
one of his favorites, James Hamilton. He was involved in County
Down of which he got the north half, nearest Scotland. He gave a
section of this to Hugh Montgomery.

They kept estate records. There are three books about early Scotch
estates:

Historical Account of the MacDonnalds of Antrim. By Rev. G. W.
Hill.

The Hamilton Manuscripts, edited by T. K. Lowery, in 1868. (In
1660 there was a list of every lease holder and military lists of
all who fought against the Catholics).

The Montgomery Manuscript published by Rev. George Hill in 1869.

The Plantation of Ulster, 1608–1830, by Rev. George Hill, was
a larger project. In Counties Londonderry and Tyrone land was
granted by James I, and the London Company was formed and was
responsible for planting this land. They subdivided it into nine sections, for weavers, vintners, ironmongers, etc. A map shows each group
and the section tells when they came. This is a genealogical goldmine.

TAX RECORDS had to do with locating people. There was a Hearth
Rolls Tax of two shillings for each hearth or fire. This tax got every
person no matter how poor he was. Many of these records were lost
in the Public Record Office fire. The Presbyterian Historical Society
has land records for county Tipperary from 1663 to 1669. The Subsidy
Roll was copied for County Down and is in the Public Record Office.
The Hearth Money Rolls in the Public Record Office in Dublin are
available since the office burned in 1922. The 1955 Report of the
Public Record Office listed all the Parish records, over 1500 pages of
records.

Wills are of two classes, Prerogative Wills and Diocesan Wills.
Prerogative wills were proved in Prerogative Court. If a man had

property of more than five pounds value his estate was settled in Prerogative Court. The Archbishop of Armagh presided over all courts. Sir William Betham, Ulster King of Arms, in Dublin, abstracted the genealogical information from the wills and Sir Bernard Burke made genealogical charts from the abstracts, many of which were in private hands when the record office burned. Burke's records are in the Genealogical Office in Dublin. The Vicar's Index lists 36,000 wills. It is in many American libraries and photostats may be obtained from the Library of Congress. Diocesan wills were burned but indexes had been made. These gave the name, place of residence, the year the will was proved, county and diocese. There are unpublished indexes for the Diocese of Connaught and the Diocese of Down. These are ·in the Public Record Office at Dublin.

The Presbyterian Historical Society, Miss Jennie L. M. Stewart, Church House, Fisherwick Place, Belfast, Ireland, has a list of every Presbyterian Parish record in Ireland, and all of the genealogies in Ireland. They charge $1.00 an hour for search. Send them $5.00 and ask them to pass it on to a genealogist, and you will receive a great deal of information. Catholic records are being filmed.

The Public Record Office in Belfast has reports of the Deputy Keeper of Public Records. Her Majesty's Stationery Office in Belfast has family manuscripts, leases, diocesan wills, deeds, and marriage records. The Presbyterian Historical Society of Donegal has a list of Protestant householders from 1740. The Public Record Office of Belfast has some records of immigration to America. The Genealogical Society of Dublin has about six hundred and fifty family manuscripts, most of which do not concern Americans. Mr. Gerard Slevin is in charge.

International Postage

How does one send return postage to a foreign country? It is sent by means of an international reply coupon. These are obtainable at the postoffice. This coupon is exchangeable in any country of the Universal Postal Union for a postage stamp or stamps representing the amount of postage for an ordinary single-rate letter destined for a foreign country. The cost is 11 cents and is an easy way to furnish return postage. When it is received the party will exchange it for postage of his country.

International Money Order. If you purchase a book from a foreign country, go to the post office and fill in an application form for an International Money Order. This will cost 10 cents for each $10.00. The post office will then mail the order to the New York Exchange Office, and they will make out the money order and send it on to the foreign country. You will hold the receipt from your post office.

If you asked a friend to send you an air mail letter from Great Britain, weighing one ounce, it would cost six International Reply Coupons, or 66 cents; therefore it would be best to send an International Money Order. Make inquiry at your local post office, as the rates change from time to time.

24. HERALDRY

HERALDRY—HISTORY—PARTS OF THE ACHIEVEMENT—CHARGES
—TINCTURES—CADENCY—HOW TO READ A HERALDIC DESCRIP-
TION—HOW TO ESTABLISH YOUR RIGHT TO THE USE OF COAT
ARMOUR.

Heraldry is not an American institution but coat armour
may properly be assumed by many Americans. Coats of arms have
been used by Americans from early colonial times. In fact, George
Washington, himself, used one. There has been prejudice against
their use by Americans, as being undemocratic, snobbish, and generally out of keeping with the American way of life.

Coats of arms came into general use about the time of the Crusades,
as a matter of expediency to recognize armored warriors in battle.
Horses and dogs also wore armor. Roman dogs were called Fidos
(meaning faithful) and that name has endured. The love of ornament
and symbolism has also played its part in the use of heraldic devices,
and today not only the United States, but every state, has its own coat
of arms and state seal. Likewise, cities have their municipal seals and
coats of arms. The propriety of the use of coats of arms on any government level is not considered undemocratic or snobbish; then why
should their use by individuals be so considered?

A popular misconception is that coats of arms were only used by
European nobility. This is not true. The Herald's College was established in England, in 1483, by King Richard III. Heralds were sent
out to visit families and record their pedigrees. These were called the
Herald's Visitations, and are published in the Harleian Society Manuscripts, by shires (counties).

Any one to whom arms were granted is entitled to the use of the
arms upon moral principles. Their use has no legal status in the

United States, and therefore, there is no penalty for using arms to which one has no right, although that would, from an ethical point of view, be plain pilfering.

The need for the use of coat armour belongs to the past. In fact, its use parallels the development of military science for the most part. After the discovery of gun powder its use declined, and certainly in this atomic age there is little need for it.

Heraldry, or armory, to give it its more ancient name, has, from the beginning of time, fascinated the minds of men who, throughout the ages, have shown a love for symbols, typified today by such emblems as national flags, state and national seals, political badges, military insignia, and trade marks which are an outgrowth of the old merchant's marks, with their familiar slogans (Progress is our most important business; his master's voice, etc.).

First, it was merely a decorative art which, from Biblical times, was used as a means of recognition (Numbers, Chapter 2, verse 2: "Every man of the children of Israel shall pitch by his own standard, with the ensign of their father's house"). Finally, in the twelfth century it emerged as a serious science of hereditary marks of recognition and of distinction.

However, the first coats of arms were assumed without authority. Armorial bearings were in general use throughout Europe long before surnames became fixed, and there is also proof that some knights assumed cognomens suggested by their own armorial devices. The work of Sir Walter Scott, the most deeply read scholar in medieval lore, made many references in his novels to the symbolism of heraldry, as did also Shakespeare, Chaucer, and Spenser. Although the use of coat armour cannot be traced to a period before the Crusades (1096–1270), it is known that the use of symbols and shields extended to the remotest antiquity. First, it was merely a decorative art which, from Biblical times, was used as a means of recognition. It is probable that to ancient Egypt, the birthplace of all the arts and sciences, may be ascribed the earliest use of symbols.

It has been said that the original use of symbols was to supplement defects in language, before writing was generally practiced. Some symbolism, like some phrases, has become universal. The cross is the symbol of one faith and the crescent of another. The lion was borne as the ensign of the Tribe of Judah, and the eagle of the Romans, the two-headed eagle of the East; the raven was borne by the ancient Danes, and the crescent and star by the followers of Mohamet, and retained by the Turkish Empire.

To really appreciate the symbolism of medieval times, one must consider the degree of illiteracy that existed. Very few people could read or write. In 1215 A. D., when the great Magna Charta of England was secured, none of the twenty-five barons who became sureties for the Great Charter, could read or write, and to this their seals, not their signatures, were affixed.

Since arms were first assumed without any regulating authority, much uncertainty surrounds the whole subject. In ancient coat armour many objects have been used which defy identification by heralds. If one wishes to study a family coat of arms, it is first necessary to study the social customs of the period in history in which it was assumed, and by learning the uses of the objects charged upon the escutcheon, he may be able to interpret something of the life of the family. The earliest coats of arms were very simple. DeClare was the first one used in England.

HERALDRY—in a strict sense, includes everything within the province of the College of Arms. (arms, pedigrees, ceremonials, etc.)
ARMORY is concerned only with arms.
ACHIEVEMENT OF ARMS refers to the shield of arms and all the accessories that go with it.
COAT OF ARMS, as the term is used, is synonymous with achievement. This term was derived from a garment that was worn over the armor, and embroidered with the coat of arms.

Personal armorial bearings are put to many uses. They may be seen chiseled in stone over the entrances to such pretentious buildings as the foreign embassies in Washington, D. C., and in colonial America were often found upon gravestones. Sometimes they are embodied in the design of a wrought iron gateway. Furniture, panelling, fireplaces and other woodwork are used to display carved heraldic designs in some homes. Household silverware is often engraved with the family coat armour. It is also seen painted upon china, carried out in needlepoint and occasionally in hooked rugs. Engraved bookplates and note paper are popular methods of depicting arms.

Parts of The Achievement

(1) THE SHIELD OR ESCUTCHEON is the important part of the achievement to which everything else is an accessory.

(2) THE HELMET is used to support the crest (although helmets may be used without crests). The type of helmet and its position indicates the rank of the bearer of the arms. (4 forms)
   1. Royal princes bear a gold helmet with six bars or grilles, affronté. (front view)
   2. Peers (Dukes and Marquises) bear a silver helmet with five golden grilles, and it is in profile.
   3. Earls, Viscounts, and Barons bear a steel helmet with open visor which has ten steel grilles, five of which are visible.
   4. Esquires and Gentlemen wear a steel helmet, in profile, with closed visor.

(3) THE CREST surmounts the helmet. It is never granted by itself. It was first granted to nobles so they could be distinguished from their followers, but it could not be worn in tournaments or battle, because it was topheavy.

(4) THE WREATH consists of twisted silk and metal placed over the helmet to support the crest. The wreath is made of the predominant metal and colour in the arms. There are always six twists and the metal is always placed toward the dexter side which is on the left, as one looks at it, as this would be on the right side of the wearer.

(5) THE MANTLING, or lambrequin, was originally a piece of cloth which hung from the wreath down the back of the helmet, and its use was to protect the back of the neck from the heat of the sun. It became ragged and mutilated from long service. As represented today, it usually appears as leaves, and is carried out in the predominant colour and metal of the shield—the metal is usually used as a lining.

(6) SUPPORTERS are figures of men, beasts, birds, or imaginary creatures which stand at either side of the shield and seem to support it. In England, their use is restricted to peers of the realm, and Knights of the Bath, Garter, Thistle, and Saint Patrick, and sometimes to untitled persons for distinguished

service. In Ireland, "Chiefs of the Name" may be granted supporters. In Scotland, they are allowed to peers, minor barons,
chiefs of clans, and the Lord Lyon may grant them to anyone
he wishes.

(7) MOTTO. In English armory mottoes are not hereditary. No authority is needed for their adoption and the choice of a motto
is left to individual taste. In Scotland the motto is the subject
of a grant and cannot be altered. In England and Ireland, the
motto is generally placed below the shield, and in Scotland above
the shield, and some Scottish arms have two mottoes, one above
and one below the shield.

AUGMENTATIONS OF HONOUR are additions to an achievement (coat-
of-arms) awarded for distinguished service.

ABATEMENTS OF HONOUR indicate some dishonourable demeanor, quality or stain in the bearer, whereby the dignity of the coat armour
is greatly abased. Such acts include revoking a challenge, coward-
ice, discourtesy to women, boasting of military prowess, killing of
a war prisoner, lying, or treachery. A traitor had his arms reversed,
and after his execution, they were forfeited. For other offenses the
shield was debruised with the tinctures of stain—Murrey and
Tenne. There is no known case of a mark of abatement having
been used, as a man would refrain from bearing arms at all rather
than to advertise his dishonour.

ILLEGITIMACY—the baton was used as a mark.

Charges

The following are the more common charges:

(1) Geometrical figures are called honourable ordinaries and are
seven in number—the perfect number—Bend, Chevron, Chief,
Cross, Fess, Pale, Saltire.
Sub-ordinaries are fourteen—twice the perfect number—Annulet, Billet, Bordure, Canton, Flaunch, Fret, Gyron, Inescutch-
eon, Label, Lozenge, Orle, Pile, Roundel, Tressure.

(2) Human figures and man-like monsters.

(3) Beasts and beast-like monsters (lion is the most important)

(4) Birds and bird-like monsters (eagle and falcon most important)

(5) Fish, reptiles and insects (bee—dolphin—pike)

(6) Vegetation—(rose—trees—trefoil)
(7) Inanimate objects (chess rooks, castles, escallops, mullets, water bougets)

Tinctures

Shields and their charges are distinguished by various colours, called, in heraldry, tinctures. These comprise metals, colours and furs.

Metals

TINCTURE	HERALDIC TERM	ABBREVIATION	MEANING
Gold	Or	or.	Generosity; elevation of mind.
Silver	Argent	arg.	Peace and sincerity.

Colours

Red	Gules	gu.	Martial fortitude; magnanimity.
Blue	Azure	az.	Loyalty and truth.
Black	Sable	sa.	Constancy and grief.
Green	Vert	vert.	Hope.
Purple	Purpure	purp.	Sovereign majesty and justice.
Reddish-purple	Murrey	mur.	A stain; mark of disgrace; rare.
Orange-tawny	Tenne	ten.	A stain; mark of disgrace; rare.

Furs

Ermine—argent powdered with sable spots.
Ermines—sable powdered with argent spots.
Erminois—or powdered with sable spots.
Erminites—the same as ermine with a red hair on each side of the black spots, or tails.

Pean—sable powdered with or spots.

Vair—formed by a number of small bells, or shields, of one tincture arranged in horizontal lines in such a manner that the bases of those in the upper line are opposite to others, of another tincture below.

Counter-vair—the same as vair, except that the bells, or shields, placed base to base, are of the same tincture.

Potent—formed of figures resembling crutch heads and arranged in the same manner as vair.

Counter-potent—potent arranged similarly to counter-vair.

The furs, vair, counter-vair, potent and counter-potent are always to be blazoned argent and azure, unless otherwise specified.

Marks of Cadency or Difference

While the oldest son, under English law, inherited his father's estate, all the sons were equally entitled to bear the paternal arms, and so a mark of difference was required. All bore the arms of the father, differenced as follows:

1. Eldest son—a label.
2. Second son—a crescent.
3. Third son—a mullet.
4. Fourth son—a martlet.
5. Fifth son—an annulet.
6. Sixth son—a fleur de lis.
7. Seventh son—a rose.
8. Eighth son—a moline cross.
9. Ninth son—a double quatrefoil.

How to Read a Heraldic Description

A blazon is a verbal description of the arms. To emblazon means to depict the arms in colour. Every blazon starts with a description of the field, followed by a description of the principal charge, then the secondary charges. If you follow the blazon exactly, paying strict attention to the punctuation, you cannot go wrong. To illustrate, the following heraldic description would be thus interpreted:

Arms—Argent, a lion rampant gules.

Crest—Issuant from a mural crown or, a stag's head, in the mouth
a branch of hawthorn, all proper.

Interpretation: the first word "Arms" refers to the shield, and the
first named colour "Argent" is the colour of the shield; "a lion rampant gules" refers to the principal charge on the shield which is a
rampaging lion, tinctured gules. Crest—"From a mural crown or,"
means that a crown is placed above the wreath which surmounts the
helmet—that it is a mural crown which means that it was granted to
one who first mounted the wall of a besieged place and set up a standard there, of gold. "A stag's head, in the mouth a branch of hawthorn,
all proper," indicates that all charges since the last colour mentioned
(which was gold, Or) are in their natural colours, "all proper." Here
it is permissible to depart from the heraldic tinctures. In other words,
on a silver shield is placed a red lion, in rampant stance. The crest is
a golden mural crown from which emerges a stag's head, holding in
its mouth a hawthorn branch, both painted in their natural colours.

When no heraldic description is given, there are certain distin-
guishing marks which indicate the colours to be used.

Or—plain field powdered with dots.

Argent—clear white field.

Gules—perpendicular lines.

Azure—horizontal lines.

Sable—horizontal and perpendicular lines crossed.

Vert—diagonal lines drawn from dexter to sinister.

Purpure—diagonal lines drawn from sinister to dexter.

Use of Coat Armour

To prove your right to the use of a coat of arms, you must first
prove your descent from the person to whom it was granted. Having
done this, submit your proof to the Committee on Heraldry of the
New England Historic and Genealogical Society, 9 Ashburton Place,
Boston 8, Mass., and make application for its registration. For a very
nominal fee, this committee will study your proofs, and if they are
found to be bona fide, will register the arms. The committee does not
register crests. The crest is an unimportant adjunct of the arms, and

was often changed or varied by a family; sometimes different branches of the same family used different crests. The shield is the important part of the arms.

The College of Arms, Queen Victoria Street, London, E.C. 4, is the official registry of coats of arms and pedigrees for England, Wales, Northern Ireland, and the British Commonwealth and Empire. They will confirm coats of arms to those entitled to them, or issue new grants to Americans of English descent, upon the payment of the required fees. They also register crests and heraldic badges. The College has much unofficial genealogical material which, with the official genealogies, constitutes one of the largest genealogical collections in the world. The Officers of Arms, who constitute the College, are members of the Royal Household. Successive officers have practiced for more than four centuries as genealogists, and the records may be consulted, through them, on payment of fees. Suggested reading: *The Records and Collections of the College of Arms* by A. R. Wagner, Richmond Herald. Inquiries regarding Scottish coats of arms should be addressed to Lord Lyon, Old Register House, Edinburgh, Scotland.

Interpretation of the symbolism of heraldry is most interesting, and sometimes throws new light upon the early history of a family. To properly interpret the meaning of a coat of arms, one must study the social customs of the time in which the person who first bore the arms, lived. The charges upon the shield may be items that were in use at the time, and it may require considerable research to determine what they are, and their significance.

25. BACKGROUND IS A GEM OF MANY FACETS

After you have checked all original sources and set up your family history based upon sound evidence, don't be content to stop there. Do not treat your ancestors merely as names and dates, for if you do, like the physician who only knows his patients by case numbers, you will have lost the human touch. Remember, it was their personalities, as well as their physical qualities, that have formulated your background and blessed you with whatever touch of genius you may possess. Your work is not finished until you reconstruct the lives of these men and women, through the solid approaches which you have so painstakingly worked out from the information you have gleaned from the many original records you have consulted.

Now is the time to do your biographical work and round out the story of the lives of those who have preceded you. Ask yourself these questions: What part in the history of this great nation did these men and women whose names I have placed upon my family chart play? What were they really like? How were their personalities affected by the times in which they lived? What were their vocations and avocations? By what diseases or illnesses were they affected? What were their religious concepts? In what sports did they participate? Were they civic, military, or ecclesiastical leaders, or just plain dirt farmers? Many other questions will occur to you.

How do you arrive at the answers to the above and other questions? There are several angles of approach to this problem. What impact did your family have upon history, and how were their lives affected by the history of the times in which they lived? In order to solve that problem you must do two things. First, you must retrospect your thinking into the era in which these men and women lived, but don't make the mistake of considering them in the light of modern times. Remember that if the telephone, the telegraph and radio had been invented, Paul Revere's horse would not have worked up such a lather on the night of April 18, 1775, and if there had been a radar system in good working order there would have been no need to hang lanterns in the Old North Church tower. Secondly, you must familiarize yourself with the national and regional history of the times in which they lived, then narrow down your investigations to find what part they played in local and national affairs.

To do this it is suggested that you set up a chart, without names, using dates and places only, and in place of the ancestor's name, substitute events current at the time. This will present a graphic picture of the times and show what wars and other important events occurred contemporary with the lives of these men and women, and also if they were of the right ages to have served. Not every man who answered the call to arms on April 19, 1775, has been given his rightful place of honor on the pages of American history, and to the average reader most of them still remain the "unknown soldiers" of the American Revolution. But, if your ancestor stood on the bridge at Concord, wintered at Valley Forge, or saw Lord Cornwallis humbled at Yorktown, then the story of his participation in the fight for liberty is, to you, one of the most important chapters in American history—for "you were there." You owe it to him to preserve the record in the family

WAR	DATES	INTERVAL
King William's	1690–1697	5 years
Queen Anne's	1702–1713	31 years
King George's	1744–1748	6 years
French & Indian	1754–1763	12 years
American Revolution	1775–1783	29 years
War of 1812	1812–1815	31 years
Mexican War	1846–1848	13 years
Civil War	1861–1865	33 years
Spanish-American	Apr. to Aug. 1898	19 years
World War I		

history. The following table will be useful in making these deductions:

For example, the immigrant ancestor's dates are 1641–1715; was of the right age to have served in the colonial wars; was an Original Proprietor of Haddam, Connecticut, and a Deputy to the Connecticut General Court. By checking the war records and town records of Haddam and the colonial records of Connecticut, you will find information on this man.

His son (1673–1747) served in colonial wars; farmer; town official of Haddam; member Congregational church; his wife's father was a Founder of Hartford, and his name is on the Founder's Monument. The clues there are colonial war records, Haddam town records, Congregational church records, and Hartford town records for wife's ancestry.

His son (of the third generation) (1711–1792), owned a stone quarry in Haddam, served in the French and Indian War, was a member of the Connecticut Legislature during the American Revolution; Congregationalist. See Bibliography, Military and Pension Records, Chapter 28—Bodge; Haddam town and church records; Connecticut colonial records.

His son (of the fourth generation) (1744–1837) inherited the stone quarry at Haddam and shipped paving stones by water as far as Louisiana; Deacon in the Congregational Church; Justice of the Peace; Representative to the Connecticut General Assembly; was 31 at the start of the American Revolution and became a Lieutenant-Colonel. Clues: shipping records; church, Justice of the Peace, Connecticut colonial, state, and military records.

His son (of the fifth generation) (1778–1863), resided at Haddam, Connecticut and Chili, New York, where he served as a Methodist minister; served in the War of 1812 and was an active abolitionist, helping many slaves to find refuge in Canada. Clues: Haddam, Connecticut, and Chili, New York, town records; church records; military records; abolitionist; Civil War and War of 1812 records; Underground railway.

In addition to charting this type of information, the same thing may also be done for other topics, such as occupation, religion, geographical locations of residence, and illnesses and causes of death of ancestors. These factors are an index to past generations that afford you a better understanding of your own. Likenesses of ancestors should also be preserved.

There is a great deal of library material not catalogued as 929 which will serve as excellent supplementary reading and which will give you a better understanding and a broader view of the times in which your ancestors lived. Follow through on this and you will come to know and understand them better. Learn to use the biographical material in your library. Locate this not alone by name, but by region, and by occupation.

Many historical novels based upon sound research have been written which cover various regions and periods of time. These portray vividly the life and times of the people. When you discover such a work that relates to the area and time in which an ancestor of yours lived, you will find it not only interesting but very instructive reading as well.

26. WHAT IS RESEARCH

WHAT IS RESEARCH?—ETHICS AS APPLIED TO GENEALOGY—
SOME LEGAL ASPECTS OF COPYRIGHT.

What is Research?

We speak of research in connection with genealogy—but just what is research? Research is defined, by Webster, as critical and exhaustive investigation or experimentation, having for its aim the discovery of new facts and their interpretation, the revision of accepted conclusions, theories, or laws, in the light of newly discovered facts.

Therefore, merely copying the work of another person is not research, and copying and publishing the work of another as one's own is plagiarism, or literary theft. The difference between a copyist and a researcher is that the copyist simply appropriates and accepts the work done by another person, while the researcher seeks original datum for the analysis and interpretation of newly discovered facts, or to throw new light upon accepted conclusions. There are many errors in published genealogies and in other material relating to genealogy, and when these are found, corrections are frequently printed in genealogical periodicals. Every so often, some one locates some buried documents, and these, too, point up errors in existing printed records. Always bear in mind that everything that is printed in books is not necessarily true. So, we agree with Mr. Webster that a copyist is an imitator, and sometimes even a plagiarist.

There are two classes of people doing genealogical research, those who are content to sit in a pleasant, air-conditioned library and freely copy the work of others, and those who, for the sake of accuracy and truth, are willing to go into stuffy vaults and delve into dusty, ill-ventilated storage rooms to uncover the truth. The beginner naturally starts in a large library and searches the published material relating to his family. This is more easily accessible than the original records found in archives, and is the most dangerous type of research for the printed pages contain many errors, and the individual who wilfully copies and republishes secondary material, is helping to perpetuate these errors. *This, definitely, is not research.*

Those who devote time to the study of scientific methods of genealogical research are doing much to eliminate the "copyist." The genealogy courses given in our universities, colleges, and adult education programs are doing a great deal to improve the quality of family histories that another generation will find on library shelves. For students in these classes learn that the only way to produce the accurate, truthful record of a family is by recourse not to printed records, but to original sources. They learn how to dig into the archives and come up with proof, and their finished work is not the result of haphazard methods, but of scientific investigations based upon proven facts. By these methods, they are able to piece together, step by step, the true history of a family. *This is research.* A family history compiled from original records not only presents a true picture of the family, but it also reflects the achievement of the compiler and sets him apart, not as one who looked upon his work as a job to be done, but as a mission to be accomplished.

Ethics as Applied to Genealogy

A genealogist should be as much concerned about ethics as should any of the other professions, for he deals with human relations, and as such, may well be termed a humanitarian.

Do not present as your own, the work of another person. If the other person gave you the idea in the first place, then the very least you can do is to be gracious enough to give him credit for the idea. This rule applies to genealogical societies, and editors of genealogical magazines, as well as to individuals.

When writing to someone to ask for information always enclose an addressed, stamped envelope, except when writing to government agencies above the county level. For this purpose, it is well to use two sizes of stamped envelopes, the commercial size and the 13's which may be enclosed within the commercials without folding. Government agencies do not like to have stamps, nor is it necessary, as their mail is sent out as "Official Business."

If you are answering queries in some magazine such as the *Genealogical Helper* or the *Hartford Times Genealogical Section,* it is a good idea to mimeograph an outline of your lineage, in the form of an Ahnentafel, if you like, enclose a sheet in each letter, and ask for corrections and additions. It saves a great deal of time and enables you to get out a great many more letters. Here's a little rhyme which sums it up:

> "When asking favors, you'll make a friend,
> If you remember a stamp to send,
> And when that friend gives help to you,
> Please send a card to thank him too."

Don't be like the lady who wrote Abraham Lincoln requesting a bit of advice, and his signature that she might have it for a keepsake. This was his reply: "When asking strangers for a favor, it is customary to send postage. There's your advice, and here is my signature. A. Lincoln."

Some people feel that they should not share information with others. I have heard people say: "This is my information—I dug it out and anyone who gets it will have to pay for it." More often than not, the person who talks that way is always seeking help from others, and is usually a copyist and not a researcher, so probably his material isn't worth much anyway.

I would say that the best measure of ethics in genealogy is the application of the Golden Rule, for it seems to me that *a candle loses nothing when it lights another candle.*

Moral Responsibility

A genealogist owes a responsibility to his client to present a true picture of his findings—and he also owes a responsibility to posterity to leave correct records. He is employed to find the truth, and he should place loyalty to the truth above all else. He should never publish erroneous material knowingly, even if a client would pay him for so doing. If a genealogist receives a fee in advance, it is his responsibility to do the work covered by that fee, within a reasonable time.

A genealogist has no right to publish work for which a client has paid, without the express permission of that client, and it should be in writing. A genealogist should have a clear understanding with his client as to the work that is to be done, and the fee he is to receive for doing it. It is well to have this in writing, and signed by both parties, even if it is only a gentleman's agreement. Confidence should always be maintained between the genealogist and his client.

The fee charged should depend upon the value of the service rendered. If you have had a great deal of experience, and know how to evaluate records, and also are thoroughly familiar with the holdings and collections of the library or libraries wherein you will work, then you are entitled to the larger fee. If you are a beginner, explain that to your client, and if he still wishes to employ you, set your fee accordingly and have it clearly understood.

Fees are often graded according to the type of work done. If you are employed to search records only, then you are entitled to a record searcher's fee. For actual research, evaluating records and library materials, compiling, editing, and publishing family histories, you are entitled to a researcher's fee, whatever that may be in your locality. For typing manuscripts, you would charge the accepted typist's fee in your locality.

Making Corrections in Library Books

If you find an item in a library book that you know, from your personal knowledge of the family, is not true, don't make corrections in the book by writing all over the margins. Take the book to the librarian in charge of the room and ask what is the policy of the library in regard to making corrections. Some libraries will ask you to type the correction on a sheet of good grade paper, giving references where the correct information may be found, or if from family records, state who owns them and where they are located, or if the correction concerns a person who was living during your lifetime, state that fact, and sign your name and address. Then the library will attach this between the pages of the book. *But, never in a book which you yourself do not own.* If the author is living, it is well to write him and give him the correct information, with references for same. He will appreciate it, and if he puts out another edition, he will make the correction. When you come across a book in a library in which the margins are written full of corrections, you have no way of knowing who is right, the author or the person who made the correction.

If someone challenges the authenticity of the material in a printed book in the Library of Congress, he is requested to write a documented letter, showing the corrections. This is placed in a *Book of Corrections* kept by the library, and a slip is placed in the book, to which the correction refers, "See Book of Corrections," page—. Libraries, like other institutions, have established certain policies and regulations regarding the use of their facilities. Find out what they are, and conform to them, and you will always be welcome.

Some Legal Aspects

In many instances matters legal and genealogical are closely allied. The genealogist and the attorney are sometimes called upon to work together, in the settlement of estates, especially where there are no direct descendants. Then the genealogist must work out the lineages of the claimants, and show their relationship to the deceased, while the attorney determines the legality of the claim, under the laws of descent and distribution of the state in which the estate is being probated. If you are employed to do family research to determine the heirs of a decedent, be very careful to stay within your own field. Do not give legal advice or even express your opinion as to the validity of a claim. Remember you are employed as a genealogist and not as an attorney.

The newspapers carry many accounts of fabulous estates in foreign countries, usually complete with castle. How is one to differentiate between the real and the phony ones? It isn't easy. Through experience I have found that the first thing to do is to determine if there is a tangible estate, or if the presumption that there is an estate is based upon a family tradition which has developed into a colorful story by having been retold through several generations. This is much easier to do if the presumed estate is within the boundaries of the United States. Then, if such an estate is found to exist, the thing to do is to submit proof (and it had better be completely documented) of the claimant's relationship to the decedent. These foreign estates, if they exist, and most of them don't, can become very deeply involved in international law.

FORM OF NAMES: A name written in any form is legal so long as it is not meant to deceive. A man may write his name James K. Brown, James Kenneth Brown, or J. Kenneth Brown. *Validity of unrecorded writing:* Legally, the presumption exists that writing over thirty years old is valid writing.

Hearsay evidence is prohibited by law; that is, oral or written statements made out of court and used as evidence. The exceptions are: declarations concerning pedigrees—the history of family descent which is transmitted from one generation to another, and which shows births, marriages, and deaths. *Exception:* the statement of a deceased person concerning a pedigree has to be made at a time when he had no motive for stating an untruth.

Recorded public documents may be placed in evidence but they are not always proof. For example, a birth or death certificate proves only the fact that a birth or death occurred. The identity of the individual must be established. In most states a school record is admissible evidence to prove age.

A letter is the property of the writer and cannot be published without his consent. Court records often contain much information on family matters; et al. on a deed signifies "and others," and always gives more information. A petition to quiet title is a valuable source of genealogical information, as it names all the heirs and gives the daughters and their husbands.

Copyright

A copyright is the exclusive right to reproduce (by writing, printing or otherwise), publish and sell the matter and form of a literary or artistic work. In the United States and Great Britain, copyright rests entirely upon statutory provisions. In the United States, the Constitution, Article 1, section 8, empowers Congress to: "promote the progress of science and the useful arts, by securing, for limited times, to authors and inventors, the exclusive right to their respective writings and discoveries." The term writings has been construed to include maps, charts, music, prints, engravings, drawings, paintings, photographs, and photoplays, as well as books, written and printed matter. The first statute was passed in 1790. The Act now in force went into effect July 1, 1909, and was amended in 1912. The term of copyright is twenty-eight years, with right of renewal for twenty-eight years. A copyright confers the right of literary property.

To obtain a copyright, write to the Library of Congress Annex for blanks. Place upon the title page of your book, *Copyright*, followed by the year, by your name. A copyright costs about $4.00.

Libraries with facilities for reproducing materials must observe the rules of copyright before reproducing material by such means as photostats, and they will not photostat material upon which the copyright has not expired. This usually doesn't interfere much with genealogical material, such as coats of arms, pedigrees, maps, and material in books.

27. DICTIONARY OF TERMS AND ABBREVIATIONS

ABSTRACT, a summary of the important points in a book or manuscript.

ABSTRACTER, a person who prepares an abstract.

ABSTRACT OF TITLE, an epitome of the successive conveyances and other facts upon which a person's title to a piece of land rests.

abt., about

Abu; Abou, literally, father; the first element in many Arabic proper names; sometimes abbreviated to Bu.

ACADIA, the original name of Nova Scotia.

ACHIEVEMENT, an escutcheon with its helm, crest, mantle, supporters and motto. (Her.)

A.D., Anno Domini.

add., addatur, L.; let there be added

ADMINISTRATION, the management and disposal, under local authority, of the estate of an intestate, or of a testator having no competent executor.

ADMINISTRATOR, a person to whom letters of administration, that is authority to administer the estate of a deceased person, have been granted by the proper court. He differs from an executor in that he is appointed by the court, while the executor is appointed by the deceased.

ADMINISTRATION WITH WILL ANNEXED, administration granted where the testator has appointed no executor, or where his appointment of an executor, for any cause, has failed, as by death, incompetency or refusal to act.

a.d.s., autograph document signed.

ADVENTURERS, in colonial United States, those men who went in advance of the settlers to locate in a town.

ae., aet., aetat. L. aetatis—of age.

AFFIDAVIT, a written or printed declaration or statement of facts, made voluntarily and confirmed by oath or affirmation of the party making it, taken before an officer having authority to administer such oath.

AFFINITY, the relationship by marriage between a husband and his wife's relations, or between a wife and her husband's relations. In common parlance, affinities are relations-in-law, as opposed to consanguinity which relates to blood relationship.

AGNATES, see consanguinity.

AHNENTAFEL, a table of ancestors.

ALIAS, L. alias dictus—an assumed name.

ALIEN, one who is not a citizen of the country in which he is living.

ANCESTOR, one from whom another is descended in direct line.

ANTENUPTIAL CONTRACT, a contract made before marriage, between a man and woman in respect to their property rights.

ANTIQUARIAN, a student of old times, through their relics, such as manuscripts, monuments, and remains of ancient habitations.

ap.—prefix, signifying son of.

APPLICATION, LAND, a formal request for rights in, or eventual title to public lands.

APPRENTICE, a person, usually a minor, bound, in due form of law, to a master, to learn from him, his art, trade or business, and to serve him during the term of his apprenticeship.

ARCHIVES, public records or documents preserved as evidence of facts, as national or family archives.

arg., L. argentum—silver. (Her.)

ARMOUR, defensive arms for the body; any covering, usually of metal, used to protect the person in battle.

ARMS, the hereditary ensigns armorial of a family; a device adopted by a government as a mark of authority, used especially on seals and documents.

ASCENDANT, an ancestor, or one who precedes in genealogical succession.

ATLAS, a collection of maps in a volume.

ATTEST, to witness the execution of a written instrument, at the request of one who makes it, and subscribe to the same as a witness.

az., azure; blue. (Her.)

b., born.

BANNS, the published notice of an intended marriage.

bap., baptized.

ben, Hebrew—son.

BEQUEST, a gift by will; a legacy.

BIBLIOGRAPHY, a list of writings relating to a given subject or author; also a list of author's or printer's works.

BIOGRAPHY, the written history of a person's life.

BONA FIDE, in or with good faith; without fraud or deceit.

BOUNTY LAND, land given by the government, as a bounty, usually in compensation for military service.

BOUNTY LAND WARRANT, a right granted for military service, involving a specific number of acres of unallocated public land.

Bu, see Abu; abou.

bur., buried; burial.

C, copyright.

c. or ca. L. circa, about.

CADASTRAL SURVEY, MAP OR PLAN, a public land survey for the purpose of registering the quantity, value and ownership of real estate, used in apportioning taxes; usually made on a scale of 25″ to the mile, or a square inch to the acre.

CANON LAW, an ecclesiastical law or statute.

CENSUS, an official enumeration of the people of a state or nation.

CERTIFIED COPY, an exact copy of a Bible, tombstone, baptismal or other record that has been attested by a notary public, as being a correct copy.

cf., confer; compare.

CHARGES, the figures upon a shield. (Her.)

CHARTER, an instrument in writing, from the sovereign power of a state or county, granting or guaranteeing rights.

CLAN, a social group comprising a number of households, the heads of which claim descent from a common ancestor, bear a common surname, and acknowledge the paramountcy of a chief.

CODICIL, an instrument made subsequently to a will, and modifying it in some respects. It must be executed in the same manner as the will itself, and forms a part of it.

COGNATES, see consanguinity.

COLLATERAL ANCESTORS, persons belonging to the same ancestral stock, but not in a direct line of descent.

COLONY, a company of people transplanted from the mother country to a new province or country, and remaining subject to the jurisdiction of the parent country.

COMMON LAW, the unwritten law that is binding because of long usage and universal reception, in contradistinction to statute law.

CONSANGUINITY, the state of being related by blood, or descended from a common ancestor, and in the law is divided into two classes —Agnate and Cognate. Agnate consanguinity applies to all relations on the father's side of the family, and cognate to all relations on the mother's side of the family.

COPYRIGHT, the exclusive right to reproduce, publish and sell the matter and form of a literary or artistic work, granted by authority of the government of a country.

CREST, a bearing or device set upon the helm and used separately as an ornament or cognizance. (Her.)

d., died or death.

D.A.R., Daughters of the American Revolution.

dau., daughter.

De, from.

DECEDENT, a deceased person.

DECLARATION OF INTENTION, a sworn statement by an alien that he intends to become a citizen.

DEED, a sealed instrument in writing, duly executed and delivered, by which one person conveys land, tenements or hereditaments to another.

DE LA; DE LE; DEL, all mean "from the," followed by place (Norman-French); as Dexter, meaning from Exeter.

DENIZEN—one admitted to residence in a foreign country.

DEPOSITION, the testimony of a witness taken upon interrogation, not in open court but in pursuance of a commission to take testimony issued by a court, reduced to writing and duly authenticated.

desc., descendant.

DESCENDANT, one who is descended from another.

DEVISEE, a person to whom lands or other real property are devised or given by will.

DEVISOR, a giver of lands of real estate by will; a testator.

DIOCESE, the territorial extent of a bishop's jurisdiction.

DISTRICT LAND OFFICE PLAT BOOKS, books of maps which show the location of the land of the patentee.

DISTRICT LAND OFFICE TRACT BOOKS, books which list individual entries by range and township in the district office of the Bureau of Land Management.

doc., document.

DOCUMENT (noun), an original or official paper relied upon as the basis of proof or support of anything else.

DOCUMENT (verb), to evidence by documents.

DONATION APPLICATION, an application for frontier land in Florida, New Mexico, Oregon, or Washington, which was given to a settler who fulfilled certain conditions.

DONEE, one to whom a gift is made.

DONOR, one who makes a gift.

DOWER, the legal right or interest which the wife acquires by marriage in the real estate of her husband.

d.s., document signed.

d.s.p., L. decessit sine prole; he died without issue.

d.v.p., L. decessit vita patris; he died in his father's lifetime.

d.y., died young.

EARMARK, a mark of identification on the ear of a domestic animal, used in colonial United States to identify unfenced stock; earmarks were registered and were hereditary.

ed., edited; editor; edition.

EMIGRANT, one who departs from a country to settle elsewhere (the emigrant from England is the immigrant to Massachusetts)

EPITAPH, an inscription on a grave stone.

ERRATUM, pl. errata—an error or errors by a printer, or author, in a printed book or manuscript. A list of such errors with corrections, is found at the end of the text. It is to the advantage of the owner of a book to make these corrections in it.

ESCUTCHEON, a shield upon which armorial bearings are depicted.

est., estate.

et. al., et alibi; et alii.; and others; on a land deed, is a clue to look for "the others."

ETHICS, is the science of moral duty.

et. seq., L. et sequens—and follows.

et. ux., L. et uxor—and wife,

EUGENICS, the science which deals with the influences that improve the unborn or native qualities of a race or breed, especially the human race.

EVIDENCE, any proof which is presented by means of witnesses, records, documents, etc., for the purpose of either establishing or disproving any alleged fact.

EXECUTOR, a person appointed by a testator to carry out the directions and requests of his will, and to dispose of the property according to his testamentary provisions, that are to be carried out after his death. An executrix is a female executor.

F.A.S.G., Fellow American Society of Genealogists.

f.e., for example.

F.I.A.G., Fellow Institute of American Genealogy (now defunct).

ff., and following pages.

f. i., for instance.

fid., fiduciary.

FITZ, used as a prefix to the father's name, means son. (Norman-French)

FOLKLORE, the comparative science which investigates the life and spirit of a people, as revealed in their customs and tales.

FRANKLIN, STATE OF, a temporary state organized in 1784, in the western lands of North Carolina, but now a part of Eastern Tennessee, which ceased to exist about February 1788.

FREEHOLDER, one who held land in fee simple, which entitled him to the right to vote and to hold office.

FREEMAN, one who took an oath to a government and church and was given civil or political liberty.

F.S.G., Fellow Society of Genealogists (London or Scotland)

G.A.R., Grand Army of the Republic. An organization of Union veterans of the Civil War.

gaz., gazetteer.

GAZETTEER, a geographical dictionary.

GENERATION, the average lifetime of a man, or the ordinary period of time at which one rank follows another, or father is succeeded by child. A generation is usually considered to be 33 years.

GHOST TOWN, a town no longer existing.

GRANT, to give or bestow, as a land grant.

GRANTEE, a person to whom a grant is made.

GRANTOR, a person by whom a grant is made.

g.s., gravestone.

gu., gules; red (Her.)

GUARDIAN, a person lawfully invested with the power, and charged with the duty of taking care of a person, and managing the property and rights of a person who, because of age or other status, is incapable of administering his own affairs.

HABEAS CORPUS, any of several common law writs having for their object to bring a party before a court or judge.

HEARSAY EVIDENCE, second-hand evidence as distinguished from original evidence; it is the repetition at second hand of what would be original evidence if given by the person who originally made the statement.

HEIR, at common law is a person who succeeds, by the rules of law, to an estate in lands, tenements or hereditaments, upon the death of his ancestor, by descent and right of relationship.

HELMET, a defensive covering for the head. (Her.)

HER., Heraldry.

HERALDRY, the art, practice or science of recording genealogies and blazoning arms.

HOLLAND DUTCH, natives of The Netherlands who settled in the United States; not to be confused with Pennsylvania Dutch who were Germans.

HOLOGRAPHIC WILL, a will made in the handwriting of the testator.

HOMESTEAD APPLICATION, an application for government land under the Homestead Act of 1862.

h.s., L. hic situs or sepultus; here is buried.

ibid., L. ibidem—in the same place.

i.e., L. id est—that is.

illus., illustrated.

IMMIGRANT, one who goes into and settles in a foreign country.

IMPRIMIS, in the first place.

INDENTURE, a mutual agreement, in writing, between two or more parties, whereof each party has a counterpart or duplicate, the parts being indentured by a notched cut for identification.

INDENTURED SERVANT, a person who engaged himself to another, for a certain number of years, to pay off a debt, usually from four to seven years.

int., intentions.

INTESTATE, not having made a will; not disposed of by will.

inv., inventory.

INVENTORY, a list of the assets in the estate of a deceased person, filed by executor, or administrator of an estate, in probate court.

ipso facto, L. by the act itself.

JURISDICTION, sphere of authority.

KINDRED, relatives by blood.

LAMELLATION, a process of preserving manuscripts or printed pages, after they have first been cleaned and sterilized, by welding cellulose acetate foil to both sides of the paper.

LAND ENTRY PAPERS, papers filed in connection with the acquisition of public land, and including bounty land warrants, donation, preemption and homestead applications, private land claims, land scrip and purchase by cash or in installments. They include the name of the person who acquired the land, his place of residence, dates when application and land were entered, and date of patent.

L.C. Library of Congress.

L.D.S., Latter Day Saints.

LEGACY, a bequest left by last will and testament.

LEGAL DESCRIPTION, the description and identification of the location of a particular parcel of land, according to the official plat of survey.

LIBER, a book in which deeds, mortgages, wills, and other public records are kept.

LINEAGE, descent in a line from a common progenitor.

LINEAL, descent in a direct line from father to son.

liv., living or lived.

ll., lines.

LOG MARKS, individual or corporation marks on ends of logs to identify ownership, and registered; used during lumbering era.

LOYALIST, an American colonist who remained loyal to Great Britain during the American Revolution.

l.s., L. locus sigilli—place of the seal.

m., married or marriage.

MAC, prefix; Irish and Gaelic son.

m. bn., marriage banns.

MIGRATION, to change residence, usually from one part of a country to another.

MORTALITY SCHEDULE, a special census taken in connection with the regular enumerations of the 1850, 1860, 1870, and 1880, listing deaths in preceding year.

MSS., manuscript; manuscripts.

mur., murrey—a stain. (Her.)

N.A., National Archives.

NAMING SYSTEMS—DUTCH, followed a pattern; the first son was named for his paternal grandfather; the second son for his maternal grandfather; first daughter was named for her maternal grandmother, the second daughter for her paternal

grandmother. This gives a reliable clue to the names of all four grandparents.

NAMING SYSTEMS—GERMAN, children were given one name for their parents, and one name for their godfather or godmother.

NAMING SYSTEM—SCANDINAVIAN, in early records before surnames were common, the son of Jan was called Janson, and his daughter was called Jansdatter.

n.d., no date.

N.E., New England.

nee., born; used in introducing the maiden name of a married woman.

NECROLOGY, a history of the dead; a register of deaths.

N.E.H. & G.R., New England Historic & Genealogical Register.

NON-CONFORMIST, one who had separated from the Church of England.

n.p., no paging.

N.S., New Style Calendar.

NUNCUPATIVE WILL, an unwritten will, having been declared or dictated by the testator in his last sickness, before a sufficient number of witnesses, and afterwards reduced to writing.

N.X.N., no Christian name.

N.Y.G. & B.R., New York Genealogical and Biographical Record.

O', a prefix to ancient Irish family names, followed by the genitive case of the name of the ancestor, as O'Neill (nom. Niall). Before surnames of females, O' is replaced in Irish by ni, daughter. It prefixes H before a vowel, as Oh-

Airt, O'Hart. The apostrophe is due to the mistaken idea that O stands for of.'

OATH OF ALLEGIANCE, an oath to bear true allegiance to a particular government or sovereign.

obit.; obiit., died.

obiit sine prole, died without issue.

O.E., Old England; Old English.

OP, out of print.

or.—Or, gold. (Her.)

O.S., Old Style Calendar.

PALIMPSESTS, parchment manuscripts from which original writing has been erased in order that the blank surfaces obtained thereby may be once more used by a later writer. The old writing may be brought to light by the fluorescent qualities of ultraviolet radiation, and photographs taken for permanent records.

pamph., pamphlet.

PAPER TOWN, a town the plans for which were drawn on paper but never developed.

passim., everywhere.

PATENT, a document which transfers legal title to public lands.

PATENTEE, a person who receives a patent.

PENNSYLVANIA DUTCH, Germans who settled in Pennsylvania, in contradistinction to the Holland Dutch.

POLL TAX, a tax levied on every male citizen over a given age.

POSTERITY, descendants.

pp., pages.

PRE-EMPTION APPLICATION, an application by a person who had already settled on unappropriated land.

PRIVATE LAND CLAIM, a claim to land granted to individuals from foreign countries prior to the cession of that land to the United States. These were in Alabama, Arkansas, California, Florida, Illinois, Indiana, Iowa, Louisiana, Michigan, Mississippi, Missouri, Colorado and New Mexico.

prob., probable; probably.

PROBATE, the process of proving a will or settling an estate.

PROGENITOR, a forefather.

PROOF, an establishment of a fact by evidence.

PROVINCE, an administrative district or division of a country.

pub., published; publication.

PUBLIC DOMAIN, public lands of the United States; comprised Illinois; Indiana; Michigan, part of Ohio; Wisconsin; Florida; Alabama; Mississippi, and all states west of the Mississippi River except Texas and Alaska.

purp., purpure; purple. (Her.)

QUAKER, a member of the Society of Friends.

q.v., L. quod vide; which see or see reference.

REDEMPTIONER, an indentured white person who sold himself as a servant for a brief term of years to defray the cost of his passage to America.

RELICT, a widow; a widower (rare)

res., residence.

REV., Revolution.

rev., revised.

sa., sable; black. (Her.)

s.a., L. sine anno; without year.

S.A.R., Sons of the American Revolution.

S.C.V., Sons of Confederate Veterans.

SEPARATIST, a non-conformist.

SHIELD, the escutcheon or field upon which are placed the bearings in coats of arms

sic., so (as copied); a word often inserted in brackets in quoted matter, after an erroneous word or date. In genealogy it infers doubt as to name or date.

s.l.a.n., L. sine loco anno vel nomine; without place, year, or name.

s.l. et a., L. sine loco et anno; without place and year.

s.l.p., L. sine legitima prole; without legitimate issue.

s. p., L. sine prole; without issue.

STATUS PLAT, a copy of the plat of survey upon which has been diagrammed and noted such information as is necessary to determine the Federal ownership of public lands and resources.

STATUTE, written law enacted by the legislative branch of a government.

S.U.V., Sons of Union Veterans.

S.V, Sons of Veterans.

TARTAN, dress of Scottish Highlanders; each clan had its own distinctive plaid.

ten., tenne; a stain. (Her.).

TESTAMENT, the disposition of one's property after death.

TESTATE ESTATE, an estate which is disposed by will.

TESTATOR, a deceased person who died leaving a will.

TORY, a person living in the American colonies during the Revolution, who remained loyal to Great Britain.

t.p., title page.

t.p.m., title page mutilated.

t.p.w., title page wanting.

TRACT BOOK, a narrative, journal-like record which is an index to and digest of all essential actions and transactions which affect public lands. District Land Office Tract Books list individual entries by range and township.

TRADITION, that which is transmitted orally through successive generations, without the aid of written memorials; any belief, custom, or way of life which has its roots in one's family or racial past; an inherited culture.

TRUSTEE, a person in whom property is vested in trust for others.

U.C., Upper Canada.

UNITED EMPIRE LOYALISTS, See Loyalists.

unm., unmarried.

uxor, wife.

v., volume.

var., various; variant.

vert., Vert; green. (Her.)

VISITATION, an official personal inquiry made by an officer-at-arms, at different times, to examine the rights of the people within his heraldic province, to bear arms;

also, a document containing a record of such inquiry.

viz., namely.

vol., volume.

V.R., vital records.

WARNING OUT LAW, a colonial law which empowered a town to warn out individuals or families that were newcomers (within 3 years) and had become impoverished and likely to become town charges, to return to the town from whence they came. No stigma was attached to this procedure; sometimes a widow with children was warned out after her husband's death, if she did not have means of supporting her family.

WAR PERIODS, (wars and events connected with them)—French and Indian and Colonial Wars, (1637–1765); American Revolution (1770–1781); War of 1812, (1812–1815); Civil War (1861–1865).

WARRANT, to guarantee to a purchaser or other grantee, the title to, or quality, or quantity of, the thing sold or granted, as a warranty deed.

WHIG, a political party which was in opposition to the Tories in Great Britain until 1832; also in Colonial America, the Whig Party was opposed to British rule and to the Tories.

wid., widow.

widr., widower.

WILL, any legally executed instrument in which a person makes disposition of his property to take effect after his death.

wit., witness.

WITNESS, an individual whose knowledge of a fact or occurrence is sufficient to testify in respect to it.

X, Christ; Christian; properly, the Greek letter Chi which is like an X. Used as a prefix to words beginning Christ.

X-mas, Christmas.

xped, christened.

Xr., Christopher.

yeo., yeoman.

28. BIBLIOGRAPHY

BIBLIOGRAPHY—(K) indicates Kalamazoo Library; (S) State Library.

Beginner's Guides

ARIZONA TEMPLE DISTRICT, Genealogical Library, Mesa, Arizona: *Practical Research in Genealogy; A Compilation of Genealogical Research Data.* Compiled by Gladys Bushby and Evelyn Fish. Mesa. 1955.

BENNETT, ARCHIBALD F.: *A Guide For Genealogical Research.* Salt Lake City. 1951. Includes appendices describing sources in Canada and in Europe, and interprets dates of different calendars. (S)

BENNETT, ARCHIBALD F.: *Finding Your Forefathers in America.* Salt Lake City. 1957. Uses case histories to discuss genealogy. (S)

DOANE, GILBERT H.: *Searching For Your Ancestors.* Univ. of Minnesota Press. 2nd. ed. 1952. (K) (S) Includes bibliographies and a "Bibliography of Lists, Registers, Rolls, and Returns of Revolutionary War Soldiers."

EVERTON, GEORGE B., AND RASMUSON, GUNNAR, comps.: *The Handy Book for Genealogists.* Logan, Utah. 3rd. ed. 1957. (S) First ed. (K)

EVERTON, GEORGE B., AND RASMUSON, GUNNAR, comps.: *Improved How Book For Genealogists.* Logan, Utah. 1959.

JACOBUS, DONALD LINES: *Genealogy As a Pastime and a Profession.* New Haven, Connecticut. 1930. (S)

KIRKHAM, E. K.: *The ABC's of American Genealogical Research.* Salt Lake City, Utah. 1954. (S)

KIRKHAM, E. KAY: *Research in American Genealogy.* Salt Lake City. 1956.

PARKER, DONALD DEAN: *Local History, How to Gather It, Write It, and Publish It.* Social Science Research Council, New York 17, New York. 1944. (K) (S)

REED, EVAN L.: *Ways and Means of Identifying Ancestors.* Chicago. 1947. (K) (S) Gives locations of records, sources, and county origins, with maps for the states east of the Mississippi.

STETSON, OSCAR FRANK: *The Art of Ancestor Hunting; A Guide to Ancestral Research and Genealogy.* Brattleboro, Vermont. 1936. 3rd. ed. Stephen Daye Press. New York. 1956. (K) (S)

STEVENSON, NOEL C.: *Search and Research. The Researcher's Handbook, A Guide to Official Records and Library.* 1951 (S) Out of print. New edition scheduled to appear in 1959. Lists libraries, records and record depositories, and reference books for every state and territory of the United States; record sources in Canadian Provinces; fifty-four page directory of family associations.

Keys to Family Genealogies

DAUGHTERS OF THE AMERICAN REVOLUTION: *Catalog of the Genealogical and Historical Works in the Library of the National Society, Daughters of the American Revolution.* Washington, D. C. 1940. (K) (S)

GENEALOGICAL BOOK COMPANY, 521–23 St. Paul St., Baltimore 2, Maryland. Occasional Catalogs. (Free)

GOODSPEED'S BOOK SHOP, Boston 8, Massachusetts. Frequently issues catalogs of genealogy and local history. ($1.00)

GRATZ, D. L., Bluffton, Ohio. Occasional Catalogs. (Free)

JEWETT, EVERETT, Rowley, Massachusetts. Occasional Catalogs. (Free)

LONG ISLAND HISTORICAL SOCIETY: *Catalog of American Genealogies in the Library of the Long Island Historical Society,* Brooklyn, N.Y. 1935. (S)

TUTTLE, CHARLES E., COMPANY, Rutland, Vermont. Occasional Catalogs. ($1.00)

UNITED STATES LIBRARY OF CONGRESS: *American and English Genealogies in the Library of Congress.* 2nd. ed. Washington. Gov't Printing Office. 1919. (K) (S). Microcard Supplement (S)

Special Tools

ARMSTRONG, ZELLA: *Notable Southern Families.* Chattanooga, Tenn. 1918–1933. 6 v. (S)

AUSTIN, JOHN OSBURNE: *Genealogical Dictionary of Rhode Island; Comprising Three Generations of Settlers Who Came Before* 1690, *with Many Families Carried to the Fourth Generation.* Munsell. Albany. 1887. Additions and Corrections by G. Andrews Moriarity, in The American Genealogist, from v. 19. (1943) (S)

BAILEY, ROSALIE FELLOWS: *Pre-Revolutionary Dutch Houses and Families in Northern New Jersey and Southern New York.* N.Y. 1936. (S) Includes documented family history.

BARDEN, MERRITT CLARK: *Vermont, Once No Man's Land.* 1928. (Families, soldiers, and grants, along the New York border of Southern Vermont.) (S)

CANDLER, ALLEN D., AND EVANS, CLEMENT A.: *Cyclopaedia of Georgia.* 3 v. Atlanta. 1906.

CHALKLEY, LYMAN: *Chronicles of the Scotch-Irish Settlement in Virginia; Extracted from the Original Court Records of Augusta County, 1745–1800.* 3 v. Rosslyn, Va. 1912.

FARMER, JOHN: *A Genealogical Register of the First Settlers of New England.* 1829. (S)

HEMENWAY, ABBY MARIA: *The Vermont Historical Gazetteer.* 5 v. (1868–1891) Index published in 1923. (S)

HINSHAW, WILLIAM WADE: *Encyclopaedia of American Quaker Genealogy.* 6 v. (1936–1950). Contains records of Quaker Meetings of North Carolina, Philadelphia, New York City and Long Island, Ohio, and Virginia. (S)

HUGHES, THOMAS P.: *American Ancestry;* Giving the Name and Descent, in the Male Line, of Americans Whose Ancestors Settled in the United States Previous to the Declaration of Independence. 12 v. Albany. (1877–1899) (K) (S)

JACOBUS, DONALD LINES: *History and Genealogy of the Families of Old Fairfield, Connecticut.* 3 v. New Haven. 1930.

JORDAN, WILFRED, ED.: *Colonial and Revolutionary Families of Pennsylvania.* vols. 1–15 to date. Philadelphia. 1933—

MEYNEN, EMIL: *Bibliography on German Settlements in Colonial North America.* Especially on the Pennsylvania Germans and Their Descendants, 1683–1933. Leipzig. 1937. Excellent for Pennsylvania German source material. The University of Michigan General Library.

NOYES, SYBIL; LIBBY, CHARLES THORNTON; AND DAVIS, WALTER GOODWIN: *Genealogical Dictionary of Maine and New Hampshire.* Portland, Me. 1928–1939. (S)

POPE, CHARLES HENRY: *The Pioneers of Massachusetts.* 1900. (S)

SAVAGE, JAMES: *A Genealogical Dictionary of the First Settlers of New England.* Showing three generations of those who came before May 1692. 4 v. Boston. 1860–1862. (K) (S)

SEVERSMITH, HERBERT F.: *Colonial Families of Long Island, New York and Connecticut.* 4 v. Washington, D.C. 1939. (5th. v. in progress)

STILLWELL, JOHN EDWIN: *Historical and Genealogical Miscellany; Data Relating to the Settlement and Settlers of New York and New Jersey.* 5 v. New York. 1903–1932. (S)

Guides and Indexes

BAILEY, ROSALIE FELLOWS: *Guide to Genealogical and Biographical Sources for New York City (Manhattan), 1783–1898.* (Printed by the Author, 60 E. 80th. Street, New York 21, N.Y.). 1954. (S)

BARBOUR, LUCIUS BARNES: *Index of Connecticut Vital Records to 1850.* In Connecticut State Library, Hartford. Microfilm copies in the Burton Historical Collection, Detroit Public Library, the Wisconsin State Library, and Western Reserve Library. (Contains 17 reels of town records and 81 reels of alphabetized vital records.)

Daughters of the American Revolution Magazine; Master Index to Genealogy. (vols. 1–84) 1892–1950. Washington, D.C. 1951. (K) (S)

DOLL, EUGENE E., ED.: *The Pennsylvania Magazine of History and Biography Index.* vols. 1–75. (1877–1951). The Historical Society of Pennsylvania. Philadelphia. 1954. (S)

DRAUGHON, WALLACE R.: *North Carolina Genealogical Reference. A Research Guide.* Durham. 1956.

HENAWINE, WAYNE STEWART: *A Checklist of Source Materials for the Counties of Georgia.* In the Georgia Historical Quarterly. 32: 179–229. September 1948.

HOYT, MAX E.; SUCCEEDED BY MRS. HOYT: *Index to Revolutionary War Pension Applications in the National Archives.* Supplement to National Genealogical Society Quarterly. March 1943—(Now in letter S.) (S)

JACOBUS, DONALD LINES: *Index to Genealogical Periodicals.* 3 v. 1932; 1948; 1953. Indexed by family name, place, and topic. (S)

MCAUSLAN, W. A.: *Mayflower Index.* 2 v. 1932. (K) (S)

MUNSELL, JOEL AND SONS, PUBLISHERS: *The American Genealogist, Being A Catalog of Family Histories Published in America from 1771 to Date.* Albany. 1900. Many editions. (S) (K has 1895 v.)

PASSANO, ELEANOR PHILLIPS: *An Index of the Source Records of Maryland—Genealogical, Biographical, and Historical.* Waverly Press. Baltimore. 1940. Arranged alphabetically by surnames, covering Maryland families chiefly, and many colonial families of Southern States. Contains some 20,000 names, cross-indexed, and has an excellent bibliography of Maryland and other state records.

PENNSYLVANIA HISTORICAL AND MUSEUM COMMISSION: *Guide to the Published Archives of Pennsylvania,* covering the 138 volumes of Colonial records and Pennsylvania Archives, with name indexes to third series. Henry H. Eddy and Martha L. Simonetti. Harrisburg. 1949. (S)

RIDER, FREMONT, ED.: *American Genealogical Index.* 48 v. Middletown, Conn. 1942–1952. (S) Index covers names in many genealogies, town and county histories.

RIDER, FREMONT, ED.: *American Genealogical Biographical Index.* In progress since 1952. Middletown, Conn. 21 v. to date. (S)

SEVERSMITH, HERBERT F.: *Long Island Genealogical Source Material.* Publication Number 9, National Genealogical Society. OP. (S)

STEWART, ROBERT ARMISTEAD: *Index to Printed Virginia Genealogies, Including Key and Bibliography.* Richmond. 1930.

SWEM, EARL GREGG: *Virginia Historical Index.* 2 v. Roanoke, Va., 1934–1936. Consult for Virginia families and Southern research. Family coat of arms references are also included. Contains 900,000 entries.

WATERS, MARGARET RUTH: *Genealogical Sources Available at the Indiana State Library for All Indiana Counties.* Indianapolis. 1946.

WILLIAMS, ETHEL W. (MRS. E. GRAY): *Bibliography of Source Material on Local History and Genealogy in Michigan.* (In process).

WILLIAMS, Ethel W. (MRS. E. GRAY): *Index to Genealogical Periodicals (1952–1957)*. Continuing from Jacobus' volume 3, above, indexed by family name, place and topic. In progress.

Published Census Records

BARBER, GERTRUDE A.: *State Census of Delaware County, New York*. 1855. 3 volumes.

Delaware; Reconstructed 1790 Census of Delaware, by Leon DeValinger. National Genealogical Society Publication Number 10. Washington, D.C. 1954.

DUBESTER, HENRY J.: *State Censuses. An Annotated Bibliography of Censuses of Population Taken After the Year 1790, By States and Territories of the United States*. Gov't Printing Office, Washington, D.C. 1948. OP Extracts published in Kirkham's "Research in American Genealogy."

JACOBSEN, EDNA L.: *New York State and Federal Census Records, An Inventory*. New York State Library. Albany. 1957.

Kentucky: Second Census of Kentucky. 1800. Tax Lists of the 42 Counties. Compiled by Garrett Glenn Clift. Frankfort. 1954.

Rhode Island: Census of the Inhabitants of the Colony of Rhode Island and Providence Plantations, Taken in the Year 1774. Providence. 1858.

UNIVERSITY OF THE STATE OF NEW YORK: PUBLICATIONS OF THE NEW YORK STATE LIBRARY: *New York State Census for 1835; 1845; 1855; 1865; 1875; 1915*.

UNITED STATES BUREAU OF THE CENSUS: *A Century of Population Growth From the First Census of the United States to the Twelfth, 1790–1900*. Gov't Printing Office. 1909. (K) (S) This is known as the *Analysis of the Census of 1790*, and contains maps of the first 13 states, showing changes in county lines; also distribution of surnames by states. The latter shows you at once in which state or states the family was most numerous at the time, thus giving you a clue as to the region upon which you should base your search. Various spellings of the surnames used at that time are also fully given, pp. 227–270.

UNITED STATES BUREAU OF THE CENSUS: *Heads of Families At the First Census of the United States Taken in the Year 1790*. U.S. Gov't. Printing Office, 1907–8. 12 v. (K) (S) Separately and very conveniently indexed volumes for the following states: *Connecticut; Maine; Maryland; Massachusetts; New Hampshire; New York; North Carolina; Pennsylvania; Rhode Island; South Carolina; Vermont; Virginia*.

Vermont: Heads of Families At the Second Census of the United States, Taken in the Year 1800, in *Vermont*. Montpelier. 1939. (K) (S)

City Directories

Are an important source. They have been published irregularly for counties and other regional areas, often as Gazetteers or Business Directories. They have been printed since 1813 in Albany, New York, since 1879 in Boston, Massachusetts, since 1832 in Buffalo, New York, since 1786 in New York City, since 1785 in Philadelphia, and since 1815 in Pittsburgh, Pennsylvania. *Directories in the Library of Congress*: published in "The American Genealogist;" 13: 46–53; 27: 142. (S)

Kalamazoo City and County Directories. 1885—(K)

MORIARTY, JOHN H.: *Directory Information Material for New York City Residents, 1626–1786; A Bibliographic Study*. Bulletin of the N.Y. Public Library. October 1942.

Published Probate Records

ANJOU, GUSTAV, ed.: *Ulster County, New York Probate Records*. 2 v. New York. 1906.

BARBER, GERTRUDE A.: has published *abstracts of wills of the following New York Counties:* Cayuga (1799–1842); Chemung (1836–1850); Columbia (1786–1851); Delaware (1797–1875); Monroe (1822–1847); Oneida (1798–1863); Otsego (1794–1851); Schenectady (1809–1845); Schoharie (1795–1863); Tompkins (1817–1833); Washington (1798–1825) plus index to wills (1825–1850); Warren (1813–1850); Letters of Administration in Delaware County (1797–1844).

CHARLESTON, SOUTH CAROLINA FREE LIBRARY: *Index to Wills of Charleston County, South Carolina, 1671–1868*. Charleston. 1950.

COTTON, JANE BALDWIN, ED.: *Maryland Calendar of Wills*. Baltimore. 1921–1928. 8 volumes of wills 1635–1743.

DELAWARE PUBLIC ARCHIVES COMMISSION: *Calendar of Kent County, Delaware Probate Records, 1680–1800*. Compiled by Leon DeValinger, Jr. Dover. 1944.

FERNOW, BERTHOLD, COMP.: *Calendar of Wills on File and Recorded at Albany, New York, 1626–1836*. New York. 1896. (S)

FISHER, CHARLES: *Abstracts of Snyder County, Pennsylvania Probate and Orphan's Court Records, 1772–1855*. 1940.

FULTON, ELEANORE JANE: *An Index to the Will Books and Intestate Records of Lancaster County, Pennsylvania, 1729–1850*. Lancaster. 1936. (S)

GRIMES, J. BRYAN: *Abstracts of North Carolina Wills*. Pub. by the Secretary of State. Raleigh. 1910.

GRIMES, J. BRYAN: *North Carolina Wills and Inventories*. Pub. by the Secretary of State. Raleigh. 1912.

HOLMAN, WINIFRED L., AND REED, GRACE W. W.: *Vermont Probate Districts* in *The American Genealogist*, 27: 65–69, April 1951. (S)

LA FAR, MABEL FREEMAN: *Abstracts of Wills of Chatham County, Georgia, 1773–1817*. National Genealogical Society Publication, Number 6. Washington, D.C. 1936.

MAGRUDER, JAMES MOSBY: *Index of Maryland Colonial Wills, 1634–1777, at Annapolis.* Annapolis 1933. 3 v.

MANWARING, CHARLES WILLIAM: *A Digest of the Early Connecticut Probate Records.* Hartford, Conn. 1904–1906. 3 v. (S)

NATIONAL SOCIETY OF COLONIAL DAMES OF AMERICA, DELAWARE CHAPTER: *A Calendar of Delaware Wills, New Castle County, 1682–1800.* n.d.

New Jersey Archives: Wills 1670–1817; First Series, vols. 23, 30, 32–42. (S)

NEW JERSEY DEPARTMENT OF STATE: *Index of Wills, Inventories, etc., in the Office of Secretary of State Prior to 1901.* Trenton. 1912–1913. 3 v. (S)

NEW YORK (County) Surrogate's Court: *Abstracts of Wills on File in the Surrogate's Office, City of New York, 1665–1801.* N.Y. Historical Society Collections. 1893–1913. 17 v.

OLDS, FRED A.: *An Abstract of North Carolina Wills from About 1760 to About 1800.* Supplementing Grimes' Abstract of North Carolina Wills, 1663–1760. Oxford, N.C. 1925.

PELLETREAU, WILLIAM S.: *Early Long Island Wills of Suffolk County, 1691–1703.* 1897. (S)

PELLETREAU, WILLIAM S.: *Wills of the Smith Families of New York and Long Island, 1664–1794.* 1898. (S)

Probate Records of Essex, Massachusetts. Massachusetts Colony Probate Court for Essex County. Salem, Mass. 1916–1920. 3 v. (S)

Probate Records of the Province of New Hampshire, 1635–1771. In New Hampshire State Papers, vols. 31–39. Concord. 1907–1941. (S)

SARGENT, WILLIAM M.: *Maine Wills, 1640–1760.* Portland. 1887.

SOUTH CAROLINA UNIVERSITY LIBRARY: *Indexes to the County Wills of South Carolina.* A separate index compiled from the W. P. A. copies of each of the county will books, except those for Charleston County. Columbia. 1939.

TORRENCE, CLAYTON, COMP.: *Virginia Wills and Administrations, 1632–1800.* Richmond. 1931.

YOUR FAMILY TREE, A CURRENT PERIODICAL BEING PUBLISHED AT INDIANA PENNSYLVANIA: *Abstracts of Wills in the following counties:*
Allegheny, 1789—; Bedford, unrecorded wills, 1770–1792; Bucks, wills and administrations, 1682–1693; Cumberland, 1752–1768; Franklin, 1784— in progress; Lycoming, 1796–1807; Northampton, 1752–1762; Washington, 1781–1811; Westmoreland, 1773–1779. In volumes 1–7 (S)

Tax Records

FOTHERGILL, MRS. AUGUSTA BRIDGLAND (MIDDLETON): *Virginia Tax Payers, 1782–1787, Other Than Those Published by the United States Census Bureau.* Richmond. 1940.

GEORGIA DEPARTMENT OF ARCHIVES AND HISTORY, RUTH BLAIR, ED.: *Some Early Tax Digests of Georgia.* Atlanta. 1926.

New York City Tax Lists, 1695–1699. In Collections of New York Historical Society. 1910 and 1911. (S)

PENNSYLVANIA ARCHIVES: *Tax Lists, 1771-1773, 1779, 1782.* Series 3, v. 17, pp. 3–898. (S)

YOUR FAMILY TREE: *Early Tax Lists of the Following Pennsylvania Counties:* Chester; Cumberland; Dauphin; Indiana; Lycoming; Venango; Westmoreland. In volumes 1 to 7. (S)

Land Records

Eighteenth Century Records of the Portion of Dutchess County, New York, That Was Included in Rombout Precinct and the Original Town of Fishkill. In Collections of Dutchess County Historical Society. v. 6. 1933.

HOUSTON, MARTHA LOU: *Reprint of Official Land Lottery of Georgia, 1827.* Columbia, Georgia. 1929.

JILLSON, WILLARD R.: *The Kentucky Land Grants.* A systematic index to all of the land grants recorded in the State Land Office at Frankfort, Kentucky, 1782–1924. Louisville. 1925. Filson Club Publication Number 30.

JILLSON, WILLARD R.: *Old Kentucky Entries and Deeds.* A complete index of all of the earliest land entries, military warrants, deeds and wills of the Commonwealth of Kentucky. Louisville. 1926.

Michigan—First Land Purchases from the Government in the following counties, have microfilmed from records in the Auditor General's Office: Allegany; Barry; Bay; Berrien; Branch; Calhoun; Clare; Clinton; Eaton; Genesee; Gladwin; Grand Traverse; Gratiot; Hillsdale; Huron; Ingham; Ionia; Iosco; Isabella; Jackson; Kalamazoo; Kent; Lake; Lapeer; Lenawee; Livingston; Macomb; Manistee; Mason; Mecosta; Midland; Monroe; Montcalm; Muskegon; Newaygo; Oceana; Osceola; St. Clair; St. Joseph; Sanilac; Shiawassee; Tuscola; Van Buren; Washtenaw; Wayne. (S)

NUGENT, MRS. NELL MARION: *Cavaliers and Pioneers—A Calendar of Virginia Land Grants, 1623–1666.* Richmond. 1934.

Oregon Donation Land Claims: Index giving land office; certificate number; acreage; Town; Range; Section. Published as a supplement to The Genealogical Forum of Portland, Oregon. (vol. 3 to vol. 7) Has also been published separately. (S)

PENNSYLVANIA ARCHIVES: *Forfeited Estates; Inventories and Sales.* Series 6, v. 12, pp. 3–919. In Colonial Records, volumes 11 and 15; in Archives, Series 1, vols. 7 and 9. (S)

PENNSYLVANIA ARCHIVES: *Land Warrantys (1730–1898);* Series 3, v. 24, pp. 3–792; v. 25, pp. 3–809; v. 26, pp. 3–905; *(1733–1896)* Series 3, v. 35, pp. 349–568; "Last Purchase" Land Warrantys *(1785–1860);* Series 3, v. 26, pp. 701–905. (S)

PENNSYLVANIA ARCHIVES: *Welsh Purchasers, 1681–1702;* Minutes Series 3, v. 1, pp. 3–24.

Suffolk County, Massachusetts Deeds. 14 v. 1880–1906. (S)

Warrants for Lands in South Carolina, 1672–1711. Columbia. 1910–1915.

Vital Records

ARNOLD, JAMES NEWELL: *Vital Records of Rhode Island, 1636–1850.* Providence. 1891–1911. 21 v. (S)

BAILEY, FREDERIC WILLIAM: *Early Connecticut Marriages as Found on Ancient Church Records Prior to 1800.* 1896–1906. 7 .v (K) (S)

BARBER, GERTRUDE A.: *Death and Marriage Records Copied from the Following Newspapers:* New York Evening Post (items cover the whole U.S.) (1801–1890); Otsego County, New York (1795–1875); Delaware County, New York (1797–1875); Cemetery Records of Orange, Sullivan, Columbia, and Rockland Counties, New York.

CLEMENS, WILLIAM MONTGOMERY: *American Marriage Records Before 1699.* 1926. (K) (S)

CLEMENS, WILLIAM MONTGOMERY: *North and South Carolina Marriage Records from the Earliest Colonial Days to the Civil War.* New York. 1927.

Connecticut Vital Records. Published for Bolton and Vernon, Mansfield, New Haven, Salisbury, Saybrook, Sharon, Woodstock. (K) (S)

CROZIER, WILLIAM A.: *Early Virginia Marriages.* 2nd. ed. Baltimore. 1953.

KNORR, CATHERINE L.: *Marriage Bonds and Minister's Returns of Charlotte County, Virginia, 1765–1815.* Mimeo. 1951.

MASSACHUSETTS. *Vital Records of Massachusetts Towns.* Vital records of most of the towns in the state have been published to 1850. List in New England Historical and Genealogical Register, 73: 53–62, Jan. 1919; also in National Genealogical Society Quarterly, 31: 83–87, September 1943. (S)

Names of Persons For Whom Marriage Licenses Were Issued By the Secretary of the Province of New York Prior to 1784. Albany. 1860. Two Supplements have been issued, one by the New York State Library; the other by the New York Historical Society. (S)

NATIONAL SOCIETY OF COLONIAL DAMES OF AMERICA, NEW HAMPSHIRE CHAPTER: *Grave Stone Inscriptions Gathered by the Old Burial Grounds Committee In the State of New Hampshire.* Cambridge. 1913.

NEW JERSEY ARCHIVES: *Marriage Records, 1665–1800.* v. 22. (S)

PENNSYLVANIA ARCHIVES: *Baptisms, 1734–1834.* Series 6, v. 6. (S)

PENNSYLVANIA ARCHIVES: *Marriages Recorded by the Register General, 1685–1689.* Series 2, v. 8; *Marriage Licenses, 1784–1786.* Series 6, v. 6, pp. 285–310; *Marriage Licenses Issued Previous to 1790,* Series 2, v. 8, pp. 1–790; also v. 9. (S)

SALLEY, ALEXANDER SAMUEL: *Death Notices in the South Carolina Gazette, 1732–1775.* Columbia. 1917.

SALLEY, ALEXANDER SAMUEL: *Marriage Notices in the South Carolina Gazette and Its Successors.* Charleston. 1902.

WESTERVELT, MRS. FRANCES A.: *Bergen County, New Jersey, Marriage Records From the Entries As Originally Made At the Court House by Ministers and Justices of the Peace of the County, 1795–1878.* 1929.

Apprentices' Indentures

COLLECTIONS OF NEW YORK HISTORICAL SOCIETY: *Indentures of Apprentices, 1694–1708, 1718–1727.* 1885 and 1909. (S)

YOUR FAMILY TREE: *Servants and Apprentices Bound and Assigned in Pennsylvania in 1745.* 6: 81–83; 7: 12–13, 51–52, 75. (S)

Military and Pension Records

AINSWORTH, MARY GOVIER: *Recently Discovered Records Relating to Revolutionary War Veterans Who Applied For Pensions Under the Act of 1792.* Abstracts from War Office Letter Book, 1791–1794, in National Archives. In National Genealogical Society Quarterly, March 1958, and continuing currently. (S)

BODGE, GEORGE M. *Soldiers' in King Philip's War.* 3rd. ed. Boston. 1906. (S)

BRUMBAUGH, GAIUS M.: *Revolutionary War Records.* Virginia Army and Navy Forces, with Bounty Land Warrants for Virginia Military District of Ohio, and Virginia Military Scrip, taken from Federal and State Archives. Washington. 1936. (S)

CANDLER, Allen D.: *Revolutionary Records of the State of Georgia.* 1908. 3 v.

A Census of Pensioners for Revolutionary or Military Services; with their names, ages, and places of residence . . . as returned in the Sixth Census, Washington. 1841. Reprinted in Baltimore. 1954. (S)

CLARK, BYRON N.: *War of 1812—A List of Pensioners.* With an appendix containing names of volunteers for the defense of Pittsburgh. Burlington, Vermont. 1904.

Colonial New York Muster Rolls, 1664–1770. Printed in the second and third Annual Reports of the New York State Historian. 1896; 1897 (S)

CONNECTICUT HISTORICAL SOCIETY: *Rolls and Lists of Connecticut Men in the Revolution, 1775–1783.* 2 v. Hartford. 1901–9. Collections, vols. 8 and 12. (K) (S)

CONNECTICUT Historical Society: *Rolls of Connecticut Men in the French and Indian War, 1735–1762.* 2 v. Hartford. 1903–1905. Collections,

CONNECTICUT: *Record of Service of Connecticut Men in the War of the Revolution; War of 1812; Mexican War.* 2 v. Hartford. 1889. (S)

CONNECTICUT: *Roll and Journal of Connecticut Service in Queen Anne's War, 1710–11.* Acorn Club. Hartford. 1916.

CROZIER, WILLIAM A.: *Virginia Colonial Militia, 1631–1776.* Baltimore. 1954.

DELAWARE ARCHIVES: *Military and Revolutionary Records.* 5 v. Wilmington, 1911–1919.

EGLE, WILLIAM H.: *Pennsylvania in the War of the Revolution, Battalions and Line, 1775–1783.* (Taken from Pennsylvania Archives) (S)

ERVIN, SARA S.: *South Carolinians in the Revolution.* With service records and miscellaneous data; also abstracts of wills (Laurens County), 1775–1855. 1949.

GEORGIA: *Revolutionary Soldier's Receipts for Georgia Bounty Grants.* Atlanta. 1928.

GODFREY, CARLOS E.: *The Commander-in-Chief's Guard.* Revolutionary War. Washington. 1904. (S)

GWATHMEY, JOHN H.: *Historical Register of Virginians in the Revolution, Soldiers, Sailors, Marines, 1775–1783.* Richmond. 1938.

HEITMAN, FRANCIS B.: *Historical Register of Officers of the United States Army, From Its Organization, September 29, 1789 to March 2, 1903.* 2 v. Washington. 1903.

HOYT, MAX E.: *Index to Revolutionary War Pension Applications*—See Guides and Indexes.

Index of Awards on Claims of Soldiers of the War of 1812. Albany, N.Y. Gives place of residence of veterans in 1860. Microfilm (S)

LOSSING, BENSON J.: *The Pictorial Field Book of the Revolution.* 2 v. New York. 1859. 1860. (K) (S)

Massachusetts Soldiers and Sailors in the Revolutionary War. 17 v. 1896–1908. (K)(S)

MATHER, FREDERIC G.: *The Refugees of 1776 from Long Island to Connecticut.* Albany. 1913. (K) (S)

Michigan in the War. George. State Printer. 1882. 1039 pages. Part 3. Registers of Commissioned Officers. (K) (S)

Michigan Volunteers in the Civil War—Record of Service, 1861–1865. 46 v. Everard. Kalamazoo. 1900: Index, v. 47 (85, 271 names) Michigan Soldiers and Sailors Individual Records. 1097 p. 1915. (K) (S)

Military Minutes of the Council of Appointment of the State of New York, 1783–1821. 4 v. 1901–2.

New Hampshire Revolutionary Rolls. 3 v. Concord and Manchester, 1885–1887. New Hampshire State Papers, vols. 14–16. (S)

NEWMAN, HARRY W.: *Maryland Revolutionary Records.* Data obtained from 3,050 pension claims and bounty land applications, including 1000 marriages of Maryland soldiers, and a list of 1200 proved services of soldiers and patriots of other states. Washington. 1938.

NORTH CAROLINA DAUGHTERS OF THE AMERICAN REVOLUTION: *Roster of Soldiers from North Carolina in the American Revolution.* Durham. 1932.

NORTH CAROLINA STATE RECORDS: *North Carolina Revolutionary Pensioners Under the Acts of 1818 and 1832, as Reported by the Secretary of State to Congress in 1835.* vol. 22, pp. 55–92.

PENNSYLVANIA ARCHIVES: *Associators and Militia Muster Rolls, 1774–1783* Series 2, v. 13, pp. 269–552; Series 3, v. 23 (1775–1781), pp. 423–443; Series 5, v. 7 (1777–1782), pp. 3–1150. (S)

PENNSYLVANIA ARCHIVES: *List of Officers and Men of the Pennsylvania Navy, 1775–1781; Papers Relating to British Prisoners in Pennsylvania.* Series 2, vol. 1. (S)

Pension List for the United States for 1813. Baltimore. 1953. (S)

Rhode Island: Nine Muster Rolls of Troops Enlisted During the Old French War; also Journal of Captain William Rice in the Expedition of 1746. Providence. 1915.

ROBERTS, JAMES A.: *New York in the Revolution as Colony and State.* 2 v. 1898. 1904. (K) (S)

STRYKER, WILLIAM S.: *Official Register of the Officers and Men of New Jersey in the Revolutionary War.* Trenton. 1872. (K) (S)

UNITED STATES PUBLIC DOCUMENTS—Serial Nos. 2078, 2079, 2080, 2081, 2082; *List of Pensioners on the Roll January 1, 1883.* 5. v. (S)

WALDENMAIER, NELLIE PROTSMAN: *Some of the Earliest Oaths of Allegiance to the United States of America.* Washington. 1944. 2000 Oaths of Allegiance.

WILSON, SAMUEL M.: *Catalog of the Revolutionary Soldiers and Sailors of the Commonwealth of Virginia to Whom Land Bounty Warrants Were Granted by Virginia for Military Service in the War for Independence.* Baltimore. 1953. From official records in the Kentucky State Land Office, Frankfort.

Immigration and Naturalization

BAIRD, CHARLES W.: *History of the Huguenot Emigration to America.* 2 v. New York. 1885. (S)

BANKS, Charles E.: *Planters of the Commonwealth.* Boston. 1930. (S) Lists of Passengers to Boston and the Bay Colony, 1620–1640.

BANKS, CHARLES E.: *Topographical Dictionary of 2885 English Emigrants to New England, 1620–1650.* Elijah Brownell, ed. 1937. Reprint Baltimore. 1957. (K) (S)

BANKS, CHARLES E.: *The Winrthop Fleet of 1630.* Boston. 1930. (S)

BROCK, Robert Alonzo: *Documents, Chiefly Unpublished, Relating to the Huguenot Emigration to Virginia and to the Settlement of Manakin Town.* Richmond. 1886. Collections of Virginia Historical Society. volume 5.

FAUST, ALBERT, AND BRUMBAUGH, GAIUS: *Lists of Swiss Emigrants in the Eighteenth Century to the American Colonies.* 2 v. Washington, D.C. 1920–1925. (S)

GUISEPPI, M. S. ED.: *Naturalization of Foreign Protestants in the American Colonies*

Pursuant to Statute 13, George II. C. 7. Publications of the Huguenot Society of London. Manchester. 1921. v. 24.

HIRSCH, ARTHUR HENRY: *The Huguenots of South Carolina.* Durham. 1928.

Holland Society of New York. Year Books, 1885. Contain early passenger lists from the Netherlands to New York. (S)

HOTTEN, JOHN C.: *The Original Lists of Persons of Quality Who Went From Great Britain to the American Plantations, 1600–1700.* New York. 1874. (K) (S)

JOHNSON, Amandus: *The Swedish Settlements on the Delaware.* New York. 1911. 2 v. (S)

KNITTLE, WALTER ALLEN: *Early Eighteenth Century Palatine Emigration.* Philadelphia. 1937.

LANCOUR, ADLORE HAROLD: *Passenger Lists of Ships Coming to North America, 1607–1825.* A Bibliography. New York Public Library Bulletin Number 41. May 1937. (S)

MYERS, ALBERT COOK: *Immigration of the Irish Quakers into Pennsylvania, 1682–1750.* Swarthmore, Pennsylvania. 1902.

Naturalizations in the American Colonies, With More Particular Reference to Massachusetts. In Proceedings of the Massachusetts Historical Society, v. 4, pp. 337–364. 1860.

PENNSYLVANIA ARCHIVES: *Immigrants, 1786–1808.* Series 2, v. 17, pp. 521–667. (S)

PENNSYLVANIA ARCHIVES: *List of Ship's Registers, 1762–1776.* Series 2, v. 2, pp. 631–671; Series 5, v. 1, pp. 384–413. (S)

PENNSYLVANIA ARCHIVES: *Ship Certificates, 1753–1761.* Series 5, v. 1, pp. 380–381. (S)

REVILL, JAMES, COMP.: *A Compilation of the Original Lists of Protestant Immigrants to South Carolina, 1763–1773.* Columbia, S. C. 1939.

RUPP, I. D.: *Collection of 30,000 Names of German, Swiss, Dutch, French, and Other Immigrants to Pennsylvania, 1727–1776.* 1876. An index was published by M. V. Koger in 1935. (S)

SIMMENDINGER, ULRICH: *True and Authentic Register of Persons Who, in 1709. . . . Journeyed From Germany to America.* St. Johnsville, New York. 1934.

STRASSBURGER, RALPH BEAVER: *Pennsylvania German Pioneers.* A publication of the original lists of arrivals in the Port of Philadelphia from 1727 to 1808. ed. by William J. Hinke, Norristown, Pa. 1934. 3 v. added title page, Pennsylvania German Society Proceedings, v. 42–44. (S)

Migrations Within the United States

BILLINGTON, RAY ALLEN: *Westward Expansion. A History of the American Frontier.* Bibliography, pp. 757–834.

Buck, Solon J., and Elizabeth H.: *The Planting of Civilization in Western Pennsylvania*. Pittsburgh. 1939. (K) (S) Excellent bibliography.

Cleaveland, Dorothy Kendall: *The Trade and Trade Routes of Northern New York*, from the beginning of the settlement to the coming of the railroad. In New York State Historical Journal, 4: 205–31. October 1923. (New York to Vermont roads).

Higgins, Ruth L.: *Expansion in New York with Special Reference to the Eighteenth Century*. Ohio State University. Columbus. 1931. Bibliography pp. 163–188. Lists New York State towns with approximate dates of first settlements.

Holbrook, Stewart H.: *The Yankee Exodus;* an account of migration from New England. New York. 1950 (K) (S) of Bibliography, pp. 364–371.

Lynch, William W.: *The Westward Flow of Southern Colonists Before 1861*. In the Journal of Southern History, 9: 313–327. August 1943.

Meriwether, Robert Lee: *The Expansion of South Carolina, 1729–1765*. Kingsport, Tenn. 1940.

Rosenberry, Lois (Kimball) Mathews: *The Erie Canal and the Settlement of the West*. In Buffalo Historical Society Publications. 14: 187–203. 1910.

Rosenberry, Lois (Kimball) Mathews: *The Expansion of New England;* the spread of New England settlements and institutions to the Mississippi River, 1620–1865. Boston. 1909. (S)

Rosenberry, Lois (Kimball) Mathews: *Migrations from Connecticut After 1800*. New Haven. 1936.

Stillwell, Lewis D.: *Migration from Vermont*. Vermont Historical Society. Montpelier. 1948. (S) Has bibliographical footnotes.

Periodicals

The American Genealogist. Quarterly. New Haven, Connecticut. Donald Lines Jacobus, editor. 1922— (S)

The Detroit Society for Genealogical Research Magazine. Quarterly. 1937— (S)

The Maryland & Delaware Genealogist. Quarterly. Washington, D. C. Raymond B. Clark, Jr., editor. 1959—

Michigan Heritage. Quarterly. Published by the Kalamazoo Valley Genealogical Society. Kalamazoo, Michigan. 1959—

National Genealogical Society Quarterly. Washington, D. C. 1912— (S)

New England Historical & Genealogical Register. Quarterly. Boston. 1847— (S) Has consolidated index to first 50 volumes.

New York Genealogical & Biographical Record. Quarterly. 1870— (S)

The North Carolinian. Quarterly. 1955— (S)

The Pennsylvania Genealogical Magazine. 1895—. Before 1948 it was titled *Publications of the Genealogical Society of Pennsylvania*. Annual. Irregular. (S)

The Pennsylvania Magazine of History and Biography. Quarterly. Published by the Historical Society of Pennsylvania. Philadelphia. 1877—. For Index to first 75 volumes see Guides and Indexes.

The Virginia Genealogist. Quarterly. Published by John Frederick Dorman. Washington, D. C. March 1957— (S)

Newspapers

BRIGHAM, CLARENCE S.: *History and Bibliography of American Newspapers,* 1690–1820. 2 v. Worcester, Mass. 1947. Lists newspaper holdings in American libraries.

GREGORY, WINIFRED, ED.: *American Newspapers, 1821–1936, A Union List of Files Available in the United States and Canada.* New York. 1937. Gives name and location of repository of newspaper files, 1821–1936.

JOHNSON, J. PERCY H., ED.: *N. W. Ayer & Sons Directory of Newspapers and Periodicals.* Published annually; contains names and locations of newspapers and periodicals in the United States and possessions, Canada, Newfoundland and Bermuda.

New York Times Index: A Master Key to All Newspapers. Quarterly. New York. 1913—

New York Times Index: A Master Key To The News. Annual. New York. New York. 1930.

UNITED STATES: *A Check List of American Eighteenth Century Newspapers in the Library of Congress.* Washington. Government Printing Office. 1936.

UNITED STATES: *Check List of American Newspapers in the Library of Congress.* Washington. 1900. Government Printing Office. This covers American files through 1900.

UNITED STATES: *Check List of Foreign Newspapers in the Library of Congress.* Government Printing Office. Washington, D. C. 1929.

END OF BIBLIOGRAPHY.

INDEX